Teacher appraisal observed

Teacher appraisal systems have been in place since 1992, bringing with them considerable controversy. But just how effective are they, and what does this mean for the classroom teacher? This major new study, led by Ted Wragg, tackles these and many other questions. It uses as its basis information gathered from all 109 authorities, 658 primary and secondary teachers and 479 appraisers, and as such represents the most extensive study of this area ever undertaken.

The issue of teacher appraisal is examined from the perspectives of all those concerned and at all levels. The main focus of the study is on teacher competence in the classroom, which lies at the heart of school effectiveness and improving pupils' achievement. Through the use of a variety of methods including intensive case studies, the book provides a unique insight into the quality of classroom practice and teacher appraisal today. It examines what appraisal means for those involved and how to use this knowledge to move on from this point.

Ted Wragg is Professor of Education at the University of Exeter and will be familiar to readers from his widespread writing on education, including his regular column in the *Times Educational Supplement*. **Felicity Wikeley** is an experienced teacher and has worked for several years in community education. She is currently Research Officer at the Centre for School Improvement, University of Bath. **Caroline Wragg** is a research fellow in the School of Education at the University of Exeter. Her research interests include classroom management, nursery education and school improvement. **Gill Haynes** is an educational researcher at the University of Exeter, and also lectures in research methodology. She has a particular interest in the teaching of literacy in primary schools.

Teacher appraisal observed

E C Wragg, F J Wikeley,
C M Wragg and G S Haynes

London and New York

First published 1996
by Routledge
11 New Fetter Lane, London EC4P 4EE

Simultaneously published in the USA and Canada
by Routledge
29 West 35th Street, New York, NY 10001

Routledge is an International Thomson Publishing Company

© 1996 E. C. Wragg, F. J. Wikeley, C. M. Wragg and G. S. Haynes

Typeset in Palatino by
BC Typesetting, Bristol

Printed and bound in Great Britain by
TJ Press Ltd, Padstow, Cornwall

British Library Cataloguing in Publication Data
A catalogue record for this book is available from the British Library

Library of Congress Cataloging in Publication Data
Teacher appraisal observed/E. C. Wragg *et al.*
    p. cm.
    Includes bibliographical references and index.
    1. Teachers – Rating of – Great Britain. 2. Teachers – Rating of –
Great Britain – Case studies. 3. Observation (Educational method).
4. School management and organization – Great Britain – Case studies.
I. Wragg, E. C. (Edward Conrad)
LB2838.T385   1996
371.1'44'0941–dc20   95-25984

ISBN 0–415–12580–4
ISBN 0–415–12581–2 (pbk)

Contents

Tables

Preface

This book describes the research undertaken during the Leverhulme Appraisal Project, a two-year research project funded by the Leverhulme Trust. There were three strands to the research. The first studied what happened in 109 English local education authorities (LEAs) when appraisers were trained by their LEA. The second was a questionnaire survey of 1,137 teachers and appraisers in primary and secondary schools in sixty-four local authorities. The third strand was a set of intensive case studies of twenty-nine primary and secondary teachers during the two years when appraisal was introduced by law for the first time.

During the project we used questionnaires, interviews and observation. We not only observed the appraisal process itself, we also observed the classroom teaching of the teachers in our sample before, during and after their appraisal. This variety of research strategies produced rich data, first of all about appraisal, but also about management, school organisation and human interaction.

The chapters in this book describe one of the few large-scale studies of appraisal in a whole country. It is to be hoped that the Leverhulme Appraisal Project will add to our knowledge of appraisal and teachers' personal and professional development.

ECW, FJW, CMW, GSH

Acknowledgements

We should like to express our gratitude to the Leverhulme Trust for supporting the Appraisal Project. We should also like to thank the many heads, teachers and local authority officers who co-operated so fully with us.

Introduction

Evaluating the work done by professional people is a difficult and challenging assignment. Society requires that those in receipt of public funds must be accountable, yet evaluation needs to be conducted in a sensitive manner, otherwise it may achieve the opposite of what is intended: resistance rather than co-operation, or poorer, rather than better performance. Evaluating what teachers do in the school generally, and in their own classroom in particular, is especially problematic. There is often disagreement about what constitutes effective teaching, and the gains sought are usually long term, rather than short term. Teacher appraisal cannot be dispensed with in a few minutes.

This book describes a two-year study of teacher appraisal in England, which was funded by the Leverhulme Trust. The Education Act 1986 had required that teachers should be appraised. In practice most schools did not immediately cease what they were doing and make appraisal their highest priority. The advent of the Education Act 1988, with its major programmes of change in curriculum, testing, school management and organisation, pushed the matter even further down the batting list. Some schools did indeed try out systematic forms of appraisal and there were various pilot studies in selected local education authorities, but in most schools the process was mainly informal.

From 1992 to 1994 all primary and secondary schools were required to undertake an appraisal of teachers on their staff. For many it was the first time this had been done in a systematic manner. There was a requirement on local authorities to oversee the preparation and training of appraisers, as well as the actual carrying out of the exercise. Teachers had to be observed teaching in their classrooms on at least two occasions, for a minimum of one hour in all, though the nature of the observation was not specified. After this they were required to set targets for the future that they should endeavour to meet.

We decided to conduct a two-year monitoring of this significant first national exercise, with particular scrutiny of the place of lesson observation. Since all teachers had to be observed, it was important to know how this was done, what appraisers did, how the teachers reacted, and what the outcomes appeared to be in the shorter and longer term. The project took place at Exeter University, funded by the Leverhulme Trust, and the four researchers were Professor Ted Wragg, who directed the project, Felicity Wikeley, Caroline Wragg and Gill Haynes, the four co-authors of this book.

In order to construct a full picture of the process, we operated through three linked project strands, allowing us to draw up both national and local perspectives. The three studies used both qualitative and quantitative methods, and were as follows:

Study 1: the local education authorities (LEA) study   Every English LEA, 109 in total, was written to, in order to elicit what training in classroom observation was being given to appraisers. A 100 per cent return was obtained, a rarity in educational research, though some responses were fuller than others.

Study 2: the national survey   A multi-item questionnaire was sent to a national sample of primary and secondary school appraisers and appraisees. A total of 658 teachers and 479 appraisers replied.

Study 3: the case studies   Intensive case studies of twenty-nine primary and secondary school teachers were carried out over the two-year period.

The data from these three studies reveal the process from inception to completion and beyond, and give an individual classroom, as well as a regional and national perspective. By observing as well as interviewing and using questionnaires, we were able to witness the processes at first hand.

Appraisal is in any case a fascinating topic to research. It actually gives a dipstick impression of life in school generally, for it offers insights into teachers' aspirations and concerns, teacher–pupil interaction, staff relationships, styles of school management and organisation, and the impact of intervention on what takes place thereafter. This research is, therefore, of much wider interest than a single study of two years of a particular initiative. It taps into the very bloodstream of school life and describes the impact, or sometimes the lack of it, of policy on practice.

The findings are described in the following chapters. In the first chapter there is an account of teacher appraisal and some of the related issues, as well as of the design of this research. Chapter 2 raises the important issue of classroom observation and what teachers do when they teach. In the third chapter we describe Study 1 of the three strands mentioned above, namely the role played by local education authorities in the training of appraisers, the framework within which the exercise of appraisal was placed. Chapter 4 reports Study 2, the findings of the national survey of teachers and appraisers, telling how they recounted their experiences.

The second half of the book concentrates on the intensive case studies of twenty-nine teachers which constituted Study 3. Chapter 5 gives an illustrative case study of one school to show how the process worked out in practice. Chapter 6 covers what teachers and heads told us in interviews about their perceptions of the process. Chapters 7 and 8 give the details of how classroom observation was carried out in the case study schools, analysing the preparation for and implementation of this important part of the process in the primary and secondary class- rooms studied. Finally, in Chapter 9 we try to make sense of the whole of what we have found and to place it in the wider context of educa- tional change and the management and development of professional skills.

There is always the problem, in a study of this kind, of writing for different audiences. Appraisal is a topic which is of general interest to heads, teachers, school governors, teacher trainers, policy makers, advisers, inspectors and politicians concerned with the spending and accountability of public funds, as well as to the research community. We have tried to write the book in such a way that it will be read by these wider constituencies. That means that we sometimes give the kind of detail or statistical analysis that might interest researchers more than practitioners or policy makers. Equally we raise issues and report events that might excite practitioners and policy makers more than researchers. We hope that we have managed to walk that difficult tight- rope without falling off too many times.

Before embarking on the main text we need to clarify the terminology we have used. In 1985 the Department of Education and Science pro- posed a set of conventions which included the following:

1 *Evaluation* – a general term used to describe any activity by the insti- tution or LEA where the quality of the provision is the subject of systematic study.
2 *Review* – a retrospective activity implying the collection and examin- ation of evidence and information.
3 *Appraisal* – emphasising the forming of qualitative judgements about an activity, a person or an organisation.
4 *Assessment* – implying the use of measurement and/or grading based on known criteria.

There was an additional comment about *staff appraisal* including 'quali- tative judgements about performance', and *staff development* being concerned with 'general matters of in-service training needs and career development' which may, or may not, be based on staff appraisal.

In general we have used similar conventions, though this can be a little difficult stylistically when the use of certain phrases piles up in the account, and in some places paraphrases or synonyms are used. Even in different parts of the English speaking world differences in terminology are commonplace, and the term *teacher evaluation* is more frequently used in the United States for what is called *teacher appraisal* in Britain.

In addition we have tried to use the following terms when possible:

Appraisee	the teacher being appraised
Appraiser	the person doing the appraising
(Area of) focus	the aspect of teaching, or work in the school, on which the teacher and appraiser decided to concentrate
Feedback	information and discussion of lesson following an observation by the appraiser
Appraisal interview/dialogue	discussion of the appraisal of the teacher's work in the school in general (not just of lessons observed)
Targets	resultant targets for future action set at the appraisal interview/dialogue

In the case of the somewhat ungainly term *appraisee* we have often simply said *teacher*, and common words like *interview* are used whenever they appear natural and appropriate, not solely in the context of the final summary appraisal interview.

Chapter 1

The appraisal of teaching

Teaching is not a single skill. Whereas in some jobs the same routine is repeated over and over, making it relatively easy to do and even easier to evaluate, teaching combines knowledge, numerous skills of management and communication, relationships, the manifestation of personal traits, values and attitudes, and intricate patterns of behaviour. Teaching is not a simple matter either to carry out or to appraise. *evaluate the Performance*

Consider an incident which was observed during a research project (Wragg 1993). A teacher, attempting to explain insects to eight and nine year old children, accepted 'spider', 'ladybird', 'worm' and 'snail' as responses to a question asking for examples of the genre. Only one of these, the ladybird, is actually an insect. During and after the lesson the children appeared confused, and most obtained low scores on a test in which they were asked to identify insects. On the surface this is a simple event to appraise: the teacher was incompetent, since he did not know himself what an insect was. As a result the children were confused and appeared to learn little or nothing.

Closer scrutiny, however, reveals that this is not the end of the matter. If this event had occurred during a lesson in which the teacher was being appraised, what might the aftermath have been? Should the appraiser have simply awarded a low grade, on the grounds that the teacher was not competent? Would the giving of a grade achieve anything? Can we be sure that lack of subject knowledge is the problem, for at one stage in the same lesson, when a child mentioned that a spider was an insect, the teacher replied, 'OK, you think of a spider. You keep the spider there'. He never revisited the matter. Could this mean that his own subject knowledge was not the central issue, but rather that his failure to return to the point and give children feedback about their answers might have confused them?

What is clear from this example alone is that the observation and appraisal of teaching, and indeed of pupil learning as well, raises many issues. These include, among others, the nature of professional competence, the purposes and intentions of teachers, what children learn or fail to learn, the strategies teachers employ, methods of observing and recording what happens in lessons, the content and style of discussion after teaching has been observed, the roles of teacher and appraiser, and what needs to happen following an appraisal to ensure that teachers and ultimately pupils benefit from the whole exercise.

APPRAISAL AND ACCOUNTABILITY

Formal systems of teacher appraisal must to some extent be seen as part of a general push for accountability. In any activity involving the expenditure of large sums of private or public money, the sponsors are likely to ask for an account to be rendered, especially if financial resources are tight. Education costs billions of pounds, and even though teachers may not always be as well paid as they deserve, salaries do constitute a significant proportion of that expenditure. Furthermore, at a time when millions of jobs have disappeared, in most cases never to return in their previous form, parents recognise that the more highly educated in society have a better chance of obtaining employment than those who leave school with few or no formal qualifications. Hence the increasing pressure on schools since the 1970s, and especially during the 1980s and 1990s, to achieve as much as possible during the compulsory years of education.

Accountability can operate at several levels, at both micro- and macro-level. Elliott et al. (1982) argue that teachers feel most accountable at a local level, to their pupils, fellow teachers and children's parents. To those wider constituencies, such as governors, committees and local authorities, accountability may be seen as more remote and thus more legal and formal in nature. Appraisal straddles these levels, since it is legally required, but conducted at individual school level. Many teachers probably see the head as the person to whom they are most accountable.

There has been increasing emphasis on financial aspects of education, so it is not surprising that the language of accountancy is not far from discussions about effectiveness. Thus terms like 'cost effective' or 'performance indicators', which sometimes do not fit well with the traditionally held view of teaching as an art suffused with a certain amount of mystique, are increasingly heard during discussions about education. There are millions of pupils and hundreds of thousands of teachers, so it is tempting to think entirely in terms of quantities: whether the teacher is in the top few per cent, obtains high marks from raters, or achieves high test scores from pupils. Quantitative aspects do have a part to play, but there is a very strong qualitative dimension to be considered.

Teachers are now compared, unfairly perhaps, with the finest communicators in the world. A lesson in a primary school on insects may be judged in the eyes of the pupils alongside television programmes presented by outstanding broadcasters and film makers, who have access to brilliantly and expensively filmed vignettes of insect life provided by a galaxy of photographers and naturalists from all over the globe. The jobbing teacher with a few worksheets, wallcharts, filmstrips and dehydrated butterflies can easily look pedestrian in comparison with the glossy images of the high-budget television series.

The definition and application of appraisal will depend on individuals' own attitudes and values. Those who believe teaching to be a refuge for life's incompetents will see it as a way of smoking out the indolent and incapable. Many who actually work in education will regard it as part of a continuous process for the improvement and extension of professional skills. Such a view sees any act of appraisal as an interim measure, both retrospective and prospective, looking back at what has or has not been achieved, taking stock of the present, and then planning some pathway that will help the teacher develop further in the future. It can be part of the development of what Wragg (1994) called the 'dynamic practitioner' in the 'dynamic school'.

The concept of appraisal, in theory a self-evident, neutral notion, can acquire overtones of retribution or support, depending on the individual's vantage point. Someone with a strong financial perspective would see it as a value-for-money exercise, addressing the question, 'Is whatever teacher X does a better investment of money than, say, buying new pieces of the most modern information technology, books, ancillary helpers, videos, and all the other things a teacher's salary might purchase?' This view frequently encompasses a comparative dimension, seeking to compare teachers with each other to discover who should be promoted or paid a financial bonus.

One term commonly used, especially in industry, is 'performance appraisal'. The word 'performance' can be widely stretched. It carries with it both commercial associations of products and profits, and theatrical notions of someone centre stage enacting a scene before an audience. There is some reluctance amongst teachers to being perceived either as an intermediary in a simple input–output industrial model, or as someone obliged to dominate the classroom when under observation because of pressure to 'perform'. A few years ago there was often embarrassment in initial teacher training when external examiners with a secondary school background, mistakenly turned loose to watch primary student teachers, subsequently announced that they were unable to judge what they had seen because the teacher had not 'performed'.

None the less, there is some value in looking at the purposes of appraisal in industry and commerce, and Whyte (1986) has written a full review of assessment objectives and procedures in these fields. One principal purpose commonly reported in commercial firms is the linking of monetary rewards and job performance, a controversial issue in teaching. Other arguments often advanced include: facilitating the more effective use of human and material resources, identifying candidates for promotion to higher responsibility, improving individuals' motivation, dismissing or demoting the incompetent, rationalising and redeploying employees, and, though this is rarely stated in explicit form, exercising control over staff. All of these are possibilities in the field of teacher appraisal, though some have been embraced more eagerly than others.

THE DEVELOPMENT OF APPRAISAL

There is nothing new about analysing the nature and effect of teaching. In various classical civilisations this was done by some of the best known teachers, who often fashioned a unique philosophy from reflections on their own observation and analysis of teaching. In ancient China, Confucius wrote in his *Analects*:

> If out of the four corners of a subject I have dealt thoroughly with one corner and the pupils cannot then find out the other three for themselves, then I do not explain any more.

Socrates was one of many Greek figures to scrutinise teaching, emphasising the importance of questioning and encouraging learners to think for themselves, while in Roman times Cicero and Quintilian analysed teaching methodology in considerable detail, and their analyses of, for example, what they judged to be successful lecturing, were very influential. In some mediaeval universities students who could demonstrate their teaching skill publicly might be accepted as members of a teachers' guild and given an early form of teaching qualification. Paris University students in the thirteenth century who could successfully argue a case before a panel of examiners would be granted the chancellor's licence to teach, and in Bologna candidates for a bachelor's degree had to have been adjudged competent to teach on the basis of lectures given to other students, in order to earn their degree.

In modern times the debate about passing judgement on teaching has been much more intricate and involved. The arguments about what constitutes effectiveness are described in the following section, but in a pluralist society there is not just one sole form of teaching which is regarded as 'effective'. Politicians sometimes have a simpler, more unclouded view of appraisal. The evolution of appraisal in England has been well documented by Hazlewood (1994), who studied its impact on the middle management of secondary schools.

The period before the Education Act 1986, which made appraisal a legal requirement, was dominated by a speech made by the Secretary of State at the time, Sir Keith (later Lord) Joseph, at the North of England conference in January 1984, when he said that appraisal was the means to 'remove unsatisfactory teachers from a profession where they can do much harm'. The aftershock of this widely reported statement, rapidly picked up by teacher unions, some of which threatened to boycott appraisal for nearly a decade thereafter, was so fierce that he mitigated what he said in later speeches, stating, at a conference in Chester in January 1985:

> To be fully effective an appraisal system would have to be complemented by better arrangements for the individual teacher's career development, including induction, in-service training. . . . [It is not the case that] I am only concerned with the need to dismiss the very small number of incompetent teachers who cannot be restored to adequate effectiveness. . . . I am concerned with the whole range of positive advantages that would flow from applying to the teaching force standards of management which have become common elsewhere.

In February 1985, the Permanent Secretary at the Department of Education and Science (DES) picked up the proposition that the DES wished to 'apply to the teaching force standards of management which have become common elsewhere'. He said he wanted soundly based decisions on such matters as staff deployment, in-service training, promotion and career development, as well as a framework for helping schools and colleges to improve standards, set goals and identify ways in which staff could achieve these communal goals (Hancock 1985).

It was the Education (No. 2). Act 1986 that made appraisal a legal requirement, and the Education (School Teachers' Pay and Conditions of Employment) Order 1987 that charged head teachers with 'supervising and participating in any arrangements within an agreed national framework, for the appraisal of performance of teachers who teach in the school'. Pilot projects were then set up in three urban and three rural local authorities, namely Croydon, Newcastle and Salford, and Cumbria, Somerset and Suffolk respectively. The county of Suffolk had already taken a lead in pioneering the introduction of appraisal (Suffolk Education Department 1985, 1987).

The next phase of evolution was strongly influenced by political issues. Despite a further assurance from the Minister of State, Angela Rumbold, in an address to the Industrial Society in February 1987 that sacking poor teachers was 'no longer in anyone's mind', two of the largest teaching unions, the National Union of Teachers and the National Association of Schoolmasters/Union of Women Teachers, refused to serve on the National Steering Group of the six LEA pilot projects for the whole of 1987, largely because a pay settlement had been imposed on the teaching profession. In the following year the Education Act 1988 began to dominate the attention of teachers and their representatives, as well as politicians.

The two Secretaries of State who were in office between 1989 and 1992 did not stay long. The first, John MacGregor, made a pragmatic decision that the introduction of the National Curriculum established by the Education Act 1988 should be the Government's highest priority. In a 1989 speech to the Secondary Heads' Association MacGregor had spoken positively of the potential that teacher appraisal had 'to strengthen and develop the quality of both teaching and of management in schools in ways that will lead to better education for pupils'. In September 1990, however, he decided that it should be voluntary.

His successor, Kenneth Clarke, came under attack from opposition parties for the delay, so in December 1990, he countermanded MacGregor's decision in a letter to local education authorities, stating that 'Regular appraisal will help to develop the professionalism of teachers and so improve the education of their pupils'. The Education (School Teacher Appraisal) Regulations 1991 embodied the law and the DES Circular 12/91 offered advice about how the exercise should be conducted.

In the same year alterations were made to the Teachers' Pay and Conditions of Service document so that heads were compelled to introduce appraisal and teachers were obliged to participate. Every teacher working for more than 0.4 of a full-time post had to be appraised between 1992 and 1994; the head teacher was responsible for appointing the appraiser; targets were to be set; the appraiser should, where possible, have management responsibility for the teacher concerned; there would also be observation of classroom teaching lasting an hour or more, with at least two observation periods.

In the wake of all the political arguments, the pressures from the introduction of the National Curriculum and other changes, and the repeated threats of boycott from some teacher unions (one union leader, Nigel de Gruchy of the NASUWT, asserting that 'professionalism amongst teachers runs the risk of being crushed once and for all'), appraisal was introduced in minimalist form. There was no national proforma, nor were grades awarded. Dismissal and promotion were not accorded a high profile, though the regulations did state that appraisal information 'may be taken into account . . . [in] the promotion, dismissal or discipline of school teachers' or in 'the use of any discretion in relation to pay'. Some latitude was, therefore, left to local interpretations of the regulations. Appraisal had become a legal requirement for the first time in England, and the various interpretations of the framework were amongst issues we wished to explore in the Lever-hulme Appraisal Project.

'EFFECTIVENESS' AND TEACHING

One assumption made by some advocates of appraisal is that what is 'effective' in teaching is uncontroversial and universal, that we can recognise it when we see it, or obversely, that we can identify ineffective teaching and take steps to make it more effective. At an individual level this is probably true, in that people do hold personal views about teaching and may defend them quite persuasively. However, the consensus which was thought to obtain in the nineteenth century, when training institutions were called 'Normal Schools' on the grounds that there was some commonly agreed 'norm' of good teaching, no longer exists. Pluralism in our society is illustrated by the many debates about so-called traditional and progressive teaching styles, teaching sign language to deaf children, the various methods of teaching reading, the systematic teaching of grammar in English lessons, the use of a predominantly oral approach in foreign language teaching and other classroom issues. In a pluralist society like our own, no single stereotype is supreme.

There is also the pressing question about what exactly is meant by the term 'effective'. For some it is strictly about what children learn, so the more factual knowledge they absorb, the more effective the teacher. Others would argue that incremental gains in pupils' learning are only one part of the story, and that the real test is approval by those competent to judge: pupils, heads, experienced observers, fellow teachers. There is no guaranteed agreement here either. Teachers may judge their fellows by their acceptability or otherwise as a staffroom colleague, and in many cases have not actually witnessed them teaching, whereas pupils see them every day in the classroom, but rarely in a social context. Heads are often dependent on indirect evidence such as plaudits or complaints from parents, the sound or absence of noise from their classroom, and more visible features, such as punctuality, dress, behaviour at staff meetings, report writing, or contribution to out-of-school activities.

There are also significant differences between primary and secondary schools. In open-plan primary schools, or where the head makes a practice of teaching alongside other teachers, professional competence or lack of it will be much more public than in a secondary school, where most teachers operate fairly privately inside their own box classroom. There are numerous significant differences between teaching and industrial processes. In teaching there is no single agreed outcome. In professional football the major objectives are to score goals and avoid conceding them; in many businesses the principal intention is to sell as many products as possible with maximum profits for shareholders and the minimum of complaints about poor quality from purchasers; doctors try to cure as many patients as they can, and dentists seek to reduce tooth decay and avoid the unnecessary loss of teeth in their patients.

Teachers on the other hand are often given numerous responsibilities. Some are specific and tangible, such as teaching basic skills in a range of fields in the primary phase or specialist subjects like mathematics, science and foreign languages at the secondary stage. Others are vague, such as 'developing responsible adults for the world of the twenty-first century', 'realising the full potential of every child', or fostering something as important but elusive as 'happiness'. Since children are influenced by their families, their friends, other adults and the mass media, it is not easy to assign either credit or blame, should these more vague hopes materialise or fail to come about.

The notion of 'performance indicators' fits more easily in some fields of endeavour than in teaching. The football team which wins consistently, unless it resorts to underhand methods, has arguably been more successful than the one which loses regularly; sales figures, profits, number of products rejected during quality control, complaints from customers and volume of repairs needed under guarantee, are all valuable indicators of 'performance' or 'effectiveness' in the commercial world. Furthermore many professional skills can be produced to order. Ask a professional musician to play the violin, time an international sprinter over 100 metres, watch a glassblower for a few seconds, and the skills are immediately obvious and demonstrable. Teaching skill on the other hand is rarely so explosive. Much of it may be painstaking, for stayers rather than sprinters. The performer who can produce a single impressive lesson when observed may be less valuable and effective with a class of children over a whole year than the quieter, less extrovert teacher who is deeply interested in individuals, marks their work meticulously and sustains the effort over several months.

During the 1950s there was a considerable amount of energy devoted to seeking the ideal teacher stereotype. Teachers were rated by observers, tests were given, pupils were polled and heads were interrogated. An American writer, Barr (1961), summarised a massive amount of this work by concluding:

> Some teachers were preferred by administrators, some were liked by pupils, and some taught in classes where there were substantial pupil gains, and generally speaking these were not the same teachers. There is plenty of evidence to indicate that different practitioners observing the same teacher teach, or studying data about her, may arrive at very different evaluations of her; this observation is equally

true of the evaluation experts; starting with different approaches, and using different data-gathering devices, they, too, arrive at very different evaluations.

More recent classroom research, especially in the United States, has begun to claim a degree of consistency. Nate Gage (1978) in his book *The Scientific Basis of the Art of Teaching* argues that the majority of systematic studies of children in the early years of schooling now show that, so far as the development of basic skills in such fields as reading and arithmetic is concerned, teachers who teach in what many would call a 'formal' style, that is with more teacher direction, less pupil movement permitted and more testing of achievement, appear to obtain better test scores than those who adopt a 'progressive' approach with greater informality and more pupil decision making.

This sounds, on the surface at any rate, as if the quest for models of effectiveness is over. Urge everyone to teach this way, it could be argued, and reading and arithmetic competence will soar. Yet if one looks at many of the studies which try to relate what teachers do in the classroom to what pupils actually learn, the problem becomes clear immediately. Most research is based on tests of short-term memory, whereas many teachers have longer-term objectives. Thus the music teacher, hoping her pupils will enjoy and practise music throughout their lives, may well find herself formally assessed in terms of whether or not they know what a minim is, or can beat 4/4 time, which may or may not be related to lifelong interest.

The messages seem to be clear enough when one is considering the question of effective teaching: there is no single way of teaching well; many different styles find favour according to context and circumstances; there will be differences of opinion even amongst those highly experienced in the profession; effectiveness as a teacher extends beyond the boundaries of the classroom, so preparation and planning, pastoral care and relationships with others such as fellow teachers and parents must be taken into account. Systematic studies of teachers have often used short-term scores of what can be readily measured. In the appraisal of teachers a longer-term perspective must also be considered.

In the absence of hard empirical evidence about effective teaching, there is no easy solution to be discovered in the research literature, though certain findings and many of the procedures used by researchers will be of interest to those involved in teacher appraisal. There will, therefore, be a strong subjective element when judgements and decisions are made. In some cases it will be power and status, or intuition and whim, that determine what these should be, rather than research evidence or the rights and wrongs of any particular case.

In one school, not included in the present research, a checklist was devised with the item 'Teacher sticks to lesson plan' as a positive 'hurrah' criterion of effectiveness. It was the view of the head that it was desirable to keep to one's initial plan. Adhering closely to, or altering one's lesson plan is a perfectly legitimate topic for discussion after a teacher has been observed, but not solely in terms of it being *invariably* desirable, irrespective of circumstances, and simply because someone in authority has strong views on the matter.

The criteria by which teachers' effectiveness should be judged, therefore, is a crucial issue. Typically those passing an opinion on teachers' classroom competence will look at one or more of three aspects: the behaviour and experiences of pupils (whether what they are doing is worthwhile, whether they appear to be absorbed in their task or are misbehaving, the extent to which the task matches the pupils' ability and previous experiences); the behaviour of the teacher (professional skills such as the ability to explain new concepts, ask appropriate questions, manage the badly behaved, prepare lessons, organise a classroom, assess and monitor progress); and outcomes of teaching (what pupils appear to have learned, including the knowledge, skills, attitudes and values they acquire as a direct or indirect result of whatever the teacher has done). We shall return to the matter of classroom observation in Chapter 2.

SCHOOL ORGANISATION AND MANAGEMENT

One oblique way of discerning how schools are managed would be to take a particular policy and monitor its development. Hazlewood (1994) studied the introduction of appraisal in three different schools and found varying styles of implementation that often reflected the management style generally within the school. The structural shape of many organisations which have formal systems of appraisal, such as the Police, the Armed Forces, the BBC, the Civil Service and numerous businesses, is usually hierarchical, often a tall thin triangle, with a considerable distance between top and bottom members and numerous ranks in between. The requirement in the regulations that all teachers should be appraised by someone with management responsibility for them, presupposed a similar superior–subordinate hierarchy. Yet in their daily business many schools, especially small primary schools, try to place more emphasis on collegiality than on rank or status.

Teacher appraisal was introduced at a time when the teaching force was ageing. All Governments from 1950 to the late 1970s sought to reduce class sizes, extend the school leaving age and improve pupil-teacher ratios. This led to a doubling in size of the teaching force in a relatively short period of time. In England and Wales the number increased from 200,000 in the early 1950s to about 480,000 by the late 1970s. Around 1970 there were over 100,000 students training to be teachers, but the impact of falling pupil enrolments reduced this to some 30,000 by the mid-1980s. In Scotland in 1979 one-third of primary teachers were in their twenties. By 1984 this had fallen to one-fifth. By the early 1990s roughly two-thirds of all teachers were over the age of forty. Thus teacher appraisal was introduced to a mature rather than novice profession. Had mandatory appraisal been brought in during the late 1960s or early 1970s, schools would have had several new-comers in their twenties, fresh from initial training and the experience of being observed and assessed by their supervising tutors and teachers.

Recognising the increasing maturity of the profession many schools, both primary and secondary, tried to minimise the distance between senior and junior teachers. The structure was often akin to that of a cottage loaf, with a senior management group consisting of head, deputies and special post holders in primary schools, or heads of departments and year groups in secondary schools, and a larger group of mainstream classroom teachers. The introduction of greater formality seemed likely when schools which had never had a regular system of appraisal introduced one for the first time. Furthermore the devolution of some powers and cash resources, which had previously been con-trolled by local education authorities, to individual schools, had strengthened the powers of head teachers and governing bodies. There was a possibility that appraisal could become a management tool that would increase this potency.

In theory schools could have a number of ways of organising the appraisal of their staff. The regulations seem to require a *hierarchical* or *superior–subordinate* model. The most logical structure for appraisal in strictly hierarchical organisations is for each person in the school to be appraised by a superior. In a pyramid hierarchy each individual is appraised by the person holding the rank immediately above. In schools this would mean that teachers on the basic professional scale would be appraised by heads, deputies or holders of special responsibility payments in primary schools, depending on the size of the school, or by their head of department in secondary schools. In turn the middle managers would be appraised by the heads, who would be scrutinised by fellow heads from other schools, local authority advisers or inspectors. These, in their turn, would be subject to review by the chief adviser, who would be appraised by the Chief Education Officer.

Supporters of hierarchical approaches argue that it is logical in an organisation, as those who are in senior positions have *ipso facto* responsibility for those lower down. Furthermore, the senior people can then, as part of their duties, ensure follow-up and support after the appraisal is over. Critics believe that appraisal not only reifies and hardens hierarchies, but also makes many teachers the unwilling recipients of management directives, as they become compelled to implement policies with which they may not concur. The obverse of this model, a *subordinate–superior* pattern, would apply if, for example, the head of a school were to be appraised by the teachers on the staff.

A second model, *peer appraisal*, occurs when two people of equal rank, such as two basic scale teachers, two deputy heads, or two heads of department, appraise each other. This is sometimes seen as a soft option. It is believed that co-equal pairs will simply confirm each other's practices, engage in mutual congratulation. Supporters of peer appraisal, however, argue that observations from a peer can effect change if they are credible with the recipient, and that collegial appraisal need not be synonymous with lack of bite.

A third possibility, *external appraisal*, is sometimes supported as a tougher, more objective approach, untainted by internal convention, an antidote to the received, and possibly ineffective, practices into which teachers may have become socialised. In order to give a broader perspective, it is often argued that outsiders must be brought in, otherwise fresh practices will never be introduced following an appraisal exercise. Critics of external appraisal argue that outsiders cannot always understand the nuances of school and classroom life, can make little impact, as they have no roots in the school, and may simply become bureaucrats, fulfilling an obligation.

State or regional inspectors who only exist to give grades are viewed with suspicion and mistrust. In France, for example, both the head and an academy inspector award an annual mark, the inspector's grade being based on the observation of a single lesson and a short subsequent conversation. In Germany, where teachers are civil servants and where there is some variety in the various Länder, a report on each teacher is usually drawn up by the head, and inspectors frequently countersign these without careful scrutiny. German inspectors have tended to concentrate on the problems of changing pupil numbers and redeployment. They tend, therefore, to see only the best and poorest teachers or those being moved to another school.

A fourth possibility is that of *self-appraisal*. Some believe that ultimately teachers must make their own decision to do things differently. Self-appraisal, it is argued, is even more important than analysis by others. Before teacher appraisal became a political and legal issue there was some development in many schools and local authorities of self-appraisal schemes, whereby individual teachers, departments and the whole school took stock of what they were trying to accomplish and how effectively they were achieving their objectives. Frequently these schemes were pioneered by local authorities, such as Oxfordshire, which asked schools to write a self-appraisal. Solihull produced a self-review checklist for its schools, and the Inner London Education Authority published three versions of a pamphlet entitled *Keeping the School Under Review*, for primary, secondary and special schools, consisting of responses to checklists under several headings. The outlines of these had often been worked out by groups of heads, teachers and administrators.

The appraisal of teachers by anyone other than educational professionals is a contentious matter. Though rare, it is possible for *lay appraisal* to take place, with pupils, parents, governors or taxpayers being asked to comment on the quality of teaching in a school. School inspections by the Office for Standards in Education began to use lay inspectors in 1992. *Pupil appraisal* is not especially common, though the research literature shows an astonishing consistency in the way pupils evaluate teaching (Wragg 1993). Pupils prefer teachers who are slightly strict, enthusiastic, interested in them as individuals and fair in their use of rewards and punishments, and who use humour which is not sarcastic. Evaluative questionnaires, staff–pupil committees and end-of-year discussions about courses are not unknown, though systematic student evaluation of this kind is more common in further and higher education than in schools.

There are many other aspects to the organisation and management of appraisal. The implementation of appraisal will often reflect the personality, beliefs and ideologies of the leaders in the school, especially the head teacher, who is a key player. Indeed, in a number of local authorities there was an insistence that head teachers should be appraised first, and that no other teacher should be considered until the head's appraisal had taken place. It would have been an attractive proposition to study the appraisal of heads themselves in more detail, but in the present research we decided to give highest priority to teachers and classroom processes, on the grounds that the direct improvement of classroom teaching is supposed to be a central precept of appraisal.

Among several important issues, not only with teachers' unions, but also with individual teachers, especially if redundancies or promotions were under consideration, was whether there should be an open or closed system. The arguments about open and closed reporting systems have been well rehearsed. In open appraisal the people being appraised see the report written about them. The arguments in favour of the open reporting system include: that people fantasise about reports they have not seen; that those in positions of authority acquire even more unchecked power if they can write secret reports; that the information recorded may be inaccurate and so the subject of the report should be allowed to check it or comment on it; that part of the value of an appraisal is that it can be discussed openly with a view to improving future practice; and that, especially with a mature teaching profession, an open system encourages trust and mutual respect.

Supporters of a closed reporting system, under which the report is secret, argue that it allows those conducting a review to be frank and honest and to pull no punches, rather than being mealy-mouthed and diplomatic; and that teachers could easily be demoralised if confronted with too blunt an appraisal, especially as the job is so demanding that all who practise it are bound to fall short of what they and others would like to achieve.

There was considerable discussion about whether a written appraisal 'belonged' to the teacher, the school or the local authority and who could have access to the report. In practice a restricted model was adopted, with teachers able to see what was written about them and limits on who else could see it and what would be done with any notes made by appraisers. As we shall report in Chapter 4, our national survey revealed a range of practices distinctly wider than what was prescribed.

STUDIES OF APPRAISAL

The subject of appraisal is a wide one to cover. It can embrace such disparate if related issues as the roles and duties of teachers, the management and organisation of schools, classroom behaviour, personality, group dynamics and interpersonal relationships, pupil learning, rewards and incentives, the relationship between process and outcome, classroom observation, and numerous other topics. There is a great deal of research into these various fields, but relatively little investigation with the act of appraisal as a major focus. It is not possible here to give an extended account of research into appraisal, so this is but a brief mention of a few key studies. Turner and Clift (1985, 1988), Lokan and McKenzie (1989), Haertel (1991), Hazlewood (1994), Medley and Shannon (1994) and Stufflebeam and Nevo (1994), have all written reviews of research into teacher appraisal.

The perceived purposes of appraisal have been studied by a number of investigators. An American study by Wood and Pohland (1983) identified four major purposes: to help teachers improve their performance, to determine the appointment of probationer teachers, to decide on staff being offered tenured posts, and to dismiss incompetent teachers. James and Newman (1985) conducted a survey of forty-six secondary schools in the Midlands and South-west of England, and found that the three most popular purposes given were: promotion of staff development, performance review and planning career development.

Turner and Clift (1985) analysed fifty-six appraisal schemes and found that most concentrated on formative matters, such as the identification of staff strengths and weaknesses, needs and interests.

An Australian study by Dimmock (1987) discovered that professional development took precedence over promotional eligibility as opportunities for promotion declined. Her Majesty's Inspectorate (HMI 1989) analysed the six national pilot projects run by rural and urban local authorities between 1987 and 1989. They described the two predominant aims as 'facilitation of the professional growth of the individual teacher and to effect institutional improvement'. This is not unlike the aims and reasons sometimes reported in other fields, and Lefton (1986), analysing the purposes of appraisal schemes in industry, concluded that the main emphasis was on understanding the nature and quality of one's own work and improving it.

One of the problems faced by researchers is the many and varied roles that teachers are asked to play. Scriven (1988) and Shulman (1991) have investigated the evaluation of teachers' fulfilment of their various duties. In a single day some teachers may be communicators of information, assessors, managers, social workers, jailers even, if they have to keep in school those who only attend reluctantly. Teachers may deploy different skills in each of these roles, even if there is a common core of competency, and some may be more effective in one role than in another.

Hoyle (1972) is one of several writers to explore a range of restricted and extended professional traits in teachers. Restricted traits include a sharp focus on the teacher's own classroom and on personal practice, whereas extended traits involve taking a wider perspective that embraces school, community and society, and an ability to link a body of theory with practice. Stenhouse (1975) criticised this view for failing to include autonomy and the ability to scrutinise critically and question the teacher's own teaching.

Some investigators have considered the actual process of teacher appraisal. In earlier studies, before appraisal was mandatory, Lloyd (1981) reported that primary heads were reluctant to make formal observations of their teacher colleagues, and Turner and Clift (1985) found that few schools made use of classroom observation in their appraisal schemes. Montgomery (1984) reported an improvement in teacher performance following the use of an approach to appraisal which involved stressing positive aspects of teaching, as well as the management, monitoring and maintenance of class control.

In later studies Bradley et al. (1989) evaluated the six local authority pilot studies. They found that teachers rated their appraisal interview most highly and the classroom observation element as least important out of four elements surveyed, the other two being initial discussion, in second place, and self-appraisal, in third place. Powney (1991) investigated the process as perceived by eighty-six teachers in middle management roles, using the same approach and some of the same questions as Bradley. His results were similar, though not identical to those of Bradley's enquiry, and the appraisal interview was again highly rated, with classroom observation in fourth place.

Some researchers have looked at the tools and methods used in appraisal. In the United States a great deal of attention has been paid to the assessment of teachers' subject and pedagogical knowledge, often under the generic heading of 'teacher competency tests'. The National Teacher Examination was one of the most widely employed, but there were criticisms of the multiple-choice pencil-and-paper nature of many of these and their lack of relevance both to classroom competence and to the teaching of specific subjects or age groups, as they were often general in nature.

Bird (1990) and Shulman (1991) have reported on the use of teacher portfolios, which contain examples of teachers' own home-made materials, lesson schemes, information about pupils' achievements and possibly audio or videotapes of lessons. The teacher's package is then scrutinised by an evaluation committee. This practice is common at the beginner stage, but less usual with experienced practitioners.

Research into appraisal is sparse in a number of areas. Few studies have followed up teachers at a later date to see what the longer-term outcomes might be. Classroom observation is a wide field with thousands of studies, but there has been relatively little enquiry into its place and effects in the context of appraisal. The topic of classroom observation is expounded more fully in Chapter 2. Despite its apparent lower standing with teachers in some research reported above, we decided to make it the central focus of our research, on the grounds that, if teaching is to 'improve', however that may be defined, as a result of appraisal, then teachers should behave differently, and 'more effectively', after appraisal has taken place. It seemed worthwhile, therefore, both to use classroom observation ourselves, in order to study teachers before, during and after appraisal, and also to investigate what happened in the classroom observation phases of appraisal, since two observations were required in the procedures set out by the DES.

THE PRESENT RESEARCH

There are several levels at which teacher appraisal might be studied. At the international level the evaluation of teaching competence is an important issue in many countries. At the national level each country that has a national scheme has its own history and rationale for whatever it does, even if responsibility is devolved to local or school level. In the present research programme this macro-scale was not something that we investigated, though we have reported on the evolution of appraisal in England earlier in this chapter.

With the principal focus on the observation of classroom processes, it was decided to investigate this at three levels. The first was national in scope, but at regional level. Since local education authorities were charged with responsibility for training appraisers and overseeing the process, we decided to survey all English LEAs to elicit how they approached training in classroom observation. We wrote to all 109 LEAs and obtained a 100 per cent response. This information provided a framework within which to locate the other two levels. This enquiry is referred to as Study 1 and is described in detail in Chapter 3.

The second investigation was also national in scope, but at individual teacher level. We wanted to see how the process was implemented in individual classrooms in primary and secondary schools, what appraisers and appraisees actually did and thought, how they perceived the process and its outcomes and the extent to which they followed, adapted or subverted the regulations and recommended procedures. Hence the large-scale questionnaire survey of 1,137 teachers and appraisers in schools throughout England reported in Chapter 4 and referred to as Study 2.

In order to flesh out the living processes and distil the essence of what happened, we decided to use a mixture of quantitative and qualitative approaches to data gathering and analysis. Originally it was intended to undertake thirty intensive case studies of teachers over the whole two-year period, but in practice twenty-nine were completed. This involved monitoring the teachers over a period of months, observing lessons and witnessing appraisal interviews, feedback sessions after lessons and even, on many occasions, sitting in on the lessons with the appraiser watching the appraisee, a risky business, as the presence of two additional adults might have affected the process, something we discuss later in the book. This set of intensive case studies constituted Study 3 and the findings are reported in Chapters 5, 6, 7 and 8.

The research was therefore undertaken within a number of research traditions, with no single ideology predominating. Our principal purpose was to investigate, describe and analyse, without too many a priori assumptions. Of course, like anyone else, we did have our individual and collective hunches, presumptions and prejudices, but we did not wish to allow consciously for any particular one of these to predominate. The quantitative and qualitative analyses are rooted in traditions described in Chapter 2, and the research was hypothesis-generating, rather than hypothesis-testing.

The blend of survey, observation, interview and case study allowed us to ground such theory as might be elicited in the data themselves. It also permitted a broader platform for explanation. As Chapter 4 will describe, our national survey was eventually to find that teachers were split roughly evenly on the question of whether they had altered their classroom practice as a consequence of being appraised. We were able to explore and illuminate the individual case detail of this overarching finding with examples from interviews, lessons and interactions of teachers we had monitored over several months.

Chapter 2

Classroom observation

At the very heart of teacher appraisal should lie the notion of change. That is because no teacher is perfect, so all teachers can, in theory at any rate, improve their practice. In order to make what they do in classrooms more effective, teachers must change their own behaviour. In turn, for pupils to learn more effectively, they too must alter their behaviour, whether directly as a result of what the teacher does, or of their own free will. Without change there could be no improvement, everything would remain the same.

That said, part of any process of change is the necessity to retain certain aspects of practice that are thought to be effective, for no teacher can change every single aspect of teaching every single day and remain sane. The logical consequence of this line of argument is the need for thoughtful scrutiny of what goes on in the classroom, certainly by teachers themselves, possibly by others. There was a requirement in the national appraisal scheme that teachers should be observed by their appraiser during appraisal for at least an hour in all, and that this should be achieved through at least two periods of observation.

Although in some of the research studies described in Chapter 1 teachers had placed classroom observation lower in importance than an interview with their appraiser, we decided none the less to make the classroom observation element of appraisal our central focus, since it had in any case become a requirement. We addressed a number of related questions. How were appraisers trained to undertake classroom observation? How was it conducted? What approaches did appraisers use? What was the reaction of teachers to it? Did they behave differently when their appraiser was present? What did teacher and appraiser discuss after the observation, and when did the discussion take place? What resolutions ensued from the observation? Did teachers feel immediately after and long after the observation that they had changed their classroom behaviour as a result? In this chapter we discuss the different approaches to and practices in classroom observation.

CLASSROOM LIFE

Classrooms can be extraordinarily busy places with hundreds of events taking place in a single day: teachers ask children questions, new concepts are explained, pupils talk to each other, some of those who misbehave are reprimanded, others are ignored. The various methods of classroom observation and the issues surrounding them have been summarised by a number of researchers, including, specifically in the context of appraisal, Medley *et al.* (1984), Evertson and Burry (1989) and Wragg (1994).

The nature and frequency of classroom interaction have been the subjects of enquiry by several investigators. Jackson (1968) reported a study in which it was found that primary teachers engaged in as many as 1,000 such interpersonal exchanges in a single day. Were this pattern repeated, there would be 5,000 interactions per week, 200,000 in a year, millions in a professional career. In a study of videotapes by Adams and Biddle (1970), there was a change in 'activity' every five to eighteen seconds and there was an average each lesson of 174 changes in who talked and who listened. One of the difficulties of observing teaching as part of an appraisal is that the job of teaching can be as busy as that of a telephonist or a sales assistant during peak shopping hours.

Prior to the advent of appraisal, and also the introduction in 1993 of a formal cycle of inspection by the Office for Standards in Education, in many classrooms the craft of teaching had been a private affair. Some teachers spend forty years in the classroom, teaching maybe 50,000 lessons or more, of which only a tiny number are witnessed by other adults. It is often difficult to obtain detailed accounts of lessons, because teachers are so busy with the running of the lesson that there is little time for them to make notes or photographic, video or sound records. By contrast practice in surgery is a much more open matter. The developers of transplant and bypass surgery took it for granted that successful new techniques must be witnessed by, and disseminated to others, through their actual presence at operations, or by means of videotapes and the written and spoken word.

During the 1980s and 1990s classroom observation became far more common than it once was. The advent of systematic teacher appraisal and lesson evaluation, the greater emphasis on developing the professional skills of initial trainees, or honing those of experienced practitioners, the increased interest in classroom processes by curriculum developers, all of these have led to more scrutiny of what actually goes on during teaching and learning. It is much more likely now, compared with twenty or even ten years ago, that one person will sit in and observe the lessons of another as part of a teacher appraisal exercise, or that a teacher supervising a student will be expected to make a more detailed analysis of lessons observed than might once have been the case.

There is now a large constituency of people who need to be aware of what is involved in lesson observation or how it might be conducted. These include teachers, heads, student teachers, inspectors, appraisers, researchers, curriculum developers and anyone else who ever sits in on a lesson with a serious purpose. Observation was presumably made a requirement on the assumption that, skilfully handled, it may benefit both the observer and the person observed, serving to inform and enhance the professional skill of both people. Badly handled, however, it may become counter-productive, at its worst arousing hostility, resistance and suspicion. Hence the emphasis placed on positive personal relationships by local education authorities, as will be described in Chapter 3.

PURPOSE AND FOCUS OF OBSERVATION

Many forms of classroom observation have been developed, partly because of the manifold contexts in which lessons may be observed and analysed: a primary teacher being appraised by the deputy head who comes for the morning to look at language and number work; a secondary science teacher watched by the head of department during a one-and-a-half hour laboratory session as part of the school's appraisal exercise; a student on teaching practice seen by a supervising teacher or tutor; a maths lesson watched by a local authority inspector conducting a review of mathematics teaching in the local authority; a class of seven year olds observed by a teacher who is also a textbook writer preparing a series of gymnastics cards for young children; a researcher studying teachers' questioning techniques watching a history class, noting down the questions asked by the teacher and the responses obtained.

In each case the observer is watching lessons, yet the purposes and approaches are diverse. The physical education textbook writer might focus specifically on pupils to see how effectively they coped with the movements the teacher was encouraging, whereas the appraisers might give much of their time to the teacher's questioning, explaining and class management, the nature of the tasks set, and pupils' learning. One might make detailed notes, take photographs, or record the whole process on video. Another might write little down, but rather reflect on what could be discussed with the teacher later.

During classroom observation appraisers need to decide what should be the focus of attention. So much happens in classrooms that any task or event, even apparently simple ones, could be the subject of pages of notes and hours of discussion. The ecology of many schools can be extremely rich and full. The main constituents of them are teachers, pupils, buildings and materials, each offering many opportunities for close study.

Most under scrutiny are teachers, the paid professionals, expected in law to act as a thoughtful parent might, to be *in loco parentis*. In order to fulfil what the law calls the 'duty of care', therefore, teachers are given certain powers as well as responsibilities. They may from time to time, for example, give punishments to children who do not behave properly, or take action to prevent injury to a pupil. Teachers' own backgrounds, personalities, interests, knowledge, intentions and preferences will influence much of what occurs, such as the strategies they employ in different situations, the timing and nature of their questions and explanations, their responses to misbehaviour, indeed what they perceive to be deviant behaviour.

As was described in Chapter 1 teachers are often asked to fill a variety of roles and carry out various duties. These can include the traditional one of *transmitter of knowledge*, but also others such as *counsellor* (advising pupils about careers, aspirations or problems), *social worker* (dealing with family issues), *assessor* (marking children's work, giving tests, writing reports) and *manager* (looking after resources, organising groups, setting goals). As classroom life can be busy and rapidly changing, some teachers may even play several of these roles within the same lesson.

During lessons pupils also take on different roles, sometimes in accordance with what is expected and required by the teacher, on other occasions according to their own choice. They are expected to be *learners* of knowledge, skills, attitudes or behaviour. From time to time they may also be *deviants* (misbehaving, not doing what the teacher has asked), *jokers* (laughing, creating humour which may lighten or heighten tension), *collaborators* (working closely with others as members of a team or group), *investigators* (enquiring, problem solving, exploring, testing hypotheses), or even *servants* (moving furniture, carrying and setting up equipment). As was the case with teachers, their backgrounds, personalities, interests, prior knowledge, intentions and preferences will influence much of what occurs. Furthermore they will be conscious of other members of their peer group, especially in adolescence, and this too may form a powerful influence on what they do.

In institutions like schools and colleges, teaching usually takes place in rectangular shaped classrooms, with furniture arranged in rows, or with pupils sitting around tables. This may not be the case in subjects like physical education or dance, however, where learning may take place in an open space, or even outdoors. Open plan areas in schools may be L-shaped, circular or constructed with some quite irregular arrangement of space. Teachers have usually had little say in the design of buildings, unless they are in a new school, so buildings often influence styles of teaching, rather than the other way round.

Despite this exclusion from the design of their classroom shape, teachers do have more choice over the use of space. Teacher A may have a room with desks laid out in rows, Teacher B may prefer groups working around tables, and Teacher C may do so much practical work and movement that neither of these arrangements is appropriate. One primary age child may spend each day as a member of a large group of eighty pupils of similar age in a three-class open plan area, another may be in a small village school built in the last century with twenty pupils of different ages. All these ecological factors, some beyond the direct control of teacher or pupil, can affect the nature of classroom interaction.

The materials which children and teachers use can be extremely varied. Herbert (1967) spent two years studying a school which had been specially designed for team teaching, and he found that the learning media being used included eleven forms of book and printed matter (e.g. textbooks, worksheets, periodicals), nine forms of reference book (dictionary, encyclopaedia, atlas, almanac), five kinds of test (textbook test, teacher-made test, standardised test), nine sorts of contentless media (paper, paint, crayon, clay), eleven forms of flat graphics (charts, posters, diagrams, magnetic boards), nine types of three-dimensional media (globes, models, toys, mobiles), and thirteen kinds of visual or audio-visual equipment (overhead projector, slide viewer, television monitor, micro-projector). Nowadays he might have found even more additions, such as micro-computers, word processors, and interactive technology. These learning media can influence teaching and learning styles, so classroom observation may focus exclusively on their use.

APPROACHES TO OBSERVATION

The several and varied purposes of classroom observation have produced many different styles of observation. Some are drawn from traditions which involve systematic measurement and careful control of the conditions under which observations take place. Others are based on the approaches developed by anthropologists studying tribal life. Some observers may be influenced by the context in which the lesson takes place, for example, the age group of the pupils, while others may concentrate on some aspect of the teaching of one particular subject, like science or English. This in turn may influence their preferred approach. The origins of many of the common approaches to classroom observation lie in the earlier part of the twentieth century.

Quantitative methods

During the early to middle period of the twentieth century educational research came strongly under the influence of the nineteenth century French philosopher Comte, who argued that human thought proceeded through three stages: the theological, the metaphysical and finally the positive or 'scientific'. There was a strong belief that systematic observation and analysis could lead to social behaviour being predicted, as relationships between one event and another became clear. An example of subsequent systematic quantitative analysis is the study by Stevens in 1912 of 100 random observations of lessons in which the focus was on the questions teachers asked in a variety of subjects. It was found that teachers talked for about 64 per cent of the time and pupils for 36 per cent, and that two to four 'lower level' (i.e. largely requiring the recall of information) questions were asked each minute.

The pattern of early quantitative work was set in the United States at a time when the 'recitation lesson', that is the formal presentation of information by the teacher standing at the front of the class, was standard. In the 1920s and 1930s there was a great deal of interest in 'attentiveness', and observers would sit at the front of the class scanning faces to see how many pupils were arguably paying attention to the teacher. This allowed profiles to be drawn up showing the high and low points of the lesson, which could be related to content matter, test scores or other measures to see when the teacher seemed to be most effective. These were crude studies, but they laid the foundation for later work.

It soon became apparent that talk was an important element of classroom life, and classroom observation switched strongly to focusing on what teachers and pupils said to each other. Early investigators concentrated on devising category systems to elicit what kind of talk the teacher engaged in, and Withall (1949) drew up a seven-category system consisting of three 'learner-centred' (reassuring, accepting, questioning) and three 'teacher-centred' (directing, reproving, justifying own actions) categories, and one 'neutral' (repetition, administration) category. Already these category systems began to take on their own values, favouring certain acts by the teacher and deprecating others, and much of the work published was highly tendentious.

The development of category systems and systematic schedules was promoted by Bales (1950), who conducted most of his own observations on small groups of adults. He devised a twelve-category system, which appealed to investigators studying classrooms, because it had such elements as 'agrees', 'gives opinion', 'asks for suggestion', and 'shows antagonism'. Each member of the group under observation was given a code number, the observers were trained until they reached a high level of agreement about which category they would assign to events, and what happened was noted down in sequence. All these became standard practice in later quantitative observation. His finding that ten to twenty different events might occur within a single minute of discussion influenced subsequent work by researchers such as Flanders (1970), who devised a ten-category system to record what was happening every three seconds.

Category and rating systems have often been divided into two classes, known as *high inference* and *low inference* measures. With high inference categories the observer has to exercise much more subjective judgement. Common examples include rating scales used by investigators such as Ryans (1960) who devised pairs of polar opposite teacher characteristics, like warm/aloof, stimulating/dull, businesslike/slipshod. The observer had to use subjective judgement to place each teacher somewhere along a five- or seven-point continuum. Low inference measures require the observer to make a decision about whether or not some piece of behaviour occurred, using categories like 'teacher reprimands pupil' or 'pupil asks question'. These are sometimes referred to as 'objective', though they are clearly not, as personal judgement is still required, and indeed the very selection of such categories can be a highly subjective process.

Quantitative observation schedules may well be informed by different ideologies. Some approaches may be influenced by the behaviourist learning theories of Skinner (1954). An appraiser using this approach might first collect baseline data, for example, how many instances of misbehaviour occur in a lesson. Next the teacher being appraised might be advised to use more reinforcement or recognition of behaviour of which she approved, so the observer might deploy categories like 'teacher praises good behaviour'.

Finally the observer might collect follow-up data to see if the incidence of pupil misbehaviour had declined. As an appraisal this would be quite a strong controlling use of observation, and those who favour qualitative approaches would criticise it for being self-fulfilling, in that the mere reduction in the frequency of pupil misbehaviour may not address the real problem. For example, a child may fidget because the lesson is boring. Reducing or eliminating fidgeting does not necessarily improve the quality of teaching and learning. Behaviourism is not the only ideology to be used by supporters of quantitative methods, nor does quantification inevitably lead to a controlling style of appraisal.

Other forms of quantitative methodology include *quality rating* and *rank ordering*. Quality rating, often using a scale from A down to E, has often been used in the appraisal of student and novice teachers, or by Her Majesty's Inspectorate. Rank ordering is rarer, but would be used, for example, if a school were looking for likely recipients of merit payments based on observed lessons, in which case the 'best', 'next best' teacher and so on, would be noted, according to whatever criteria were being employed.

The conviction at the centre of quantitative approaches is that the effectiveness of teachers can be improved if a body of knowledge is established which shows that they should do more of some things and less of others. Though this has an appeal, it has to be said that there are relatively few research findings that can be said to be of wide general concern. There are some quantitative studies that are of general interest, such as the one by Jackson (1968) which found that teachers can engage in over 1,000 interpersonal transactions in a single day.

Other enquiries that considered specific aspects of teaching may be of interest to teachers, such as research by Brophy (1981) showing infrequent and haphazard use of praise, by Deutsch (1960) revealing that some inner-city teachers in American schools had spent up to 75 per cent of their day trying to keep order, by Rowe (1972) who found that teachers allowed on average one second between a pupil answer and their own statement, or by Wragg (1993), showing that 57 per cent of primary teachers' questions were related to class management, 35 per cent to information recall and only 8 per cent required a higher order of thinking. Although, in the process of teacher appraisal, quantitative observation data from other people's research findings may offer relatively little that is generalisable to the classrooms of individual teachers, the methods used may be of interest to individuals wanting feedback about their own teaching.

Qualitative methods

Interesting insights from quantitative observation schedules fall far short of telling the whole story of classroom life. Consider the following statement: 'Haven't you started yet?' An analysis of the lesson that concentrated entirely on event counting might note that this was one of thirty-seven questions asked by the teacher during the lesson observed. In a category system it might be coded as 'managerial', or 'addressed to individual pupil'.

However, the teacher may have uttered the words in a loud and rough voice, following it up with a punishment. This might provoke a reaction different from the one that would have followed a gentle chiding voice. If the pupil was a sensitive child, then one more reprimand might be the final straw. Such context factors may override in importance the fact that the teacher's statement was the seventh of fifteen managerial questions.

Approaches to classroom observation that concentrate on such factors as the significance, meaning, impact and individual or collective interpretation of events, are rooted in a different tradition from that of the positivists described above. One strong influence is the work of cultural and social anthropologists, and this style of observation is often given the generic label 'ethnographic'. It attempts to address the problem that most people find when observing in a classroom, namely that it is such a familiar location. Most observers have themselves spent some 15,000 hours in classrooms as pupils. Indeed most appraisers are themselves teachers. It is easy to look straight through events that might hold significance, because they are taken for granted.

There are several influences on ethnographic approaches to observation. Mead (1934) advocated the study of the symbols that are part of the interaction between people, their language, appearance and gestures. Some observers have taken a particular political or ideological stance. For example, Sharp and Green (1975) studied an infant school in a working class area from a Marxist perspective. Their conclusion that teachers act as an agent of social control on behalf of a capitalist society is then to some considerable extent pre-determined by their initial assumptions.

Bryman (1988) has summarised the main influences on qualitative approaches under five headings: *phenomenology* (influenced by the German philosopher Husserl, which concentrates on how we explain the phenomena in the world around us); *symbolic interactionism* (as described above); *verstehen* (the German word for 'understanding', used by the German sociologist Weber (1947) to describe the way in which particular acts and intentions are understood, for example, the teacher's use of different voices); *naturalism* (studying natural rather than experimental settings); and *ethogenics* (careful analysis of sequences of events, without quantifying them, to understand how successive episodes interlock).

Many of these qualitative approaches stem from the methods used by anthropologists. They must detach themselves from the familiar and, like intelligent Martians, probe behind the surface of what happens. If they arrive in some location where their assignment is to study the life in a particular tribe, they may initially understand little of what they see. However, by building up a picture of tribal life, noting down certain events, interviewing members to hear their explanations, and matching one happening or explanation against others, they can soon establish a framework of understanding. A dance that appeared meaningless at first can be seen later as part of a series of rituals connected with fertility and growth, related to the planting of crops, the harvest, beliefs about the weather in general, or rainfall in particular.

Other approaches

Another perspective on classroom life comes from ethologists who have studied animal behaviour. Many colonies of creatures show interesting patterns of behaviour when younger and older members are together. Indeed, teaching and learning can often be witnessed, even though they may not take place in such formal institutions as schools. Certainly different kinds of social learning – knowing your place, respecting your elders, staying on your own territory and not straying on to that of others – take place regularly in animal communities.

The seminal book by Lorenz (1966) *On Aggression* looks at the manifestations of aggression, like bared teeth, or the bristling mane, to see how and why they occur. Pupils can sometimes be aggressive with each other, pushing and shoving often taking place when children are jostling for facilities, perhaps trying to get to the micro-computer or the science experiment first. This raises questions such as whether boys or girls as a group, or certain individual pupils, are more aggressive when it comes to securing equipment, materials or the teacher's attention, and how, if at all, the teacher responds.

The establishment and maintenance of dominance amongst animals has also been studied by ethologists, and this too has some relevance to classroom life, especially if one is studying class management. Infant teachers, who normally crouch alongside children when monitoring or discussing their work in order to minimise the height difference and reduce anxiety, may suddenly switch to maximising the difference in their height by towering over them if they are telling them off for misbehaviour.

The spoken word has often been a central focus during classroom observation, and it can be enhanced by variations in voice, when teachers use a loud or soft tone, emphasise certain words, or change from a high to a low pitch. However, although a great deal of attention has been given to what teachers and pupils say to each other in the classroom, there are important non-verbal aspects of classroom life that observers will often find of interest. Teachers often amplify an explanation with gestures, pointing a finger or spreading their arms, to make a point more clearly or emphatically. Another important element can be movement, when the teacher walks towards somebody or away from a group. Body language generally signals important messages, as when the teacher leans casually on the desk, or when a new teacher underlines his anxiety and uncertainty by holding his hands tightly under his armpits.

In research, though far less frequently during appraisal, observers wanting to conduct a detailed analysis of what is said in the classroom sometimes record and transcribe lessons. Although a written transcript is time-consuming to compile and leaves out a great deal of what happened, especially the non-verbal aspects, it does allow much more detailed analysis of events than many other methods. Time constraints usually rule this out in teacher appraisal.

OBSERVERS

When someone new comes into a classroom to observe, then the very presence of an additional adult who is not normally present may itself influence what happens. It is not easy to say exactly how things might change, because this will depend on many factors, such as how common it is for visitors to arrive in the room, the status of the person concerned, and even such matters as the age, dress and sex of the observer. The class of a student teacher might be unusually well-behaved if the head teacher arrives to observe; a group of adolescent boys or girls in a single sex school might react differently depending on whether the observer is of the same sex as themselves. A class in an open plan school well used to parent helpers, numerous unannounced visitors and the presence in the same area of more than one teacher, would be less likely to change its behaviour radically than a class in a school which rarely saw any strangers.

There have been studies of the effects of observers on classroom interaction. Samph (1976) planted microphones in classrooms and then sent observers either announced or unexpected some weeks later. He found that teachers made more use of questions and praise and were more likely to accept pupils' ideas when someone was present. Teachers and indeed pupils may attempt to provide what they think the visitor expects, and this will vary according to the impression or stereotype they form of the observer concerned. They may be irritated or excited by a visitor and behave differently from normal, hence the need for observers, where possible, to study a series of lessons rather than a single one.

Appraisers are usually members of the school, often teachers in it. There are differences between what in the literature on classroom observation are called *participant* and *non-participant* observers. Insiders can sometimes find it difficult to detach themselves from their own prior knowledge, beliefs, commitments and prejudices about a place they know very well and have seen every day for years. On the other hand they often understand the significance of events that might elude strangers. Outsiders are sometimes able to be more emotionally detached about what they see, but may occasionally be bewildered by it, or even misinterpret events through their unfamiliarity.

Non-participant observers usually need to look beneath the surface of what happens, and discuss their perceptions with others, including the teacher. It is equally valuable for participant observers to shed the worst of their prejudgements, approach observation with an open mind and ask themselves what, if anything, might get in the way of their seeing things objectively. Even matters such as dress and positioning may matter. Minimising the intrusion, not overplaying the 'status' card, making contact with the teacher beforehand, and clarifying the purpose and likely outcome of the observation, are all matters for consideration when an insider observes a lesson, if what is seen is to be as natural and unstaged as possible.

Observers have some choices about what sort of record should be kept of a lesson, and some may choose to keep none at all. Many will at least keep notes, and the assumption, in the appraisal exercise we were studying, was that these would be destroyed after post-lesson discussions had taken place. There are other possibilities. Small compact video cameras and sound cassettes offer further options beyond written notes, though teachers and pupils who are not used to being video-recorded may be inhibited by their use.

There were clearly many issues to be considered in the observation of teachers' lessons during appraisal: different traditions, various methods and approaches, numerous possible aspects of classroom life on which to focus, several means of recording events and matters for discussion, the decision to be a participant in the lesson or not, and many options for post-lesson discussion and feedback, or target setting. These were amongst the issues the present research project wished to explore further, and the research findings and conclusions are described in the following chapters.

Chapter 3

The role of the
local education authority

Local education authorities (LEAs) underwent dramatic changes in the late 1980s and early 1990s. At the same time that the role of local and regional Government was being discussed within the European Community and other international bodies under the heading of 'subsidiarity', that is the level at which decisions are taken, successive Education Acts in the British Parliament changed the very nature of LEAs. Radical changes in schools forced LEAs to modify their functions and purposes, as well as their relationships with schools and their governors.

The Education Act 1986 ensured that each school had a governing body with certain powers over the conduct and curriculum in schools. The Education Act 1988, which the then Secretary of State, Kenneth Baker, described as devolving power from the hub of the wheel to the rim of the wheel, actually moved power away from LEAs and towards both the schools and the Government itself. The Government acquired control over the curriculum and testing, while school governors took on many of the powers of hire and fire previously exercised by LEAs, though LEAs still remained, technically, the employer. The establishment, in the Education Act 1988, of grant-maintained schools which had opted out of local authority control, and city technology colleges, which also received their funding directly from the Government, further weakened the position of the LEAs. In the same Act, open enrolment, the process whereby parents could, in theory, choose any school for their child, reduced the ability of LEAs to direct pupils into schools.

Yet local education authorities did retain a number of functions. They had to ensure that enough places in schools were available for those children seeking them; they had to pass money down to schools; they were responsible for transport, special educational needs, medical and dental checks, careers advice, religious education and the implementation of the National Curriculum. Responsibility for the day to day running of individual schools was passed down to head teachers and governors, but important residual functions for the LEA remained.

As a consequence of the devolution of powers and funding to schools, many LEAs reorganised themselves in the late 1980s and early 1990s. The former paternalistic relationship with schools, which the LEAs had effectively 'owned', had to be modified to suit the political changes that had taken place. Some LEAs turned their advisers into 'business units', selling their services back to the schools that used to get them anyway. Others tried to function as they had done previously, sometimes getting into difficulties in the process. At the time when we conducted our research into appraisal, some LEAs had adapted significantly, while others were still reeling from the aftershocks of legislation. Indeed, if anyone had wanted to study the state of English LEAs in the early to mid-1990s, one insightful approach would have been to select one particular LEA function and see how it was being discharged. Our research into the role played by LEAs in the appraisal of teachers became in part a study of the functioning of LEAs generally.

Local education authorities had been given explicit responsibility for the appraisal of teachers. Under the requirements of Circular 12/91 the local education authority was identified as 'the appraising body for county, voluntary controlled, voluntary aided, special agreement and maintained special schools'. The governing body was the appraising body for grant-maintained schools. As the appraising body, the LEA was responsible for all the aspects of appraisal set out in the Education (School Teacher Appraisal) Regulations 1991. LEAs were asked to play the central role in interpreting these regulations and the guidance issued in Circular 12/91, and thereafter disseminating advice and training to schools.

The major aim of Study 1 in the Leverhulme Project, therefore, was to discover the type of approach being adopted, the guidance being issued to schools and the nature and amount of training being offered by LEAs. This would map out the background against which appraisal in schools was taking place, as well as set the information collected from Studies 2 and 3, our national questionnaire survey and individual case studies of teachers, in a wider context. There was particular interest in whether a uniform approach to teacher appraisal was emerging throughout England, or whether different LEAs were exhibiting different attitudes and priorities, especially towards classroom observation.

METHODOLOGY

In October 1992, at the beginning of the project, a letter was sent to all 109 English LEAs. It requested information about materials produced for teacher appraisal and the approach adopted in the training and preparation of appraisers and appraisees in classroom observation.

Respondents were asked to complete a proforma giving the name, title and address of the person within the LEA responsible for teacher appraisal whom we could contact at a later date, if required.

Within three months responses had been received from ninety-four of the 109 LEAs. It was our intention to achieve a 100 per cent response, despite this being a rarity in educational research. The remaining LEAs were contacted again by letter and telephone, and eventually some kind of response was received from all 109 authorities. In the case of the last few replies, five letters had been needed.

The responses received varied considerably in size and content. Despite our letters requesting information on the materials produced by the LEA and the training provided for appraisers and appraisees in the classroom observation component of the process, nineteen LEAs returned only the proforma. Some explained they were not prepared to distribute their materials free of charge. This was either because they were unwilling to send out free copies, or because the documents had been produced for sale to schools or other authorities – a reflection of the business ethos which had begun to prevail in some LEAs.

Some local authorities, having devolved the funding they had received from the Government, were dependent on schools 'buying them back in'. The appraisal co-ordinator of one London borough wrote: 'Appraisal is part of our livelihood and therefore I am reluctant to release our training materials'. Others indicated that the information relevant to classroom observation was dealt with on their training days and were either unwilling to or did not make available copies of their training materials. Four of these nineteen indicated that they were making use of the training materials produced by the Cambridge Institute of Education. The remainder gave no information at all.

Of the ninety LEAs who made a fuller response, some sent only their main policy documents. The length of these varied from eighteen pages to 154 pages. The amount of space devoted to classroom observation also varied – and not always in relation to the document's overall length. Some LEAs responded exactly to our request and provided photocopied extracts of the sections on classroom observation from their policy documents, while others sent some of their training materials for classroom observation, but did not send the policy document which set the classroom observation component in the wider context of the whole process. A number of LEAs did make available a large amount of materials, which typically included the main policy document, a 'Teacher's Handbook', and training materials.

The variety in amount and type of response to our request for information meant that we could not be sure we had all the literature produced by the LEA. None the less, we took what we had and examined the materials with a number of key questions in mind:

1 What was the nature of the LEA documents?

- Which documents provided by the Department for Education were included
- The overall 'ethos' portrayed in the documentation

2 Did the documents give specific guidance on:

- The appraiser/appraisee relationship?
  (e.g. whether a hierarchical or peer model was recommended; how appraisers were to be appointed; whether consideration was given to interpersonal skills)
- The purposes of classroom observation?
- The planning and preparation for the actual classroom observations?
- The identification of areas of focus for the classroom observations?
- The methods of recording during the observation?
- The feedback session – context and content?

An early analysis of the first individual teacher case study data had revealed these particular stages to be key components in the appraisal process, so it was considered crucial to discover the content of the LEA guidelines in these areas.

3 What training was being offered by LEAs?
   Early indications from our case studies indicated some criticisms of the adequacy of training, so it was important to study LEA courses and training literature.

THE DOCUMENTATION PROVIDED TO SCHOOLS

All the materials received were carefully scrutinised by members of the research team in the light of the specific questions listed above. Conclusions were first drawn up by one member, and then corroborated or refuted by other members of the team on a 'negotiate until agree' principle (Bennett *et al.* 1992). This analysis is an important first step in the research, because it reveals how information from the political centre begins to pass through a succession of filters before reaching the individual teacher. Along the way to the classroom, LEA documents and training programmes, in-school documents and training procedures and the actions and words of head teachers, appraisers and professional colleagues, can all give a spin to what was originally prescribed or intended by the Government.

The influence of the DES documents

Very different approaches were adopted by different LEAs in the production of their appraisal materials. Some were little more than a reproduction of the DES documents, making extensive use of quotes from both the regulations and Circular 12/91 with little interpretation or 'home grown' input. Others contained paragraphs taken verbatim from the DES documents, without any indication of their source.

Some LEAs, however, offered a considerable amount of reflection. One urged its appraisers and appraisees always to refer back to its own scheme, to ascertain LEA requirements, 'since there are some important differences of emphasis between the LEA scheme and the guidance in Circular 12/91 from the DES'. A notable difference, in this case, was the statement that appraisal records should *not* be used for disciplinary procedures or in pay and promotion matters. This was more prescriptive than paragraphs 68 and 70 of Circular 12/91, which prohibited *direct* use of appraisal records for disciplinary procedures and matters of promotion and pay, but did allow for this information to be taken into account by a head teacher when considering such issues.

Some LEAs reproduced the DES documents in appendices, which allowed them to develop more comprehensively and coherently their own local approach towards appraisal within the main body of their policy document. In a number of cases there was a specific effort to localise the process and strip it of its imposed 'national' framework.

Localising a national process

Important messages about how the LEA perceived and transacted its role are to be found in the documents. Some LEAs clearly considered that their role was to lay down a very firm framework for appraisal and be tightly prescriptive about the content of the process. The majority, however, produced documents which 'recommended' or 'suggested' rather than 'prescribed', except when there were statutory requirements.

One interesting example of the attempt to humanise and localise appraisal occurred in the matter of the 'initial meeting' between teachers and their appraisers. The official version of the initial meeting, in Circular 12/91, stated only that 'it may be helpful for appraisal to begin with a meeting between the appraisee and the appraiser to plan and prepare for the appraisal . . .', but the majority of LEAs made the initial meeting a compulsory stage in the process. The same commitment towards teachers appraising themselves, however, was not in evidence. Only a few LEAs made self-appraisal compulsory. Most 'recommended' it should take place, rather than insisted on it.

Highly prescriptive guidelines were rare, but one LEA laid down strict parameters for the classroom observation component of appraisal, stating that two thirty-minute observations should occur within a two-week period, and that no observation should take place before the October half-term. Furthermore, appraisers and appraisees were required to complete a 'classroom observation record', and a 'negotiated classroom observation summary'. In explanation, the LEA pointed to the need to ensure some degree of uniformity.

Differences could also be identified in the target and tone of documents. Some documents were directed at the head or appraisal co-ordinator within the school, while others provided information specifically for the two teachers implementing the process, the appraiser and appraisee. The intended audience could affect the language register of the document. Some LEAs used formal, neutral language. Others seemed concerned to make the process more personal and addressed the appraiser or appraisee as 'you'. These documents consequently seemed friendlier and more immediate. The two examples below show this contrast:

> Observation must take place on sufficient occasions to give a representative view of teaching performance. The regulations state a minimum of two occasions. . . .
>
> The purpose of the observation is the collection of adequate data to inform the Professional Development Review, to be used in supportive and developmental discussion in which strengths are acknowledged and problems solved collaboratively.
>
> If it is agreed that notes should be taken, the appraisee should receive a copy of these immediately after the observation.
>
> (Extract from a local authority 'Handbook')

> Classroom observation is an essential part of the appraisal process, in order to share and develop the teaching expertise you have.
>
> You will normally be observed at work in the classroom for a total of at least one hour spread over two or more occasions. The timing of the occasions and their focus will be decided by agreement with you. . . . You will normally be given a brief initial feedback within one working day of an observation taking place. Your appraiser will also provide you with a copy of the written record of the observation at least a week before the appraisal discussion.
>
> (Extract from a local authority 'Personal guide for teachers')

Both these extracts are businesslike in tone, and both make the same kinds of comments about procedures. The first local authority, calling its document a 'Handbook', uses grammatically impersonal language ('Observation must take place . . .', 'The regulations state . . .', 'If it is agreed that notes should be taken . . .'). The second local authority, opting for the more intimate title 'Personal guide', favours direct address to the reader through use of the second person singular ('. . . in order to share and develop the teaching expertise you have', 'You will normally be observed . . .', 'Your appraiser will provide you with . . .').

Most LEAs were well aware of the sensitivity of a first-time compulsory appraisal exercise, so they signalled strongly that appraisal was a tool for professional development, rather than an instrument of assessment. One of the local authorities that had taken part in a national pilot scheme for appraisal, went so far as to rename the process 'Review and Development'. Another LEA, in its introduction, stated 'The local authority firmly believes that it is the positive aspect of appraisal that must be continually stressed'. Almost all LEAs played down the matter of quality grading. Only one LEA produced sample observation schedules on which the appraiser had to grade a teacher as 'outstanding' or 'satisfactory' in the activity observed.

There was a very wide variety in the impact made on the reader by the LEA literature. A minimalist policy statement could easily give the impression of an authority whose intention was to do no more than implement its statutory obligations. Not only was the content sparse, but the presentation of the document was often unappealing, leaving the reader with the feeling that it had been produced as cheaply as possible.

By contrast, documentation which appeared professionally designed and produced, with a contents table and well organised sections, was more likely to offer comprehensive treatment of appraisal, giving the impression that a great deal of planning had taken place in order to construct an approach consistent with the ideology of the LEA and its schools. These LEAs often had staff development schemes in place prior to the introduction of statutory appraisal, and said they considered the personal and professional development of their staff to be a high priority. One of the LEAs providing slender documentation advised its appraisers that four-and-a-half hours of their time would be required, while another producing a comprehensive set of materials talked in terms of twelve-and-a-half hours of appraiser time.

Personnel and staffing appeared to offer a further clue about the degree of importance different LEAs attached to appraisal. While some LEAs appointed a full-time appraisal co-ordinator or even set up a 'team' to co-ordinate appraisal, others merely extended the job description of a senior inspector or adviser to include responsibility for appraisal. The new responsibility was sometimes seized with enthusiasm, and sometimes embraced reluctantly. In a few authorities the task had been given to a school head or deputy.

The size of authorities may offer an explanation for these different organisational strategies, though this does not provide the whole picture. Comparable shire counties, for example, differed in their approaches, and the level of priority given by an LEA to appraisal seemed a relevant factor. Local authorities need to consider carefully the messages which the nature of their training materials and their internal organisation transmit to teachers.

THE RELATIONSHIP BETWEEN TEACHERS AND THEIR APPRAISERS

The statutory regulations merely make a fairly bald statement that the head teacher is responsible for the appointment of appraisers. Circular 12/91 adds detail:

> Wherever possible the appraiser should already have management responsibility for the school teacher. . . . [Where this is not the case] the head teacher should appoint as appraiser a person who is in a position by virtue of his or her experience and professional standing to ensure that the appraisal serves the needs of both the school teacher and the school.
>
> (DES 1991b: para. 21)

Nearly all LEAs reproduced this wording either verbatim or in a paraphrased form, reinforcing the view that the appraiser/appraisee relationship should be a hierarchical one. It was not surprising that very few mentioned the possibility of peer appraisal, although evidence from the national questionnaire survey data reported in Chapter 4 suggests that this did take place in some schools.

When we analysed LEA responses, we already had some preliminary evidence from the national questionnaire survey and case studies that the appraiser/appraisee relationship was a crucial factor in the effectiveness of the appraisal. Most LEAs stressed the need to foster rapport between appraiser and appraisee during the initial meeting between the two. This is another example of LEAs trying to humanise and localise what might otherwise have been seen as a set of cool bureaucratic Government prescriptions.

One LEA's documentation argued that head teachers, when appointing appraisers, should 'consider the quality of the existing professional relationship between appraiser and appraisee'. However, our analysis of the case studies and national questionnaire data in later chapters of this book will show that, in secondary schools, the pairing of teachers from different curriculum areas was not uncommon, especially where the teacher might sometimes distrust the appraiser's ability to undertake effective and relevant observation.

Several LEAs recommended that head teachers should draw up a list of four appraisers for each appraisee and allow the appraisee to identify any appraiser who would be unacceptable – a practice which our national questionnaire data suggest was fairly widely adopted. One LEA explicitly stated that 'it is not important [for the appraiser and appraisee] to like each other . . . but professional respect is needed'. This implied a separation of personal relationships from professional relationships – not how the two teachers got on socially, but whether professional trust and respect was present.

Examples of humanising and mitigating language abounded in sections on relationships. Notions like 'empathy', 'trust' and 'respect' received a high profile in documents. One LEA, in its 'Notes to Appraisers', recognised that trust must be present, 'in order to ensure an honest and frank approach'. Another advised that 'considerable tact and diplomacy may be required from both people, together with a willingness to be honest without being destructive'. It was generally stressed that if classroom observation was to be worthwhile there had to be trust and tolerance on both sides. 'Professional partnership' was another term that was commonly used. The emphasis was on making appraisal a positive experience for the teacher, in which the appraiser's role is seen as facilitator and supporter, rather than an assessor or judge.

Who should take responsibility for the process was an issue addressed by many LEAs. The majority appeared to consider that it was the role of the appraiser to take the lead. But it was also common for LEAs to stress two democratic principles: the need for 'negotiation' and 'agreement' at each stage. One LEA altered the terminology to make this point, renaming the initial meeting, the 'negotiating meeting'. Another stated that 'negotiation of the aims, focus and procedures of the classroom observation . . . will help to establish the essential professional partnership that should exist between the appraiser and the appraisee'.

Some LEAs tried to ritualise this procedure by requiring an appraisal contract to be completed and returned to the head teacher, signed by both teacher and appraiser, formally accepting each other, as well as agreeing the time and date at which the initial meeting would take place. This is an interesting example of a hybrid – on the one hand an attempt to localise and democratise, on the other a formal quasi-legal contract.

THE PURPOSES OF CLASSROOM OBSERVATION

The role of classroom observation in appraisal is a statutory one and yet no explicit explanation is given within the statutory regulations, or within Circular 12/91, for its presence within the appraisal process. This may well explain the absence, in nearly a third of LEA documents studied, of any discussion of the purpose of classroom observation and why a small number of LEAs do no more than refer to the regulations: 'In appraising a school teacher who is not the head teacher the appraiser shall . . . observe the school teacher teaching on at least two occasions' (DES 1991a: para. 9 (2)).

Some LEAs merely touched on the purpose implicitly, by quoting from the pamphlet *Education Observed 3*: 'The one undisputed require-ment of good education is good teaching, and performance in the class-room lies at the heart of the teacher's professional skill and of the standards of learning achieved . . .' (DES 1985).

For some of these LEAs, the appraisal interview seemed to be the key component of the appraisal process. Classroom observation was only talked of in terms of informing that interview. Indeed, a significant number stated that the main purpose of classroom observation was 'to provide information for the appraisal interview' without giving any further details, though some did acknowledge that it was 'a useful exercise in its own right'. However, the majority of LEAs illustrated their positive stance towards it by actually listing advantages. These included:

- Offers teachers feedback.
- Offers teachers an extra pair of eyes.
- Encourages collaboration between colleagues and exchange of ideas.
- Encourages more reflection.
- Encourages better lesson preparation.
- Ensures appraisal interview is based on 'knowledge of a teacher's real work'.
- Can lead to a common 'school' focus.
- Breaks down classroom isolation.
- Provides support.

Many LEAs stressed the benefit of classroom observation as the first opportunity for teachers to receive 'official' feedback on their teaching since their probationary year. One took this a step further by quoting from the ACAS Working Group (1986) report that teachers have a 'right' to have their work observed. A number of LEAs pointed to the opportunity to highlight success in the classroom, in the words of one of them, 'to identify and celebrate existing strengths'. Many more recog-nised the chance to identify areas for development and 'help teachers to set new goals'.

Nearly all LEAs placed great emphasis on the use of benign language when describing lesson observation, stressing the need for the feedback to be 'constructive' and for the appraiser to aim to support the teacher in a 'positive' way. One LEA stated that 'a critical friend can be a powerful ally in the improvement of classroom practice . . .' and the term 'critical friend' was one which was encountered again in the case studies described in later chapters. Another LEA referred to 'the aid of a *skilled* observer' (our italics). There was evidence from all our studies that appraisers did not always feel that they had the appropriate skills. The quality and quantity of training provided for appraisers in classroom observation will be discussed later in this chapter and in subsequent chapters.

The sharing of expertise was a popular theme among LEAs, tied in with the belief that classroom observation would remove barriers and break down isolation. One LEA claimed that classroom observation 'is a natural process from which appraisee and appraiser can learn from each other', and stressed that 'observation and the sharing of experiences should take place as often as time and circumstance permit'. An appraisal co-ordinator, in a written communication to us, put the point even more strongly: 'classroom observation will in our view be of pivotal importance in assisting teachers to move from a state of "autonomous isolation" to interactive professionalism'.

Many LEAs said they encouraged reflection and self-evaluation by teachers. Circular 12/91 states that '. . . school teachers should be encouraged to recognise the value of self-appraisal and to carry it out. Self-appraisal is not compulsory . . .' (DES 1991b: para. 34).

Self-appraisal was rarely made a compulsory stage of the appraisal process by LEAs, but a large number did recommend that it should take place at the beginning of the process and provided a proforma for this purpose. Several of these suggested that the areas of focus for the classroom observation should arise directly from this exercise. Some also pointed to the need for self-appraisal following the classroom observation stage of the process.

Classroom observation was perceived by LEAs as a means of ensuring that the discussion taking place during the appraisal interview was based on 'knowledge of a teacher's real work'. A small number acknowledged, however, that observation could only provide a 'snapshot' of a teacher's performance. On the other hand, one of these claimed that, despite the drawbacks of using evidence from a small number of observations, actual lesson data did provide more reliable information than general and casual impressions. This view was supported by another LEA which pointed out that classroom observation should provide 'a systematic approach to the analysis of professional practice . . . [and] . . . allow(s) for decision making based on objective data rather than subjective inferences'.

Many LEAs stressed that teachers and their appraisers should take account of available resources and their school development plan, when discussing the appraisee's needs. Some stressed that support for the teacher does not necessarily mean going out of school to attend the LEA's in-service courses, arguing that pilot schemes had shown that the majority of a teacher's needs could be met in school. The principal message was that appraisers should not raise expectations which could not then be met.

While many LEA documents put forward the advantages of classroom observation, few addressed the possible disadvantages. This was in keeping with their general stress on the positive aspects of appraisal. One LEA, however, produced as part of its training materials a list of both the pros and cons of classroom observation. The disadvantages identified were that:

- It can be threatening.
- It can prompt 'show' lessons.
- It can be costly in terms of time and cover.
- It can take the observer away from his/her own classes.

In summary, the consensus among LEAs seemed to be that classroom observation offered the best chance to stimulate discussion based on a teacher's actual performance in the classroom. Important elements in this process included self-appraisal before observation took place, and further reflection afterwards on constructive comments from the appraiser. The subsequent interview should then identify areas for development – the ultimate goal being an improvement in classroom practice. There was a widespread belief that classroom observation could support whole school approaches to curriculum and policy making, and enhance personal and professional relationships between teachers and appraisers. There was a general consensus that if classroom observation was carried out in a constructive manner, it should lead, in the words of one LEA, to 'greater team spirit among staff with teachers feeling committed, confident and comfortable'.

PLANNING AND PREPARATION FOR OBSERVATION

The regulations required that observation should take place on at least two occasions. Circular 12/91 provided guidelines on the duration of these observations: 'School teachers should normally be observed teaching for a total of at least one hour, spread over two or more occasions' (DES 1991b: para. 35).

Most LEAs quoted or made reference to this paragraph. Only one appeared to deviate slightly from the guidelines by advising shorter observations of twenty to thirty minutes. Some LEAs considered two observations to be the minimum, while one stated that it was the maximum, although no explanation was given for this limit. One LEA stated that three sessions would be necessary, all of which were to take place in the spring term.

This insistence on the spring term was double edged. One benefit was that teachers had already had one term in which to get to know their pupils. Another, particularly for secondary schools, was that the spring term is not disrupted by examinations, unlike the summer term. The disadvantage, however, and this was confirmed by our national questionnaire data and case studies, was pressure on time, especially that of the appraiser. In primary schools it was not uncommon for heads and deputies to have responsibility for up to four appraisals each. Condensing all appraisals within one term might seriously disrupt the normal day to day running of the school.

The role of the appraiser

If the goal of appraisal is the improvement of classroom practice, then the role of the appraiser during the classroom observation stage of the process must be considered a key element. It was not surprising, therefore, to find that most LEAs mentioned the need to clarify the appraiser's role before the observation began. One LEA underlined the need for 'full discussion by appraisee and appraiser so that mutual understanding of the procedures for the classroom observation is present' while another talked similarly about the need for the 'ground rules' to be established.

It was common for appraisers to be reminded that there was no single view of good teaching and that interpretations of lessons needed to be negotiated. Other LEAs recognised that classroom observation was the greatest source of apprehension and tension for many teachers, and one set out a list of things which it said classroom observation was *not*. This included '*not* teaching practice' and '*not* an inspection'.

Some LEAs stressed that the information gathered was for the teacher's benefit and not the appraiser's. The role of the appraiser was to be 'neutral', assisting a colleague to gather data. Many LEAs provided guidelines for appraisers on classroom observation. A list of the most common points made in documents is given below.

Appraisers should:

- Be objective not subjective.
- Look at performance, not personality.
- Be supportive not judgemental.
- Be sensitive.

One briefing document used alliteration to sum up the qualities it required in an appraiser: 'punctual, polite, prepared, professional'. It was also recognised by LEAs that effective communication skills were crucial. Among those identified were:

- Clarity of expression.
- Active listening.
- Questioning.

- Negotiation.
- The ability to facilitate others' expressions of feelings.

Most LEAs stressed the need for the areas of focus and methods of recording information to be clearly defined and agreed beforehand, so there would be no mystery for the teacher about the appraiser's role during classroom observation. Trying to collect information from pupils was recognised by some LEAs as a particularly sensitive issue and appraisers were warned against undermining the teacher's position with the class. Several took a prescriptive stance, insisting that appraisers should not interact with pupils or join in the lesson. In general, however, teachers and their appraisers were to agree between themselves the appraiser's role during observations. Only a small number of LEAs discussed whether pupils should be informed about the role of the appraiser in the classroom.

Teachers' preparation

For teachers, the most common form of preparation advocated was self-appraisal, and many LEAs provided a proforma for this purpose. This was then to be discussed with the appraiser at the initial meeting. Some recommended that the areas of focus should arise directly out of this self-evaluation exercise. A small number of LEAs also proposed that appraisees should keep a pre-observation diary, or make a video or audio recording of themselves in a pre-observation lesson. Two LEAs suggested that a 'dry run' could be beneficial to both teacher and appraiser, especially where classroom observation was not a normal occurrence in the school. Only one suggested that teachers might prepare for their own observation by observing their appraiser.

Appraisers' preparation

Circular 12/91 is explicit about the requirements for appraisers' prep- aration: 'Observers should have a clear understanding of the context in which an observed lesson is given. They will need to ensure that they are fully briefed by the appraisee before observation begins' (DES 1991b: para. 36).

Our own case study evidence suggested that appraisers did not seem to be receiving in-depth briefing before the observations. Analysis of the LEA documentation showed that emphasis was placed by the majority of LEAs on the need for the appraiser to be advised of the context of the lesson by the teacher in advance. The word 'context' had varying meanings attached to it, but nearly always included the aims and objectives of the lesson, an explanation of the lesson's place within

programmes of study or schemes of work, and, occasionally, the characteristics of the children.

There appeared to be some ambiguity in many LEA documents over
this briefing on lesson 'context'. One LEA advised that teacher and
appraiser should meet for about fifteen minutes before the observation.
It was also suggested by two LEAs that teachers could give their
appraiser notes instead of having a meeting. Another provided a
sample proforma for teachers to give to their appraiser at the briefing
meeting as a basis for discussion.

The identification of areas of focus

Only general advice is given by Circular 12/91 regarding the identification of areas of focus for appraisal.

> Appraisal is likely to be more purposeful if it focuses on specific areas
> of a school teacher's work. This will be particularly so with the
> appraisal of head teachers, deputy heads and other teachers with a
> wide range of managerial duties.
>
> (DES 1991b: para. 20)

The lack of guidance concerning identification of areas of focus for
classroom observation was reflected in some LEAs' documentation.
A number of LEAs either failed to mention the matter of focus at all,
or merely stated that this had to be agreed at the initial meeting, with
no advice as to which aspects of a teacher's work might be appropriate.

Many LEAs did advocate particular combinations of 'general' and
'specific' areas of focus for the two observation sessions. The most
popular recommendation was that the first session should be a general
observation, out of which specific areas of focus for the second session
might emerge. One LEA explained the reasoning behind this approach,
claiming that a general observation offered 'a broad, wide lensed view
of the teacher's work within the classroom, which should provide an
all round perspective of the teacher's performance and help to narrow
the focus for the specific focus observation'.

Although it was unusual for LEAs to be prescriptive regarding focus
identification, one did specify that the first observation should have as
its focus an area of school priority for development, while the second
should have a specific focus that had been negotiated. Most LEAs did
not recommend a maximum number of areas of focus, but of those
that did, three areas seemed to be the highest acceptable number.

This strong commitment by LEAs to a general observation followed
by a specific observation was particularly interesting as there was little
evidence from the case study and national questionnaire data that this
did, in practice, take place. Most teachers either opted to identify a

specific focus for both observations at the initial meeting, or if a general observation was preferred, this too tended to be used for both lessons.

LEAs which discussed whether the area of focus should be general or specific were likely to make detailed suggestions. These tended to fall under the following headings:

- Lesson planning and preparation.
- Classroom management.
- Learning environment.
- Use of resources.
- Teaching method/skills.
- Recognising children's needs.
- Relationships.
- Assessment and recording.

Few LEAs recommended whether teachers should choose a strength or weakness as the focus, though one insisted that 'the area of focus must be genuine'. No definition of 'genuine' was given, although this issue may have been discussed at training days. There was very little guidance generally about the process for selecting a focus. Only two LEAs appeared to provide models for identification of areas of focus. Of the others, one stated that 'the approach adopted will depend on how the school sees the purpose of appraisal'. Another implied that the choice of focus rested with the appraiser, quoting from Circular 12/91: 'The appraiser is entitled to appraise performance across the full range of professional duties undertaken, including temporary responsibilities' (DES 1991b: para. 19).

Very few LEAs discussed how 'observable' these areas of focus might be. One which did, actually listed its suggested areas of focus under the heading 'Observable areas of teaching', but its list did not differ from most other LEAs. There is evidence, from our case study data, that the identification of areas of focus for the classroom observation component of the appraisal process proved difficult for many teachers. It may be that more detailed guidance and training from LEAs would have been beneficial.

METHODS OF OBSERVING AND RECORDING

As was described in Chapter 2 there are numerous ways of recording and analysing what happens in classrooms. Evidence from our own case studies shows that very few teachers or appraisers gave much detailed consideration to how the observation should be undertaken, or what should be recorded. Furthermore, our national questionnaire survey indicated that most appraisers preferred taking freehand notes of the observation, with only a small percentage making use of structured observation schedules.

Methods of recording information gathered during classroom observation is not an issue addressed in the DES documents. The wording used in Circular 12/91 when discussing feedback is stripped of any requirement for structured or systematic observation: 'Observers should also discuss their impressions of the lesson with the appraisee after the observation' (DES 1991b: para. 36).

With lack of advice from the DES in this area, the responsibility lay with LEAs to develop guidelines. Examination of the documents we received suggested that the majority of LEAs offered little or no training in observation methods, although some did address the advantages and disadvantages of different methods of recording and their suitability to particular areas of focus and considered qualitative and quantitative methods.

External help

Of the few LEAs offering comprehensive guidance on methods of recording, the majority had apparently based their documentation on a pack called 'Training for appraisal', produced by the Cambridge Institute of Education. In the classroom observation section of this pack are examples of five types of observation schedule: an open recording sheet with headings such as 'presentation', 'questioning strategies', 'subject matter' and 'feedback'; a tally system; a timed section; a sheet containing prompting questions; and a classroom observation diagram, on which details such as pupil involvement can be recorded. There is a strong emphasis on the use of low inference measures and observers are urged to record only factual and descriptive information when using the 'open recording' and 'prompting questions' schedules.

The schedule for the tally system takes as its focus 'teacher talk', and the observer is required to make a mark each time a particular category of teacher talk occurs. These categories include: 'teacher tells', 'questions whole class (open)' and 'teacher praises'. For the timed system schedule the Flanders Interaction Analysis system is used. The classroom observation diagram maps the location of each pupil and observers assign a code number to pupils becoming involved in the lesson in any of four ways: answering a question voluntarily, answering a question when asked, volunteering a comment, making a disruptive comment. No use is made of quality rating in any of the schedules.

Home-made approaches

Some LEAs drew up their own training materials. It was not always possible to determine the origin of these, although a number seemed to be derived from what the pilot authorities had developed, but only a few placed much emphasis on preparation for classroom observation. One LEA provided its own unusually full set of documents, which included a 'General Pre-Observation Sheet', requiring the observer to record details regarding the gender and ethnicity balance and the structure of the pupil groupings within the class. Space was also made available on the form to record the role of other adults in the classroom. A second sheet, to be completed by the teacher prior to the observation, detailed the teacher's aims and organisation of the lesson to be observed.

There were three schedules related to the observation itself: a dot to dot framework on which the layout of the classroom could be recorded, a sheet on which the activities of teacher and pupils could be logged at specific intervals, and a schedule recording the 'purpose, relevance and practicability' of the task set. The appraiser was to focus on three pupils for the time log and the task assessment. Following the observation, appraisers had to summarise their observations on a schedule containing the headings: 'purpose', 'relevance and practicability', 'differentiation', 'organisation of space, time and materials', 'teaching style' and 'relationships'. This LEA stressed that the choice of schedules would depend on the areas of focus.

In general LEAs discussed only one or two types of schedule, often time logs or recording schedules. Many of the time logs had two general headings, 'time' and 'observation', and contained no guidance on what to write down under the 'observation' column, although a few attempted to be slightly more specific. One suggested the headings: 'time', 'evidence of pupil activity related to focus', 'evidence of teacher activity related to focus' and 'comments or questions to be asked'. Two LEAs provided sample schedules which noted non-verbal communication between teacher and pupils. There were also instances of schedules recording whether pupils were involved in their work.

Recording schedules could be split into those which had only the headings 'area of focus' and 'comment', and those which provided lists of areas to be considered, with room for notes to be written. These lists typically covered issues such as 'planning and preparation', 'classroom management', 'organisation of learning' and 'class environment'. Some schedules were more detailed than others. One schedule contained headings like 'classroom management', 'relationships', 'questioning and explaining', 'pupil response and participation', 'appropriateness of topic and teaching strategies' and 'match of work'.

Some of the statements on observation schedules appeared to stress subjective judgements. A statement found in one schedule was 'the aim of the activity was clear to pupils'. No guidance was given in the training materials as to whether the appraiser should question the pupils about this, or make a personal judgement. One schedule required similar high inference responses, like 'resources are clear and helpful; deployed to meet the learning requirements of the pupils; ease of access to resources in classrooms and resource centres', which could only be substantiated if a careful scrutiny of pupils' movements were undertaken.

Two significant issues emerge. First, a large number of LEAs appeared to offer little or no training, for either appraisers or appraisees, in the many different methods of observation and recording available to them. Second, where information and training had been provided, it was sometimes perceived by appraisers to be insufficient for their needs. These two factors may explain why so many appraisers in practice chose to use unstructured freehand notes as their method of recording. There may not have been much expertise on classroom observation available at all in some LEAs.

LESSON ANALYSIS

Observers should . . . discuss their impressions of the lesson with the appraisee after the observation. They should normally aim to do this within two working days of the observation.

(DES 1991b: para. 36)

The majority of LEAs concurred with this guidance in their documents, but there were differences between them over the need for immediacy. Some advocated full feedback within twenty-four hours of the observed lesson. Reasons for this time scale included, 'it will allay anxieties and concerns', 'there is a need to retain a freshness of events' and 'the most effective feedback is immediate'.

But a contrasting view was held by several authorities who identified the need for both the appraiser and appraisee to have some time for reflection before discussing the lesson. The most commonly advocated strategy was that the appraiser should make an immediate brief comment to the teacher at the end of the lesson and then provide a full feedback session within two working days. A positive comment at the end of the lesson was generally considered to reduce anxiety, though one LEA cautioned appraisers to take care over their first reaction, warning them, 'Do not flatter to deceive'.

The purpose of feedback in the process

The importance attached to feedback after the classroom observation differed between LEAs. Most advocated discussion after each observation. One or two talked of a single feedback session, to follow the second observation. The ingredient commonly identified as essential if 'successful' feedback was to be achieved was the allocation of sufficient and uninterrupted time. In general half an hour was considered to be sufficient. 'It should be brief – it's not the interview!' said one. Despite the emphasis on time to be made available for an uninterrupted discussion, examination of our case study data indicated that many appraisers, in reality, had to conduct feedback sessions at lunch time or after school.

The tone of the feedback

Of the LEAs committed to a full debriefing, a small number provided a sample agenda for the meeting. It was, however, much more common for LEAs to discuss the atmosphere and setting of the meeting and the appraiser's role during the discussion. Many stressed again the need to ensure the correct democratic 'tone' for the meeting, underlining the need for 'genuine discussion'. Appraisers were encouraged to emphasise the positive by analysing the lessons' strengths and celebrating good things; to share not advise; to describe not judge; and to offer support but not to mislead.

A large number of LEAs stressed the need for teachers to be given the opportunity to give *their* opinion of the lesson observed. Two LEAs stated that the first comments on the lesson should be made by the appraisee. One local authority placed the responsibility for interpretation firmly with the teacher, stating: 'Ideally it is the appraiser who should provide the objective evidence and the appraisee who should make the judgements'. Appraisers were urged to use open-ended questions which would help teachers draw their own conclusions, 'to offer choices not imposed solutions'. Some LEAs gave examples of the type of questions appraisers should ask. It was evident from the materials received that a number were providing specific training on 'how to give and receive feedback'.

Areas for discussion

A small number of LEAs stressed the need for the content of the feedback session to be firmly located in a whole school context. These tended to be those authorities which, from the outset, had located appraisal within the arena of whole school policy development. It was common for LEAs to recommend that the appraisee should be given some form of written record of the observation.

Most LEAs suggested that teachers should receive either a copy of the observation notes, or a summary, within twenty-four hours of the observation and definitely before the feedback session, enabling the appraisee to reflect on and interpret the observations, and thus play a fuller part in the feedback discussion. In line with the emphasis on confidentiality in most LEAs' documentation, appraisers were generally required to give their copy of the observation notes to the teacher at the end of the process, or to destroy them.

Target setting

The outcome of the feedback discussion was considered by most LEAs to provide information for the appraisal interview, so several advocated the production of a written summary of the feedback session for that purpose. As our evidence from the case studies shows, this rarely occurred. In a small number of LEAs, an official 'negotiated summary' proforma had to be agreed and signed by both the appraiser and appraisee. Some suggested that the main purpose of the feedback session was to allow teachers and their appraiser to set targets for classroom practice. In most cases, however, target setting was seen as the purpose of the appraisal interview, not the feedback session. Many LEAs used an acronym, stating that targets should be SMART:

- Specific.
- Measurable.
- Attainable.
- Relevant.
- Time constrained.

Despite the statutory requirement for observation of the appraisee's classroom, there was no evidence of any LEA making it compulsory for teachers to identify targets related to their own classroom practice. This must have implications for the extent to which appraisal will eventually affect a teacher's performance in the classroom, an issue which we investigate in greater depth later in this book.

TRAINING PROVISION

There were some organisations, often from higher education, involved in the production of a large proportion of the training materials. A number of LEAs had training programmes which were designed in conjunction with, or in consultation with, the Counselling and Careers Development Unit at Leeds University. Two London boroughs had been working with the Roehampton Institute. Several LEAs appeared to be making use of the LEAP materials, a package of videos and printed information produced for a consortium of local authorities. Others had adopted, if not as a total package, aspects of some of the training manuals produced by LEAs which had been involved in the national pilot scheme. The major single influence on LEAs' documents and training materials appeared to have been the distance learning packs 'Ready for appraisal' and 'Training for appraisal' produced by the Cambridge Institute of Education.

The way training was organised differed between LEAs. Some ran courses centrally for their teachers. A very small number offered residential courses. Others provided training in school, on in-service days or after school. The targets of the training also varied. In some LEAs, appraisers could expect to receive centrally based LEA training. In others, senior staff of a school might receive training, but they would then be responsible for cascading this training down through their school. One LEA justified this approach: 'Training will be provided using the cascade model as the only practical way of meeting training requirements effectively with the very limited funds available from the DES'.

The LEA in which teachers worked did affect the amount and type of training they received. The information from LEAs suggested that most offered only modest provision for teachers themselves, mainly 'awareness raising'. In most cases this was a single day, based in their own school, designed to 'create the climate' for appraisal, to equip teachers with a knowledge of the background to appraisal, the legal requirements, and the way it was envisaged appraisal would be carried out in their school. Some LEAs claimed to include observation skills training as part of an awareness raising course, although the amount of time available for this within a single day was minimal.

A number of LEAs placed great emphasis on joint training for teachers and appraisers, as recommended by the CIE Report on the Evaluation of the School Teacher Appraisal Pilot Study (CIE 1989). Those expounding the merits of joint training usually provided both teachers and appraisers with training in skills development. In general, this tended to include such topics as self-appraisal, negotiation, interviewing techniques, classroom observation methods, the giving and receiving of feedback, and the writing of the appraisal statement. The classroom observation component of the process seemed to be dominated by the use of video material of classroom scenes, although role play was also used.

Most LEAs promoted appraisal as a partnership between the teacher and appraiser, yet teachers did not receive equal access to training. This could hinder them in their negotiations with their appraiser. If teachers have not received guidance in the methods of observation, they may not feel competent to discuss or argue the issues about observation and its aftermath with their appraisers, as will be shown in later chapters. Appraisals then become a manifestation of power and control, something 'done to' teachers by trained appraisers, contrary to the partnership ideal espoused by so many LEAs in their literature.

Where joint training did take place, teachers could expect to receive two days of appraisal training – one day for 'awareness raising' and one day for 'skills training'. Little of this was devoted to classroom observation. Where joint training was not carried out, courses seemed, typically, to be two days for appraisers and one day for appraisees, although the actual range was from one to four days.

In contrast with the picture of universal training portrayed by the LEAs in their literature, our national questionnaire survey data indicated that in over half of the sixty-three LEAs from which we received appraiser responses, there were appraisers who received no classroom observation training at all before starting their first appraisal. In those LEAs providing information on specific skills training in classroom observation, the sessions seemed to vary in length from one hour to half a day, although one LEA did offer a three-day course for both appraisers and appraisees. During the project one appraisal co-ordinator reported to us that training for observation had been 'squashed' to one hour, from half a day, because of other pressures on schools. This low priority accorded to classroom observation in training does raise questions about appraisers' ability to analyse lessons effectively.

It is clear from the data collected in the case studies and national questionnaire survey that not all aspirations for training were realised in practice. The experience of the individual teacher or appraiser may be very different from that recommended in the policy documents. A number of LEAs stressed the need for training to take place as near as possible to the appraisal process, yet most teachers and appraisers attended courses as much as a year or more before appraisals actually took place. When we interviewed our case study teachers at the beginning of their appraisal, it was common for them to confess they were unable to remember much about training, as it had taken place so long ago.

CONCLUSION

Local education authorities were given responsibility for appraisal at a time when other powers and responsibilities were actually being taken away from them. Many were in chaos following the change in their status and duties, and most were being reorganised internally. In these circumstances our review of training documentation and procedures was like a litmus paper test, offering a fascinating insight into the very soul of these institutions in transition. Some seized the opportunity to take on a significant new assignment, eager to demonstrate their willingness to support schools, while others floundered in uncertainty.

One Chief Adviser, replying to our fifth letter asking for information, simply wrote an apologetic note saying that the advisory service had collapsed completely in that LEA and been disbanded.

The messages in the documentation were often unambiguous. Many LEAs sought to mitigate what might otherwise be seen as a cold and distant bureaucratic process. While some merely reproduced official regulations and circulars, others personalised and localised them. There was often great emphasis on the collegiality of the exercise, with stress on personal relationships between teachers and their appraisers, the need for sensitivity, positive rather than negative comments, and negotiation. There was also great variety in the degree of prescriptiveness, with some LEAs taking a permissive stance and others spelling out in detail what they required. It was a most interesting snapshot of the varied histories, traditions and aspirations of LEAs in transition, and of the different kinds of relationship they sought to maintain or establish with schools.

The variety in the amount and type of documentation received from LEAs was discussed at the beginning of this chapter, and our principal purpose has been to provide a framework for our study of appraisal in practice, as well as to indicate where similarities and differences lie and discuss uniqueness where it occurs. There is no doubt that the overwhelming view of LEAs is that appraisal must be seen as a 'positive experience', so heavy emphasis was placed on the professional development of the teacher. Thus it was rare to find LEAs explicitly recommending that areas of weakness should be selected as areas of focus. There was a general lack of guidance to teachers about choosing an area of focus, and it may be useful for this issue to be addressed in future training.

The appraisee/appraiser relationship has been identified as a key element in ensuring 'successful appraisal'. Many LEAs listed the qualities and skills an appraiser requires. Some of the communication skills may be gained or enhanced through training, but personal qualities may be less easily fostered through this medium. In view of the need for empathy, trust and respect within the relationship, the benefit of strict adherence to a hierarchical system of appraisal, without reference to the appraiser's competency in personal and professional relationships, may in future need to be questioned.

That appraisers must be briefed about the context of the lessons to be observed was stressed by the majority of LEAs. Yet this was not always what apparently happened in practice. In many instances it was difficult to tell whether LEAs were advising that such briefings should take place during the initial meeting, or whether a separate occasion should be used to inform the appraiser of the lesson context. If a pre-observation meeting were officially included in the process structure by all LEAs, it might help to avoid situations where the appraiser observed a lesson without being aware of the teacher's aims and objectives or the lesson's place within schemes of work, and without knowledge of relevant facts about the pupils.

While a small number of LEAs did appear to be addressing the issue of matching closely the methods of recording and observing with the area of focus identified, the majority discussed only one or two methods, mainly open recording or simple tally systems, or did not discuss classroom observation properly at all. Lack of observation and recording skills was identified as a matter of concern by a large number of appraisers, and was one area which LEAs may need to reassess in the light of what is reported in this research.

The following chapters of this book will examine Studies 2 and 3 of the Leverhulme Project, in which the actual experiences of teachers and their appraisers were scrutinised in considerable detail through questionnaires and intensive case studies of primary and secondary school teacher appraisals. There will also be an analysis of the extent to which the policies of the local education authorities described in this chapter were put into practice.

Chapter 4

The national perspective

Whenever a national initiative such as the appraisal of teachers is introduced, there are bound to be individual teacher and school variations, just as there were differences in the approaches of local education authorities. Over 400,000 teachers in some 24,000 primary and secondary schools were appraised during the two-year period which we were studying, so we wanted to capture a series of snapshots of what took place. The second part of the research involved drawing up a description of appraisal practice in a variety of primary and secondary schools in different parts of England, and this constituted Study 2 of the project. The principal objective was to elicit how classroom observation was actually being used in the process, so we surveyed a national sample of teachers and appraisers in both primary and secondary schools using mailed questionnaires.

Questionnaires can produce large samples of respondents. They also offer the opportunity for teachers to reflect on their practice and give considered replies. Two major disadvantages of mailed questionnaires are first that they often generate a low response rate, and second that the researcher is not able to probe behind the replies in the same way as during face to face interviews. On the other hand, questionnaires do permit the views and experiences of more people to be examined and analysed than would be possible with interviews. They also give the investigator access to teachers in different parts of the country. Oppenheim (1992) has written extensively on questionnaire methodology.

Two questionnaires were constructed, one for appraisers and one for appraisees, which covered several aspects of the appraisal process. For appraisers these included: teaching experience, position held in school, training received, observation methods used, role, feedback and targets set. For appraisees information was requested on teaching experience, position in school, how their appraiser was chosen, reaction to being observed, focus of appraisal, feedback, targets set, and what they saw as the benefits and the perceived effects on classroom practice.

THE SAMPLE OF TEACHERS AND APPRAISERS

A sample of primary and secondary schools was selected, partly from lists provided by local authorities, partly from volunteers who had read about the project. We also took a random one in 200 sample of all schools. Every effort was made to sample large and small schools, urban and rural communities, and to cover all parts of the country. Schools were written to and telephoned to discover how many teachers were willing to complete the questionnaire. As is usually the case with mailed questionnaires a genuine random sample of the total population being studied is not possible, as teachers cannot be compelled to fill them in. Inevitably, therefore, whatever steps are taken to ensure randomness are confounded, since only volunteers will reply. Some schools are better than others at persuading teachers to complete questionnaires, sometimes regarding the kind of reflection that takes place as a valuable piece of professional development for teachers. Others may request twenty questionnaires, but return three.

The total sample was split approximately 40/60 across primary/secondary. On average roughly four teachers and three appraisers responded from each school that took part in the survey, though the totals were higher per school in the secondary sector than in primary. Table 4.1 shows the sample breakdown.

Table 4.1 Sample of respondents in primary and secondary schools

	Primary	Secondary	Total
Number of schools	75	94	169
Number of teachers	265	393	658
Number of appraisers	166	313	479
Teachers and appraisers	431	706	1,137

A final sample of 658 appraisees and 479 appraisers responded to the questionnaire. The respondents were drawn from 169 schools, seventy-five of which were primary and ninety-four secondary. This large sample offers a broad picture of how the appraisal process was under-taken in schools throughout England. A more fine grain analysis of appraisal at school level will be given in later chapters which describe the twenty-nine case studies undertaken.

The sample of schools was drawn from a range of sizes and geo-graphical location. In addition to representing both the North, Midlands and South of England, with schools responding from sixty-four of the 109 LEAs, schools which replied also represented a mix of rural and urban settings. Differences in school size were also evident and the range covered both small and large primary and secondary schools and covered the 3–18 year age range. Some grant-maintained schools responded, but independent schools were not included, as appraisal was not mandatory within the private sector, though many schools undertook it using similar procedures to the local authority schools. Table 4.2 shows the location and size of schools from which the sample of teachers and appraisers were drawn.

Table 4.2 Location and size of schools from which national sample came

Location (L) and size (S) of schools	Teachers/appraisers in sample (%)
L1 Rural	9
L2 Urban	57
L3 Mixed	34
	100
S1 Primary (under 250 pupils)	15
S2 Primary (250 or more pupils)	23
S3 Secondary (under 800 pupils)	18
S4 Secondary (801 to 1,199 pupils)	22
S5 Secondary (1,200 or more pupils)	22
	100

The number of male and female appraisers responding was almost equal, but the split amongst teachers was almost two-thirds female to one-third male. The majority of teachers had many years of experience, and some 51 per cent of appraisees and 74 per cent of appraisers had been teaching for sixteen years or more. This raises a very important issue, which is that appraisal was being applied to a mature teaching profession. The pattern of recruitment during the 1960s, when over 100,000 student teachers were in training, was different from that of the 1990s. In the 1960s there were large numbers of teachers in their twenties and thirties. However, as birthrates fell during the 1970s, so too did the number of trainees. By the beginning of the 1980s only some 30,000 student teachers were preparing to enter the profession. As a result, by the late 1980s, when appraisal was introduced as a legal requirement, about 60 per cent of the teaching profession was aged over forty. Hence the large number of teachers and appraisers in the sample with over sixteen years of experience.

Head teachers were not included within the sample of appraisees, even though many heads in the sample did some teaching, as a different system of appraisal was in use for them, in which an observation of teaching was not required and their appraisers were external to the school. Table 4.3 shows the distribution of the sample. Roughly half the teachers held a scaled post, with extra payment for additional duties, including those who were heads of departments in secondary schools, or who took responsibility for some aspect of the curriculum in primary schools. About a quarter were in senior positions, and another quarter were on the basic professional scale. More than half the appraisers were in senior positions, and almost all the rest held a middle management position. This distribution confirms the principally hierarchical nature of the exercise. Most teachers were indeed appraised by someone who held managerial responsibility for them within the school.

Table 4.3 Position in school of teachers and appraisers (percentages of sample)

Position in school	Teachers	Appraisers
Head	0	18
Senior management	23	38
Scaled post holder	51	41
Main scale	26	3

Teacher and appraiser views on appraisal are initially dealt with separately, as the two groups responded to different questionnaires, offering two perspectives on the process. There are some areas in which similarities and divergences in the two groups' views can be discussed, and this will be dealt with later in the chapter.

TEACHERS' EXPERIENCES

The most common amount of time occupied by an appraisal was half a term. Nearly three-quarters of appraisals took place within half a term, though a few were spread over a shorter or longer period. As Table 4.4 shows about 8 per cent took a week or less. Another 11 per cent lasted a whole term, and a further 10 per cent went on for more than one term.

Table 4.4 Length of time appraisal occupied

Length of time	Percentage
A week or less	8
Half a term	71
A whole term	11
More than a term	10

Most appraisals, according to teachers' own reports, appear to have followed the recommended process, which involved an initial meeting, some form of self-appraisal, information gathering (the appraiser talking to other agreed people), observation, feedback and/or an appraisal interview, a statement (summary of appraisal interview), target setting and a review meeting (follow-up at a later date). However there were some variations in the suggested process. Table 4.5 illustrates that in over a third of cases the appraiser did not gather information from others. The low figure of 19 per cent reporting they had had a review meeting, is partly explained by the timing of the national questionnaire, which was given before the end of the two-year cycle. Some teachers may have had their review meeting after they completed the national questionnaire, but the figure still looks to be on the low side, given that all the respondents had already been appraised.

Table 4.5 Percentage of teachers having each part of the recommended process

Stage of process	Percentage
Self-appraisal	88
Initial meeting	100
Observation	100
Feedback	98
Information gathering	63
Appraisal interview	99
Statement	95
Targets set	95
Review meeting	19

Circular 12/91 states that teachers should have at least two occasions of classroom observation, an 'appraisal interview, in which targets for action are established', an appraisal statement and a review meeting. Implicit within this is the assumption that there should be discussion and feedback after any observations, but the other parts of the process appear to be optional. It is the collection of information from other sources, the application of self-appraisal, and the review meeting that appear not to have occurred in the manner in which the DES intended. Other guidelines seem to have been followed.

There was, however, one important area in which a significant number of appraisals were deviating from the process. Despite the requirement for at least two observations, Table 4.6 shows that in over a quarter of cases, teachers were only observed teaching on one occasion, and that over two-thirds were seen for the basic minimum of two sessions. The reasons for this minimalist approach will become clear later in this account.

Table 4.6 Number of observations

Number of observations	Percentage of sample
One observation	28
Two observations	68
Three observations	2
Four or more	2

Teachers and their appraiser

Each teacher questionnaire asked for information about the managerial relationship between teachers and their own appraiser. The evidence in Table 4.7 shows that in most cases the hierarchical model presupposed in the guidelines, had in practice been adopted. A superior–subordinate model, whereby a more senior member of staff is responsible for appraising a more junior member of staff, is not the only possible form of appraisal, as was described in Chapter 1. Although peer appraisal, where someone of the same status to the teacher, acts as appraiser, was not encouraged by the DES, in some cases there may be no alternative. Only one teacher in nine was appraised by a peer in the present sample, and only one in every 200 was appraised by someone of lower status.

Table 4.7 Managerial relationship of appraiser to teacher

Status of appraiser	Percentage of sample
Head	23
Senior management	40
Line manager	25
Same status teacher	11
Other manager	0.5
Subordinate	0.5

Since formal appraisal was for many schools a new initiative, senior management teams often wanted to operate a system where appraisal cascaded down through the school, so that those in more senior positions would lead by example. This was particularly the case in schools where heads sought to allay the fears of staff who were apprehensive about the first cycle of appraisal, by saying, 'Well, I've got to be appraised as well', which was seen as a strong card to play. In any case, some LEAs insisted that the head had to be appraised first, before the process could even start for the remainder of the staff. This ruling held up some schools if the head was on a long waiting list for external appraisal. Another issue was whether the burden of appraising others should lie with those staff who were already remunerated for carrying additional responsibilities. This was a particularly important matter for those who felt that appraisal was underfunded and time consuming.

The case studies, which will be reported in later chapters, provide further evidence on what teachers perceived to be the advantages and disadvantages of peer and hierarchical models of appraisal, but some wrote comments in the freehand sections of the national questionnaire. The main advantage of peer appraisal is often thought to be that it is less threatening, but hierarchical appraisal may offer teachers a chance of getting things done, since the appraiser may carry responsibility for their support and career development. A number of teachers said it was important to respect their appraiser as an experienced and competent practitioner whose opinion they valued, as these two written comments show:

Appraisal will only work if the appraiser commands the respect of the appraisee. This does not happen automatically because one is senior to the other.

I feel the appraisee should have the chance to participate in the choice of appraisers. Also that peer appraisal should be available if felt to be useful. No choice other than line management puts certain implications on the whole process.

The idea of respecting the appraiser's teaching ability was an important one. One question asked teachers about the appraiser's knowledge of the class observed. In the primary version of the questionnaire, appraisees were asked to indicate whether their appraisers had knowledge of the year group they were observing. In the secondary questionnaire they were asked if appraisers had experience of the subject taught in the lessons observed. Nearly two-thirds of teachers stated that the appraiser had knowledge of the class or subject, but in over a third of replies (37 per cent) the appraiser was considered not to have this specific knowledge. LEA guidelines often stated that appraisers should be able to place the lessons observed in context and should be given information about this when discussing the observations. This is perhaps of greater significance if over a third of appraisers do not have relevant experience of the class. Case studies described later in the book give specific examples of this issue of familiarity with the class and subject matter.

Choice of appraiser

In a system where trust and respect appear to be important factors, the interaction between teachers and their appraiser becomes crucial. How the two key individuals are brought together is a vital matter. In theory head teachers were supposed to take responsibility for selecting an appraiser, but when respondents were asked how their appraiser was chosen, an interesting range of practices emerged. Perceptions, even if mistaken, can be as important as 'reality' in this type of process.

Teachers were asked to indicate how their appraisers had been chosen. Table 4.8 shows the responses. Roughly half said that their appraiser had been imposed, about a quarter stated they had made their own choice, and another quarter felt they had in some way negotiated who their appraiser should be.

Table 4.8 Teachers' choice of appraiser

Choice of appraiser	Percentage of sample
No choice, appraiser imposed	51
Teacher's own choice	23
Negotiated	26

Teachers who had had their appraiser imposed were asked whether they had had an opportunity to veto the appraiser assigned to them. Nearly 80 per cent of respondents said that they could have refused the person allocated to them, though 12 per cent did not know whether they could have exercised the right of veto or not. The feasibility of this putative right of veto, however, was queried by a number of teachers in their written comments, illustrating the problem of publicly rejecting a colleague and then living with the consequences:

No element of real choice. How would a deputy express negative preference for the head and still be able to work in the school?

The right of veto would have strained relations in the department if it had been exercised.

I was not given a negative preference before my first appraiser was chosen. I then had to declare my negative preference and my appraiser was changed to one I was happier with. However, this caused ill feeling and embarrassment.

Veto would have been difficult as the appraiser was announced publicly.

Those teachers who had had an appraiser imposed upon them were asked who made the selection. The most common answer, from 80 per cent of respondents, was that the school's senior management had made the decision. Other replies included the appraiser (4 per cent), the LEA (4 per cent) or a co-ordinator or working party (7 per cent). Some 5 per cent claimed not to know.

All appraisees were asked what criteria they believed had been used when making the choice of appraiser. It would take too long to describe every reply in terms of sub-groups, so Table 4.9 shows the total responses, but does not distinguish between teachers whose appraiser was imposed and those who had negotiated or made the choice.

Table 4.9 Criteria believed by teachers to have been used in the selection of appraisers

Criterion	Percentage
Trust	41
Teaching experience	36
Seniority (position of responsibility)	64
Respect	40
Subject knowledge	24
Other	10

Although trust, respect and teaching experience featured strongly, the largest category was seniority, as one would expect from a hierarchical model of appraisal. A number of respondents mentioned more than one category.

One crucial question asked of teachers was whether they were happy both with the process and with their own appraiser. The result was that 82 per cent of teachers said they were happy with the process by which their appraiser had been chosen. Only 2 per cent of teachers stated that they were not happy, but 13 per cent said that, though they were generally content with the process, they did have reservations. In some of these cases they were happy with the process because it had worked for them, but could see what might have transpired:

Imposition of wrong person could have caused problems if head's judgement had been wrong.

I was very happy with the appraiser, but if I had not been there could have been difficulties in a small school.

My appraiser was acceptable, but other possibilities were not.

The overwhelming majority, over 90 per cent, were happy with their appraiser both before and after, this comment being typical of many:

> I believe my appraiser did a superb job and was meticulous in his work. I have borne in mind all the points that were made to me.

Only a very small minority was disappointed, though a few teachers expressed satisfaction with reservations.

Table 4.10 Percentage of teachers happy with the choice of appraiser before and after appraisal

	Before	After
Yes, happy	92	91
Yes, but reservations	7	6
No	1	1
Missing data	0	2

In the cases where teachers were not happy, they were asked to articulate their reasons:

> I believe he has serious failings as a man manager and I find his integrity suspect at times.

> My first choice was someone else.

> The appraiser was not comfortable with his role. I knew this before.

These three examples show the diversity of reasons why the complexity of the appraisee/appraiser relationship is so important, covering the professionalism of the appraiser, a preference for someone else who was unavailable, and the contagion of the appraiser's own unease. There were many reasons why appraisees had reservations about the person appraising them. These included the subject knowledge of the appraiser, the way in which the appraiser had carried out the process and also the issue of peer versus hierarchical appraisal. The following pairs of comments from teachers illustrate the contradictory nature of their reactions. What pleases one does not please another.

Peer versus hierarchical

'I needed to have a line manager to get a balanced view of my role'.

'I was unable to separate my appraiser from my boss'.

Subject versus non subject specialist

'He had no concept of subject matter and therefore saw problems where none existed'.

'I felt it might have been advantageous to have an appraiser who was not considering subject specifics'.

Feelings about the way the process was carried out

'I thought beforehand that it would be more long winded and time consuming than necessary with this person'.

'[I] felt appraisal was rushed and inadequate'.

One further issue, mentioned by several respondents, will be discussed in the later chapters describing the case studies. It related to the point we made in Chapter 3 about the power relationship between teachers and their appraisers when the latter had been trained and the former had not. Most LEAs advocated a process that was based on negotiation and agreement, yet training in these types of skills was primarily given to appraisers. A combination of training and their higher status within the school placed them in a stronger strategic position when negotiating the process.

As with other issues surrounding appraisal, there was a mixture of opinion as to whether the process should be led by teachers or their appraiser. Some of the objections raised about appraisers were based on their influencing the process too strongly. The case studies did, however, indicate that some appraisees wanted direction from their appraiser, but it was common for teachers to object if their appraiser was too focused on self:

> [My] appraiser allowed his comments to be influenced by his own priorities.

> [The] process was not carried out at my convenience; appraiser was unprepared to focus on my requests.

At its strongest this reservation emerged as a belief that appraisers should be so self-effacing that the whole process would be a normal part of their job, not a special ritual:

> It is a time consuming 'waste of time' which no doubt will fall apart. I feel if people in responsible positions do their job well they know exactly where the strengths/weaknesses are in an individual teacher and should deal with them without having to go through this long drawn out process putting more stress on teachers and those in management.

Classroom observation

Since the classroom observation element of appraisal was the central focus of the research, a number of items about it were included in the national questionnaire. These covered: who chose the focus of the observation, what it was, and why this aspect was chosen for special scrutiny; how many observations were carried out and for how long; teachers' reactions to being observed; what happened after the lesson; and what targets were set. Table 4.6 above showed that 28 per cent of teachers were only observed on one occasion, and a mere 4 per cent of the sample had been watched more than twice, so it is perhaps hardly surprising that the results reveal a very mixed picture.

Focus of observation

We asked teachers to describe the focus of their total appraisal. The results are shown in Table 4.11. The numbers in Tables 4.11 and 4.12 add up to more than 100 per cent, as some selected more than one area of focus. Many chose an aspect of school management:

Table 4.11 Most common topics of focus during total appraisal

Area of focus	Percentage choosing
School management	40
Class management	26
Teaching methods	25
Differentiation	13
Curriculum	7
Assessment	4

When asked specifically about the classroom element of their appraisal, similar concerns emerged, though, with the more specific focus, the large category 'school management' obviously disappeared. Table 4.12 shows some of the more frequently stated topics mentioned as matters teachers wanted to concentrate on during classroom observation.

Most 'class management' responses referred to the management of pupils, though a few mentioned resources. Almost all 'personal relationships' replies added that these were between teacher and pupil, though some were 'pupil–pupil' relationships. In retrospect 92 per cent of teachers felt their choice of focus had been appropriate, and only 5 per cent that it had not. The most common reason cited was that it had

Table 4.12 Most common topics of focus during classroom observation

Area of focus	Percentage choosing
Class management	37
Teaching methods	32
General focus, unspecified	25
Differentiation	19
Personal relationships	13
Curriculum	8
Assessment	4

been of personal benefit. Of the few that were not happy with their choice, most felt it had been too vague.

Some teachers went into detail about whether they had chosen to focus on a strength or weakness. The first quote below comes from a primary teacher who chose music as a strength, but wondered about the wisdom of this, while the second teacher (secondary) selected personal and social education, hoping to improve a weak area. The third teacher, also primary, explained her reluctance to reveal a weakness in what might become a competitive environment, given the possibility of merit payments and redundancies:

> I chose music as it was my strength and I felt confident. It may have done my professional development more good to have chosen a weak subject I could have been helped with.

> [I have] not had Year 9 for many years, never taught personal and social education before. Therefore it made me focus on that area of development.

> Until the process of appraisal is viewed more genuinely as a chance for open discussion and development, I would not feel happy highlighting to others my weakness when others are presenting what they know they do well.

The following two secondary teachers illustrate the extremes, one balancing areas of focus in consultation with the head of department, the other cynical about the whole exercise:

> I chose one strength [teacher–pupil interaction] and one weakness [differentiated learning]. This balance was suggested by my head of department which I thought sensible as the weakness would provide me with some basis of growth.

Given that we were both 'jumping though hoops' to placate outside authority, almost anything would do.

Selection of lesson

There was considerable variation in the amount of time spent observing lessons. The most common period was between forty-five minutes and an hour, but a quarter of the sample reported a half hour or less, and three teachers claimed to have been watched for under ten minutes.

Table 4.13 shows the breakdown of the first period of observation, as 28 per cent of the sample were not seen a second time. In the second lesson observed, the distribution was similar.

Table 4.13 Length of time teachers were observed in their classroom (first lesson)

Length of observation	Percentage of teachers
10 minutes or less	0.5
11–30 minutes	25
31–45 minutes	29
46–60 minutes	34
over 60 minutes	11.5

The choice of lesson to be observed was commonly negotiated between teachers and their appraisers. Table 4.14 shows the large extent of teacher negotiation, both in the area of focus and the lesson to be observed. These were not usually determined by the appraiser. In over half the cases (53 per cent) the selection of lessons was made through negotiation.

The two most common reasons given by teachers to explain why particular lessons were selected for observation were first that the lesson was appropriate to the area of focus (57 per cent), and second that the time was convenient (41 per cent). Almost all teachers (96 per cent) believed, in retrospect, that the choice of lesson to be observed had

Table 4.14 Who decided area of focus and lesson to be observed (percentages)

Who decided	Area of focus	Lesson observed
Teacher	55	38
Appraiser	2	4
Negotiated	37	53
Other	6	5

been appropriate, and 89 per cent said that it had been 'representative' of their everyday teaching:

> I wanted my appraisal to focus on as normal a teaching day as possible.

> A normal lesson – class input followed by group activity where children were working co-operatively and independently.

Some teachers chose their two lessons for specific reasons, and this secondary teacher treated the exercise almost like a controlled experiment, so that the appraiser could help determine how well different styles of teaching appeared to work:

> Two different subjects, two different classes [both Year 12 A level], but the same focus. Two different approaches to achieve learning. Was one more effective than the other? Why?

In many cases choice was constrained by time, and occasionally teachers claimed that there was only one lesson that could possibly have been observed as they matched their timetable to that of their appraiser. Sometimes this caused dismay:

> In the time scale it was the only lesson that could be chosen. The lesson I would have preferred to be observed – Year 10 – it was impossible to do so.

> We agreed one lesson – through pressure of time another was observed. The wrong one was chosen!

Teachers' views on their observation

Teachers were asked to rate, on a five-point scale, whether they believed their teaching was affected by the presence of an observer, and how they felt about being observed. Relatively few teachers responded at the negative ends of the scales, as Table 4.15 reveals. About two-thirds chose the two most positive categories in each five-point scale, whereas 10 per cent or fewer responded at the two most negative points.

In their comments teachers differed about the effects of the observer, many reporting some slight impact, a few confessing to more disruption to their teaching:

> They [the lessons] went reasonably well and the children were not affected by the appraiser's presence.

> I was very much treating it as a 'special performance' even though I tried not to. The children were also on their best behaviour.

Table 4.15 Five-point scales showing whether teachers were affected by the presence of an observer and teachers' feelings at being observed

Affected by presence of observer?	Percentage	Feelings at being observed	Percentage
1 (Not at all)	24	1 (Very unhappy)	2
2	43	2	4
3	23	3	34
4	8	4	35
5 (Considerably)	2	5 (Very happy)	25

I was too aware of my appraiser. The question/answer part of the lesson did not go well. This unsettled me. My thought patterns and the rest of the lesson was muddled.

We were curious to know whether there was any difference between the reactions of teachers in the light of whether or not they had chosen their own appraiser. The results are fascinating. Analysis of variance and Scheffé gap tests were used on the average scores on each of the two five-point scales, to see if there were differences that were significantly different. On the question of how happy teachers were at the presence of an observer there were no significant differences. But in reply to the question about whether their teaching was affected by the presence of an observer, the average scores were: 'appraiser imposed' (2.33), 'own choice' (2.08), 'negotiated' (2.09). The higher the average score, the more affected the teachers. The highly significant F ratio of 5.31 would have occurred by chance less than once in 200 occasions, and Scheffé gap tests confirmed that the teachers whose appraisers were imposed were significantly more affected by their presence than those who had chosen or negotiated their own appraiser.

About three-quarters of appraisers were said by teachers to have played no part in the lesson, but nearly a quarter (23 per cent) did participate. The behaviour of the appraiser during observation will be covered in more detail in the case studies later, but in a small number of cases there was so much participation it was questionable whose lesson the appraiser was assessing, and indeed whether full attention was being given to the appraisal process.

Almost all teachers said they knew what their appraiser was doing during the observation. Teaching is a busy job which demands full attention, so it is not always possible to see what an adult in the far corner of a classroom is doing, but methods of recording were either clarified beforehand or in the discussion after the lesson. Teachers' impressions of how their appraiser recorded what was happening are shown in Table 4.16.

Table 4.16 Methods of recording teachers
believed were used by their appraisers

Method of recording	Percentage
Observation schedule	7
Timed segments	8
Video	0
Freehand notes	89
None	4
Don't know	3

The totals add up to more than 100 as some responded in more than one category. Only one teacher ticked 'Video', so the zero figure in Table 4.16 is actually 0.15 per cent. The major preference was for free-hand notes, rather than systematic schedules or checklists.

Feedback and discussion

Once the observation was finished, in over 90 per cent of cases teachers and appraisers arranged a de-briefing session during which the lesson could be discussed, though in 9 per cent of cases there was written feedback only. Relatively few (16 per cent) of these feedback sessions took place immediately, and 17 per cent of teachers reported a delay of over forty-eight hours. The same question was asked of the appraisers in the national questionnaire, and it is interesting to compare the two sets of perceptions. Although the sample of appraisers came from the same schools, it should be remembered that they could not be matched exactly to each individual appraisee in the sample, as all questionnaires were anonymous, so one would expect some differences in the accounts of the two groups. Also the appraisers' returns show more missing data. However, teachers tended to estimate that feedback took place somewhat later than did appraisers, as Table 4.17 shows:

Table 4.17 Teachers' and appraisers' estimates of the timing of feedback

Timing of feedback	Teachers' estimate	Appraisers' estimate
Immediately	16	22
Within 24 hours	33	32
Within 48 hours	26	15
Longer	17	7
Missing data	8	24

There are differences in the perceptions of teachers and appraisers when it comes to the fate of notes made during the lesson observation. Notes made by the observer should have been destroyed, according to the guidelines, and one would expect differences between teachers and appraisers here, as teachers cannot be expected to know for sure what happened to notes. Table 4.18 reveals these discrepant views. The major difference between the two groups is in the 'Destroyed' category, where 41 per cent of appraisers say this is what happened. If one adds the 17 per cent of teachers who say 'Destroyed' to the 14 per cent who don't know, and adds in the 11 per cent difference in the category 'Appraiser keeps' (31 per cent compared with 20 per cent), then this may explain what appears to be a large discrepancy. Perhaps 40 per cent or so of appraisers did in fact destroy their notes, but teachers either did not know this happened, or assumed that they must have kept them.

Table 4.18 Fate of observer's notes on lessons – teachers' and appraisers' views

Fate of observation notes	Teachers' view	Appraisers' view
Appraiser keeps	31	20
Teacher keeps	22	26
Both keep copy	11	8
Destroyed	17	41
Don't know	14	0
Missing data	4	5

The next stage in the process was for an actual appraisal interview to be arranged. We asked teachers to say how long their appraisal interview lasted, how close it was to their classroom observations, how much related to classroom observation, and whether targets for future development were set. A wide range of responses accrued. Although some 10 per cent of teachers had their full appraisal interview within twenty-four hours of their classroom observation, most were spread evenly across the categories 'Within a week' (42 per cent) and 'Within half a term' (42 per cent). Most frequently the actual appraisal interview lasted between half an hour and one hour (62 per cent), but about one teacher in six had an appraisal interview lasting under thirty minutes (16 per cent) or longer than one hour (17 per cent).

The question about how much of the appraisal interview was spent discussing the classroom observations produced an average of 54 per cent, but there was a flat distribution across the ten points on the scale in the questionnaire, shown in Table 4.19.

Table 4.19 Amount of appraisal interview spent discussing classroom observation

Time (up to)	10%	20%	30%	40%	50%	60%	70%	80%	90%	100%
Teachers (%)	2	7	10	10	7	17	7	11	11	8

The figures add up to ninety, as 10 per cent of teachers did not respond. It may be that estimating how much of an interview is devoted to one element of an appraisal is open to wide interpretation, but equally there might in practice have been a genuine variation.

Target setting

Since appraisal was meant to be both retrospective, looking back at previous achievements, and prospective, making decisions about the teacher's future professional development, one final outcome of the appraisal interview should have been the agreement of targets for the teacher. When asked if targets had in fact been set, 90 per cent of teachers answered 'Yes'. On average there were two targets, but 3 per cent of teachers set five or more.

Most commonly the targets reflected the areas of focus identified in earlier parts of the questionnaire. School management (43 per cent) and class management (22 per cent), as well as teaching methods (18 per cent), predominated. A smaller number opted for differentiation (7 per cent) and aspects of the curriculum (7 per cent), and only a few selected personal relationships (4 per cent) or assessment (5 per cent). Only about one teacher in six mentioned that the targets they set grew out of the classroom observation of their lessons. Many were less clear when it came to identifying what their targets actually were. About a third of teachers did not respond to the invitation to describe their targets, some stating that these were in any case confidential, others claiming that they had forgotten what had been agreed:

> Cannot remember – I have not seen them and have not asked to see them.

> I can't remember – no record available.

> Can't remember. Most addressed management skills. Forms filled in, filed and forgotten!

This cheery forgetfulness, which was also characteristic of some appraisers as well, though not the norm for the majority of teachers, is a notable feature of a significant minority, who seem to have seen appraisal more as an imposed distraction than an important piece of professional development.

The outcomes of appraisal

One crucial set of questions that had to be asked of teachers was about the aftermath of appraisal, what were thought to be its effects, and about what, if anything, had changed. The fact that teachers had been appraised did not mean that practice had improved, nor even that it had changed at all. There is a difficulty in relying on people's written reflections on their own behaviour. Teachers may change how they do their job, but not recognise, or even realise that they have done so. Equally, they may not change their practice, but genuinely believe that they have. Furthermore, it is possible for teachers to change, but not be able or willing to ascribe any modification of what they do to a particular cause or source of inspiration. We are not always psychologically able to distinguish the roots of our own behaviour, especially if there are emotional barriers to accurate perception. For example, it is possible that a teacher who has a low regard for her appraiser might be reluctant to assign any credit for improvement in her teaching to a person she does not esteem.

The result of our question to teachers about whether they believed they had changed what they did in their classroom as a result of appraisal is shown in Table 4.20. It reveals a roughly 50/50 split between those asserting that they did modify their teaching and those believing that they did not. Indeed slightly less than half the sample answered 'Yes'. On the other hand nearly 70 per cent believed that they had derived personal benefits from appraisal.

Table 4.20 If appraisal had affected classroom practice/ offered personal benefits

	Affected practice	Personal benefits
Yes	49	69
No	50	27
Missing	1	4

These findings may, of course, be interpreted in different ways, depending on one's starting point. A Department for Education official, when told of the findings, replied, 'That's good news. If appraisal had not taken place it would have been zero per cent who would have changed what they were doing, so 49 per cent is not bad'. It might equally be argued that appraisal should help everyone modify practice, so if 50 per cent say they did not, then this is a high failure rate. Optimists see a half-full bottle, pessimists a half-empty one.

Closer inspection of some of the comments made by teachers in their written responses shows the nature of this 50/50 split. Those who did change often mentioned the advantage of having a 'mirror' in which to see oneself, and many referred to improved planning. Negative responses sometimes reflected lack of respect for the appraiser's judgement, but more experienced teachers often commented on the brevity of the whole exercise, setting one hour's observation against a lifetime of experience.

Comments from those who did change include:

The feedback was of immense benefit to me as this is how you improve your classroom practice. It is difficult to know sometimes whether you're getting it right, when you don't have time to reflect upon your teaching. Appraisal gives you this time.

Appraisal made me focus on my weaknesses and try to address them. Therefore I worked on my planning and have thus been more successful because of my efforts.

Lessons in PE and Art are more carefully planned and I feel more confident in these areas.

The following comments were made by respondents who did not change their practice:

The pressures of time and lack of enthusiasm from my appraiser meant the process became a form filling exercise in which I was being reported.

How can having someone sit in on two half-hour lessons be expected to give an overall picture of my teaching, focusing on a specific feature of it, and produce meaningful observations informing future practice?

My classroom practice in a science lab has been developed over many years as a result of experience in that area. Observation by a non-specialist for sixty minutes will not change it.

The difference between the 49 per cent who say they altered their teaching, and the 69 per cent who claim they derived personal benefits, is an intriguing one. How can people feel a process to be beneficial if it does not alter and improve what they do? To some extent this may be due to the 'managerial' type of focus that some 40 per cent of teachers set themselves, as was shown in Table 4.11. If they set themselves goals that related to school, rather than classroom processes, then their actual teaching may not have been directly affected.

The second explanation may lie in the statements that teachers made about the appraisal. Many mentioned a 'boost' simply through being given attention, whether this had pay-off in classroom terms or not; some saw career development opportunities that might not otherwise have materialised; others enjoyed the therapy of an intimate conversation:

> The busy schedule of school allows no time for self-reflection. This was the first time that I had actually sat down and thought about my teaching style and had an opportunity to discuss my aims with another member of staff.

> I found it reassuring in that a colleague from outside the department had the opportunity to see and comment in total confidence. I now feel much more appreciated as a person by my appraiser, although we got on well before.

> Half costs paid for timetabling course, and 'preparing for deputy headship' course provided. Would this have been provided through staff development in the normal way?

> Got everything off my chest!

Although there was enthusiasm about personal benefits from the great majority of teachers, some 27 per cent felt that they had not themselves gained a great deal from appraisal. Many of the sceptics clearly had not enjoyed good personal relationships with their appraiser, but some were simply cynical about the general value of the exercise, concerned about the introduction of performance-related pay on the back of appraisal, or felt they were too old to learn new tricks:

> I found it frustrating and depressing due to feedback given, which seemed totally impersonal.

> I am disappointed that I found it a negative experience due to the manner in which it was carried out. I should like to change my appraiser before the next process begins.

> How could it [benefit me]? I have been teaching more than 30 years! Early retirement?!

> Nothing will come of it because there is no money to do anything about it.

> There is obviously a widespread fear that appraisal will be tied to pay. One can trust an Education Minister as far as one can throw one. . . . Watching colleagues teach in a situation where the spirit is one of inquiry and learning among equals can do nothing but good. Where is the money to allow this? Wasting money on ill-conceived schemes erroneously patterned on the business world makes me hopping mad. . . . We are, as ever, classroom lions led by donkeys. There – I'm glad to get that off my chest!

So far the responses of teachers to the national questionnaire have been analysed as a single group. We shall now consider briefly some of the differences between groups, such as primary and secondary, and male and female teachers. Further comparisons will be made in the case studies described in later chapters.

Some group differences

It would have been possible to compare numerous sub-groups on every question which we asked. This kind of data dredging would probably have produced some significant relationships by chance, as invariably happens if several hundred such comparisons are made. Also it would have been extremely difficult to report such a volume of findings in a comprehensible and parsimonious way. It was decided, therefore, since our principal focus was on observation, to concentrate group comparisons on the two key questions about the perceived effect of an observer's presence and the teachers' feelings about being observed. One-way and two-way analysis of variance and Scheffé gap tests, as well as two-tailed t-tests for two-group comparisons, were used to discover whether the scores of various sub-groups showed differences that were statistically significant.

Table 4.21 shows the mean scores of different sub-groups' responses to the question about how much their teaching was affected by the presence in the classroom of their appraiser. The possible range of scores is from 1 (not at all) to 5 (considerably). The higher the score, therefore, the more the teachers claimed to be affected. Without tests of significance the trends in Table 4.21 seem to be clear. In general primary teachers claimed to be *more* affected by an observer's presence than did secondary teachers, and female teachers said they were more affected than male teachers.

Closer inspection of the data, however, shows a somewhat different picture. The major effect lies in the difference between the scores of primary and secondary teachers. When t-tests were performed on them, a highly significant t value of 5.22 was obtained, which showed that this kind of difference would have occurred by chance fewer than once in every 10,000 occasions. The difference between male and female teachers produced a t value of 2.58, which was also statistically significant, but on a lower scale, likely to occur by chance once in every 100 occasions.

However, whereas there were approximately equal samples of male and female secondary teachers, there were over five times more female than male teachers in the primary sample. As this imbalance could have distorted the results, we did a two-way analysis of variance on the scores, which took in both the primary/secondary and male/female

Table 4.21 Teachers' perception of the effect of appraiser's presence on teaching

Group	Mean score[1]
Male teachers	2.08
Female teachers	2.28
Primary teachers	2.45
Secondary teachers	2.05
Male primary teachers	2.49
Female primary teachers	2.45
Male secondary teachers	2.00
Female secondary teachers	2.10
Female teacher/female appraiser	2.30
Female teacher/male appraiser	2.26
Male teacher/female appraiser	2.18
Male teacher/male appraiser	2.01

[1] Five-point scale – the higher the mean score, the greater the perceived effect.

dimensions. This confirmed that it was the primary/secondary dimension that was significant, and that the male/female dimension was not. Table 4.21 shows, for example, the very small differences between male and female primary teachers, who averaged 2.49 and 2.45 respectively on this scale. By contrast, male primary teachers (2.49) and male secondary teachers (2.00) were well separated.

When the scores in Table 4.21 were analysed in terms of the pairing of appraisers and appraisees, there was a very clear order, with teachers in all-female pairs most affected, teachers in all-male pairs least affected, and mixed pairs in the middle. These differences were subjected to analysis of variance to elicit any statistical significance. A significant F ratio of 2.86 was obtained, which would only have occurred by chance once in thirty times.

The second key question asked how teachers felt at being observed in their classroom by someone. This question is related to the one above, but it addresses a different aspect. It is possible, for example, that a teacher might say that, although she was affected by the presence of an observer, she was none the less quite happy about being observed. One would expect a negative correlation between the two measures (the more their teaching is affected by an observer's presence, the less happy teachers are about being observed). A highly significant inverse relationship was indeed found between the two scales, the product moment correlation being $r = -0.34$, likely to occur by chance less than once in 10,000 occasions. This correlation, though highly significant, is not especially large. The square of the correlation ($R = 0.12$) gives the

common factor variance. This shows that only 12 per cent of the variation in scores on the one scale is 'explained' by the scores on the
other, so the two scales do appear to be measuring separate, if related
matters.

Table 4.22 shows the mean scores recorded by the various groups
on a five-point scale ranging from 1 (very unhappy) to 5 (very happy).
The higher the score, the happier the teacher claims to be. The pattern
of these responses is very similar to the answers to the previous question. Again, on first inspection, it is the secondary teachers, the male
teachers, and the male teachers with a male appraiser, who claim to be
happiest about being observed. The use of t-tests confirms some of
these surface conclusions. The scores of primary teachers and secondary
teachers are as markedly different as in the previous question, producing a highly significant t of 4.97, which would have occurred by
chance fewer than once in 10,000 occasions. In these responses, however, the sex differences were more significant than those in the
previous question. The t-test gave a value of 3.7, a result which might
have occurred by chance only once in every 5,000 occasions. Two-way
analysis of variance similarly confirmed that the male/female differences
were less significant than those between primary and secondary
teachers.

The scores in Table 4.22 were also analysed in terms of the pairing of
appraisers and appraisees, and there was the same clear order as in the
case of the previous question. The teachers in the all-female pairs were
least happy with being observed, teachers in all-male pairs felt most
happy, and mixed pairs were in the middle. When these differences

Table 4.22 Teachers' feelings about being observed

Group	Mean score[1]
Male teachers	3.96
Female teachers	3.67
Primary teachers	3.54
Secondary teachers	3.93
Male primary teachers	3.73
Female primary teachers	3.50
Male secondary teachers	4.01
Female secondary teachers	3.85
Female teacher/female appraiser	3.63
Female teacher/male appraiser	3.71
Male teacher/female appraiser	3.87
Male teacher/male appraiser	4.02

[1] Five-point scale – the higher the mean score, the greater the happiness at being observed.

were subjected to analysis of variance, a highly significant F ratio of 5.45 was obtained, which would only have occurred by chance once in 1,000 times. Scheffé gap tests confirmed that the most significant difference was between all-male and all-female pairs.

In summary, primary teachers reported being more affected by, and less happy at the presence of an observer, than secondary teachers. Female teachers were more affected and less happy than male teachers, though this effect is weaker than the primary/secondary one. Male teachers who had male appraisers were distinctly more happy at being observed and less affected by the presence of an observer than was the case with all-female or mixed pairs. Although this can partly be explained by the fact that most all-male pairs were in secondary schools, there may also be a male bonding 'buddy culture' effect at work here.

APPRAISERS' EXPERIENCES

As was stated earlier in this chapter, the sample of 479 appraisers who responded to the national questionnaire was split almost exactly half female and half male. In 97 per cent of cases, they were in middle or senior management positions. About three-quarters of them had sixteen or more years of experience. The questionnaire to appraisers concentrated on their experience, training, observation methods, the role they played, the feedback they gave to the teacher and target setting. Some of their experiences were reported earlier in this chapter, when teachers' perceptions and experiences were discussed.

Training

Almost all, 98 per cent of appraisers, said that they had received training, most frequently provided by local authorities. The great majority (83 per cent) said that they felt their training was sufficient. Nearly three-quarters (74 per cent) mentioned some training in observation. This, on the surface, largely positive looking picture needs to be qualified, however. When asked about the nature of their training, many did not respond. The elements of training courses mentioned by appraisers are shown in Table 4.23. The most common approach was the use of videos, though a few courses used role play to simulate the experience of appraising and being appraised. Only 5 per cent of the sample described specifically the type of classroom observation skills they had learned.

As was shown in Chapter 3, the training for appraisers was relatively short. Few courses devoted more than an hour, if that, specifically to observation. Some respondents gave specific detail of the nature of training, rather than just their general reaction to it:

Table 4.23 Elements of appraiser training courses

Elements of appraiser training	Percentage
Video	16
Role play	6
Handouts	1
Discussion	1
'Live' observation of lessons	1
Combination of above	22
No response	53

It [the course] showed a video of a class being observed, and each little group had to employ a different method of observing a certain aspect of the lesson. It raised awareness of observation skills.

We practised note taking, while watching a lesson on video.

[The course covered] situations through role play; importance of focusing on specific areas; observing groups of children; timed segments.

Some appraisers who had taken part in role play described it as 'not real' or 'false'. Some felt that they had not learned about how to appraise until they had actually done some appraisals. Many appraisers were aware of the limitations of what they had received:

Feel confident but not skilled, feel my training is not consistent with colleagues [especially appraisees]. Feel I need to go away and read up on focuses chosen, e.g. questions, techniques used by teachers etc.

Very little advice on how to deal with negative, obstructive appraisees. Rather too theoretical, i.e. what the [LEA] scheme involves.

Too much to cover in one day's course. Should have had more practice and feedback on technique.

Appraisers need more guidance as to what to look for in class observations.

More needed on effective classroom observation, identifying areas with appraisee, identifying achievable targets with appraisee.

Personal relationships

The high premium put on personal relationships by many local authorities was described in Chapter 3. Teachers showed in their comments above that the relationship between them and their appraiser was regarded as an important matter, and that mutual respect and under-standing were crucial. Similar concerns emerged from appraisers' comments:

> The appraisee and myself got to know each other better and I gained a greater understanding of another side of school life.

> Appraisal works only in schools where a high level of inter-staff trust is already established.

> I found the whole process quite rewarding as it gave me the oppor-tunity to learn about the day to day problems of another subject area/colleague.

Not all relationships were smoothly positive, however. Just as some teachers tended to blame their appraiser for mishaps or poor inter-personal relationships, so too a number of appraisers assigned blame to their appraisees:

> The appraisee involved had a very negative attitude to appraisal which made the appraiser's role a difficult one. She was ill-prepared and unwilling to accept any suggestion of implied criticism. I resented the time I had invested in her appraisal as a result, even though it had positive outcomes.

> An appraisal between myself as Head of Faculty and a teacher within one department of the faculty was much more difficult. The differ-ences and difficulties seemed to relate to age and a negative view of the appraisal process. It proved to be very difficult to set targets especially when the appraisee has consistently performed poorly and was not motivated sufficiently to improve his performance.

As some appraisers gained more experience through undertaking several appraisals, they often became more aware of the range of possi-bilities and problems. They were then able to make comparisons between teachers and situations, as well as see how they themselves were learning about the process. The last comment below reflects a clearly hierarchical view of appraisal. More frequently appraisers took a more collegial, co-equal stance:

> My second appraisal now in progress is going well. I feel I am getting better in helping the appraisee settle on areas of focus etc., having had one previous appraisal plus my own one. Hopefully this gets easier with practice.

> I have now done three and have found it is becoming easier for me to put colleagues at ease. Most successful have been the two where appraisees have a clear idea of what they would like to be their focus.

Appraisal was valuable where there was a genuine desire for career/ personal development and where the appraisee was open to constructive criticism/advice etc. Where this was lacking appraisal was just 'going though the motions' and was largely a waste of time.

Some staff are more able to reflect and be self-critical and analytical. Others find this difficult and have entrenched views. We see appraisal as developmental, but some staff simply want a pat on the head.

Classroom observation

The sample of appraisers, as was pointed out earlier in this chapter, is not an exact match with the sample of teachers. Since the replies were confidential it was not possible to match individual appraisers and teachers, even though, in most cases, they were from the same schools. Exact matching was only possible in the case studies reported in later chapters. One would, therefore, expect from appraisers similar, but not necessarily identical accounts of the process to those given by the teachers.

Teachers' and appraisers' accounts of the timing of feedback and the fate of notes compiled by observers were compared earlier in this chapter. Table 4.24 shows some further comparisons between appraisers' versions of what happened during classroom observation and those of teachers reported above.

Table 4.24 Comparisons between the accounts of classroom observation by appraisers and teachers

	Percentage of appraisers	Percentage of teachers
Teacher chose area of focus	52	55
Appraiser chose area of focus	1	2
Area of focus negotiated	40	37
Focus thought to be appropriate	96	92
Teacher chose lesson observed	48	38
Appraiser chose lesson observed	1	4
Lesson observed negotiated	47	53
One lesson observed	21	28
Two lessons observed	73	68
Observation lasted under 30 minutes	20	26
Observer made notes	89	89
Observer used observation schedule	14	7
Observer timed lesson segments	15	8
'Happy' or 'very happy' about observation	78	60

These two versions of events, given that there is not an exact match between the two groups, are fairly congruent. There is quite close agreement on the choice of an area of focus, and appraisers feel slightly more positive than teachers about the appropriateness of the choice. As was the case with other topics, like the timing of feedback, reported earlier in this chapter, appraisers' estimates of certain events that reflect perhaps more on them than on teachers are more favourable to themselves. Appraisers report that 48 per cent of teachers selected the lesson to be observed, for example, whereas teachers' accounts suggested it was 38 per cent. Similarly appraisers stated that 21 per cent of teachers had been observed only on one occasion, instead of the required minimum of two observations, whereas teachers put it higher at 28 per cent. They also reported that only 20 per cent of observations had lasted thirty minutes or less, compared with the higher estimate of 26 per cent from teachers.

There are some differences between the accounts of observation techniques. Although the figure of 89 per cent for use of freehand notes is identical for both groups, appraisers report a higher frequency of use of timed segments and observation schedules than do teachers, who were perhaps not always aware if these were being employed. On five-point scales, appraisers were more likely to rate themselves 'happy' or 'very happy' (78 per cent) at observing another teacher in the classroom, than was the case with teachers (60 per cent) putting themselves in the same two highest categories on a five-point scale about being observed. It is not surprising that the 'victim' appears the more apprehensive, though the great majority of both groups, it must be said, see themselves as fairly relaxed about the process.

While comparisons between appraisers' and teachers' perceptions are of interest, one major purpose of the appraiser questionnaire was to obtain their first-hand accounts of the process from their unique vantage point. There was very close agreement between appraisers and teachers about the participant or non-participant role of the appraiser. About a quarter, 23 per cent according to teachers, 25 per cent according to appraisers, participated in the lesson in some way. Some found it difficult to change their normal role:

[I] . . . provided support for SEN pupils as this is my usual role with these groups.

[I] . . . helped children by questioning to understand their maths task and actually worked with them, spurring them on.

[I] . . . played the role of support teacher and 'secretively' made freehand notes at appropriate times.

[I] . . . talked with students – asked about enjoyment of task and usefulness of lesson. Questioned their understanding of the instructions they had been given.

[I] . . . spoke to the teacher. Spoke to the pupils about their task. Sat at the back of the room and listened to explanations. Sat at the front of the room when he saw individual pupils. Walked round the room looking at work and asking questions.

These responses raise interesting questions. The first is the extent to which, if appraisers are appraising someone else, the lesson actually becomes significantly their own if they play a prominent part in it. The second is the place of pupils' perceptions, especially in the last two responses quoted above, when the appraisers systematically went round the class checking pupils' work, and in one case asking their opinions of the lesson. This can be seen as thorough or intrusive, depending on one's point of view. Some 30 per cent of appraisers said that they had talked to the pupils during the lesson.

When it came to making a record of the lesson observed, the approach tended to be informal rather than highly structured. Most appraisers (89 per cent) reported that they used freehand notes, though about one in seven said they made use of some kind of lesson observation schedule, or that they timed lesson segments. The three appraisers quoted below appear to have been meticulous in what they recorded. They used varying degrees of structure and focused on different concepts, depending on the context, the third one being a secondary science class. The second appraiser reports having negotiated the observation agenda with the primary teacher concerned:

I noted the procedure of the lesson and listed pupil activity and teacher activity including lesson introduction, pacing, nature of materials/task, appropriateness for pupils of differing abilities, close of lesson, nature of homework, place of lesson in general scheme of work.

I observed a group of children as agreed between myself and the appraisee. We had agreed on criteria for observation. I made notes of what the children said and did in the context of the agreed criteria and reported these accurately back to the appraisee. The information was accurately recorded, non-judgemental and attributable to the child and task as appropriate.

I completed a checklist which recorded the activities of the groups in the classroom focusing on their ability to work co-operatively on the task, their use and care of resources, and the class teacher's availability for direct teaching, general supervision of the children and recording their progress during science investigation.

One critical question we asked was about the extent to which the appraiser was familiar with the year group, in the case of primary, and the subject, in the case of secondary appraisers. Although about 56 per cent of appraisers said they had 'a great deal' of personal experience of teaching in the same context as the teacher they were appraising, a quarter of appraisers said that their experience was 'none or almost none', while some 18 per cent described it as 'occasional'. Thus a certain lack of familiarity with the context in which the teaching took place applied to about 43 per cent of appraisers, which could sometimes be a problem, as these accounts reveal:

As Head of Science . . . appraising Head of Creative Arts . . . I was distinctly aware of a lack of specific knowledge and skills related to his teaching area.

One appraisal was observing a colleague who teaches outside my subject area. This was interesting but harder to offer constructive strategies for improvement [in response to appraisee's request].

[The teacher] was dissatisfied with choice of me as appraiser since I did not have year/age group experience of class she taught – what could I offer her?

The shared lack of confidence in appraisers' judgement, when they do not have comparable background and experience to the teachers they are observing, is a matter of some concern. This is a point which will recur in the case studies in later chapters.

Feedback

Appraisers, like teachers, described the nature of their attempts to arrange for a post-lesson discussion in circumstances when both were busy. Some schools made arrangements for this to take place properly, others did not. There did not seem to be a great deal of difference between primary and secondary schools, it looked to be more a case of will and organisation:

Both appraisee and appraiser were given non-contact time immediately after the classroom observation to give immediate feedback. The discussion focused around the specific areas of observation with both appraisee and appraiser saying how they felt the lesson had gone.

[At the] . . . end of [the] school day – dialogue between the two staff concerned in an amicable way. There were no time pressures and no interruptions – we used the classroom that the lesson had just taken place in.

No time built in for this. Feedback given on informal basis during breaks and at end of day.

Over lunch – with hastily scribbled notes of main points and implications.

There were some status issues here, as well as matters to do with the type of building in which the school was situated. Some schools have virtually no private facilities, most areas being public. Others have several possible spaces that offer privacy. Senior staff sometimes had their own room, and so were able to withdraw from the hearing and gaze of others for a confidential conversation, whereas more junior appraisers did not have their own room. On the other hand, some senior appraisers, including head teachers, deliberately did not hold the de-briefing in their own study, preferring to 'play away' and talk in the teachers' classroom after pupils had departed.

Evaluation

Many senior staff are well used to evaluating processes in their school, so they were very articulate in their final analysis of their appraisal experiences. Their views, however, were as varied as those of teachers. Many felt extremely positive about appraisal, especially those who had been close to the design of the procedures, seeing it as a good way not just of implementing school policy, but of securing teachers' professional development:

It provides, sensitively handled, a neutral and non-threatening forum for open discussion of staff concerns and aspirations and a means of motivating, challenging and fulfilling teaching practitioners. It puts an onus on the school and its structures to be seen to be supporting staff and their own professional development.

Appraisal allows all staff to focus entirely upon themselves and their teaching and to discuss it in a professional manner – something many staff previously would have been unable to do. It also allows staff to discuss their concerns, strengths and weaknesses [something most teachers are far more concerned about]. Most professional teachers are committed to improving the quality of their work. Appraisal allows them to contemplate, discuss and set targets to allow them to do this.

Those who held a more negative view after the process typically commented on the shortage of time and resources, or were concerned about the impact on their colleagues, or simply cynical about the likely outcomes of appraisal:

I found that I simply did not have the time to fully appraise as I would have wished to. I have not followed up certain targets for the same reason, nor have I found time for the review meetings.

I can see how valuable this process is but I still feel that my main role is that of a teacher, year head, PSE co-ordinator and therefore on the list of priorities appraisal is not that high.

One teacher went completely to pieces during the lesson observation. She was quite open about it with the staff but the lesson did not go according to plan. . . . We have wondered if the classroom observations should be done more often and not related to appraisal.

The process is a worthwhile experience but often does not match up to expectations. It now feels like a farce. Lots of hype, admin, training, discussion. Now the statements sit in a drawer. There is no inset co-ordinator to help ensure targets are met. I can only do so much since as appraisal co-ordinator I should not really see the targets of those other than people I have appraised myself. Colleagues at school are off on 20-day courses unrelated to their appraisal targets but those who went through the process are neglected. Now the process in my school lies dormant and I am powerless to keep the wheels turning.

The national questionnaire helped us compile a picture of how appraisal was seen to have worked out in practice by the teachers and appraisers who took part in it. It offers the views and experiences of well over a thousand teachers and appraisers in 169 primary and secondary schools all over England, an important perspective in its own right. However, it also provides a national framework within which the twenty-nine intensive case studies that were undertaken of primary and secondary teachers can be seen, and it is to these that we now turn in the following chapters.

Chapter 5

Appraisal in Casewell School

THE CASE STUDIES OF TEACHERS

The study of local authorities and the national questionnaire surveys, Studies 1 and 2 of the Leverhulme Appraisal Project described in earlier chapters, established the framework within which Study 3, the case studies of twenty-nine individual primary and secondary teachers, were located. Case studies can put flesh on to the bones of surveys. We wanted to see at first hand what actually happened in different kinds of primary and secondary school, as experienced by those directly involved in appraisal.

This meant we had to spend considerable amounts of time interviewing and observing not only teachers, but also their appraisers and other staff in the school who were concerned with the process. The case studies are described in this and the following three chapters. It is not always possible to make a clean separation of general and specific matters, and there is bound to be overlap, but this chapter describes the experience of appraisal as observed during the research project in a secondary comprehensive school to which we have given the fictitious name Casewell School. Chapter 6 concentrates on teachers' general experiences, while Chapters 7 and 8 deal principally with the classroom observation and behaviour aspects of appraisal.

In order to witness the events from beginning to end there were certain key moments when teachers needed to be observed and interviewed. These included the very start of the cycle, when teacher and appraiser met, the times when lessons were observed and discussed, the setting of targets, and the final appraisal interview. We decided to follow up some months later with an interview aimed at checking what, in retrospect, teachers felt they had gained or how they had changed what they did.

The sample of teachers

It is neither desirable nor feasible to compel teachers to take part in intensive case study research, so the twenty-nine teachers in the sample were all volunteers. Schools of different types and size were approached in various parts of the country in both urban and rural areas. The teachers came from fourteen primary and secondary schools in four LEAs. Most were experiencing their first appraisal, but some had been involved in official or unofficial pilot schemes previously. There were eleven primary and eighteen secondary teachers. It is sometimes believed that only the more robust teachers will volunteer to be observed, but, as the accounts below will show, this is not always the case.

Classroom observation

Three independent observations of each appraisee's practice were carried out by the researchers as part of the case study. If possible these addressed the same aspect of the teacher's practice that was going to be focused on during the appraisal, though this information was not always available in the initial stages. The researchers took freehand notes, recorded any 'critical events' and studied the extent to which pupils were involved in their task or were being deviant (Wragg 1984).

The purpose of these observations was threefold: first, to assemble a picture of classroom climate; second, to detect changes over time; third, to corroborate or refute what came out of interviews and other kinds of evidence. The observations were conducted before the appraisal process started, immediately after the completion of the main part of the process and again a term later. On each occasion two half-hour observations were undertaken. As far as possible they shadowed the observation carried out by the appraiser as part of the appraisal process, but the structured observations were carried out on each occasion to allow comparisons to be made and the effects of appraisal to be assessed.

We also tried to be present at some of the observations carried out by appraisers. There is, of course, a risk that the presence of two adults may affect the lesson even more than the presence of one, but that was a risk we were prepared to take. As far as possible the focus and method of recording used by the appraiser was replicated and in addition the researchers recorded on/off task and deviancy measures on each occasion. There will be further analysis of what was seen in lessons in Chapter 7. Regardless of the role played by the appraiser during the lesson, the researchers were non-participant observers during these periods.

Observation of meetings

By careful negotiation with the participants the research team was also able to observe a large number of the meetings that were part of the appraisal process for each of the teachers. The researcher was non-participant and resisted any attempt to be drawn into the discussion, or to act as a reference for either the appraiser or appraisee's perceptions of the procedure. The dialogue at these meetings was recorded on audiotape, although in three case studies this was not done, as the person concerned would have found it too stressful. In two of these cases the appraiser asked for the conversations not to be recorded and made a similar request when being interviewed alone. In the third case the appraisee seemed to be finding the recording of the first interview so stressful that the researcher offered not to record any future meetings. The researchers also made a note of the timing, tone and atmosphere of the meetings and, when not recording, took detailed notes of the interaction between appraiser and appraisee. The tapes were transcribed and analysed as soon afterwards as possible.

INTERVIEWS BY THE RESEARCHERS

Members of the research team interviewed appraisees, appraisers and head teachers at various points throughout the process. The interviews followed a similar pattern, although with different emphases. Interviews were semi-structured to allow the interviewees to expand on any aspect they felt to be important. Head teacher interviews focused on the effect appraisal was having, or could have, on the school as an institution. Appraiser and appraisee interviews were more focused on their attitudes and experiences. As with the appraiser/appraisee meetings, all interviews were recorded unless the interviewee had expressed a desire that this should not happen.

Appraiser/appraisee interviews

The first interview we did with appraiser and appraisee covered the collection of background information about their professional lives, their previous experiences of appraisal (if any), their training for their respective roles and their opinions on a variety of aspects of the process. Questions were asked in terms of the principle of appraisal and included questions about the teacher's opinions of the purpose of appraisal, its advantages and disadvantages, the main components of any scheme, and the relative merits of a peer or hierarchical system.

Both appraisers and appraisees were asked about their expectations as to how the process would be conducted, any anticipated concerns and what they expected to gain from the experience. Appraisees were also asked if they expected their own classroom practice to be affected by appraisal and what, if any, other benefits they thought they would gain. The appraiser interview placed more emphasis on their role and the training they had received for it with particular reference to any training in observation skills.

The interviews carried out after the main part of the process had been completed focused on the appraisers' and appraisees' experience. As the main focus of the research was on the classroom observation element of appraisal there were more questions in this area covering the teacher's feelings about being observed, any difference in the method or type of observation carried out and the main points identified in the feedback. The rest of the interview compared their actual experience with their previously expressed expectations in the areas of time taken, benefits gained and perceived change in practice.

The final part of the cycle was the follow-up interview. Appraisees were interviewed a term after their appraisal had been completed, though before their review meeting. The interview was short and concentrated on their retrospective feelings about certain aspects of their experience of appraisal. They were also fed back answers they had given in the first interview and asked if their opinions had changed in light of their experience of the process. Specific aspects, such as the appropriateness of their classroom observation focus, the key components of the process and their current view of appraisal were also investigated. Finally their perceptions as to whether their approach to future appraisals would be affected by their present experience were sought.

Head teacher interviews

The head teachers of the schools in the sample were interviewed twice: before and after the school's involvement in the case studies. The interviews were unstructured, covering general areas of interest, such as staff perceptions, the head teacher's own views of appraisal, and LEA involvement and support, rather than specific issues.

In the first interview general background information about the school and its catchment were elicited as an introduction to a more specific discussion about the school's planning for, and implementation of, appraisal. This included the amount of LEA support they had received in the way of training and finance for supply cover. The last interview was constructed in a similar way and the topics included: how the implementation of appraisal had related to their expectations, including any changes they were planning to introduce in the next cycle and how the targets set were affecting the school as a whole;

how their and the staff's views had changed, if at all; and the role the LEA was now playing.

Analysis of data

The case study data were mainly in qualitative form, though the two measures covering pupils' involvement in the task and deviancy were based on an index devised by Wragg (1984). These two sets of scores can range from zero (no child on task, or no child deviant) up to 100 (all children on task, or all children deviant). The observation data were analysed in three different ways. The on/off task and deviancy scores for each observation period were recorded and analysed. They were then compared to try and ascertain any effect which might be due to the presence of the appraiser, or any change which appeared to be an outcome of appraisal.

In the tradition of grounded theory (Glaser and Strauss 1967) the criteria for analysis were taken from the interviews themselves. The text under the main headings was then analysed further for sub-categories of data. A first analysis involved the Ethnograph computer programme to analyse the interview data, and codes were attached to segments of text. As the analysis proceeded in greater depth the increase in the number of codes being used became unwieldy, so the researcher compiling each case study analysed the data collected in terms of categories and sub-categories, meanings and interpretations. Two researchers then compared analyses to ensure a common approach. As a further validity check, a third researcher analysed a sample of both sets of case studies and contributed to the discussion. A tree diagram was constructed of the issues arising from interviews to illustrate the relationships between them.

To show the whole appraisal process at work, the experiences in one of the case study schools are described below. This case is not being cited as a paragon ideal, and it is a secondary not a primary school, so it cannot be said to be 'typical' of all the schools we studied. It is simply used as an illustration because its appraisal programme was carefully organised. School and teacher names are fictitious, though the events are all real.

CASEWELL COMPREHENSIVE SCHOOL

Casewell School is a relatively small, urban comprehensive in a mainly residential area. The 900 pupils have mixed backgrounds, with a slightly higher proportion coming from the lower ability range, as the school has a special facility for children with severe learning difficulties. The head,

Mrs Cooper, had held responsibility for appraisal in her previous post and was very committed to the concept. We conducted three case studies in this school, and all three teachers were quite experienced. Interestingly all appraiser–appraisee pairs were mixed sex. One involved an appraisal by the head teacher. The remaining two were conducted by middle managers, one of whom was a subject specialist, while the other had some pastoral responsibility. As shown below, two of the case study teachers taught in the same department, whereas the third, appraised by the head teacher, taught in a different department and was also a member of the senior management team.

Appraiser
Mr Abel (head of science)
Miss Baker (head of year)
Mrs Cooper (head teacher)

Teacher
Mrs Duke (science teacher)
Mr Edwards (science teacher)
Mr Foster (languages, appraisal
    co-ordinator)

Establishing policy – the introduction of the appraisal scheme

Mrs Cooper, the head of Casewell, faced a problem from the very start. She had already had some previous experience of appraisal when she arrived at the school and was very keen to implement a scheme immediately. The staff on the other hand, as in many schools during that period, were already feeling pressurised by a plethora of changes.

> When I came here, obviously there were a number of things to do, but I felt very committed to appraisal and presented it to the Policy Committee. Unfortunately, with all the changes I was bringing, they weren't at that time ready to take on such a big initiative.

The introduction of appraisal was deferred and a working party was formed to 'look at the climate in which appraisal would best flourish'. The minutes of its deliberations were posted in the staff room so that all were informed about its progress. The preference was for the appraiser to act as 'critical friend', as well as for an 'open classroom' approach. It was felt that support from the top, seizing the development opportunities that appraisal offered, discussing how those opportunities could be met, were all important. By the time the Department for Education regulations were published, the school had completed its in-house consultations and was ready to implement a scheme. It was involved in helping set up the local authority's guidelines and, when these were produced, was already in a position to adapt its own scheme to meet LEA expectations. Mrs Cooper explained that 'our guidelines are based on the [LEA's] programme but we have elaborated – to try and give interpretations for staff as exemplars'.

Hierarchical model

It was decided to adopt a hierarchical model. Early on the head and senior management team had themselves been appraised and were embarking on the appraisals of middle management staff. Mrs Cooper explained why a hierarchical approach had been selected:

> The reason why, I suppose, we went for the senior managers was really that, as members of the Policy Group, they were acutely aware of the school framework – which was a key part of our appraisal process – that we wanted all development to come into line with the institutional needs. We haven't the resources to support, I'm afraid, other aims.

She later explained why she had supported a hierarchical rather than other kind of model. The fulfilling of institutional aims was given as a major reason. It was a case of who could influence future events. She indicated that she was not particularly opposed to the idea of peer appraisal, for example, but felt that 'there was the possibility of a greater likelihood of (fellow teachers) not being able to deliver what was promised, because they are not empowered to, whereas . . . managers are'.

Choice of appraisers

The Policy Committee had made the decision that, although staff would have a right to ask for an alternative appraiser, initially their appraiser would be appointed by the head and appraisal co-ordinator, who also indicated when appraisals would take place. Mrs Cooper explained that she wrote to all staff indicating who had been appointed as their appraiser and asking them to contact her if they had any objection to the selection:

> This had already been put to staff. I told them that this was the most effective way of handling a very delicate situation. . . . And they have been given all the details of how to appeal in the guideline booklet.

Appraisers were not told who they were to appraise until the appraisee had had the opportunity to accept or reject them. Since the scheme's introduction only two teachers had asked for alternative appraisers, and this was regarded as an indicator of success. This structured approach also avoided any single person being overloaded with appraisals.

In large departments in which the head of department could not possibly appraise all the staff, other criteria were used to select appraisers. For example, people who had already demonstrated skills within the pastoral area of their work were matched with their head of year. Mrs Cooper felt that the way in which the process had been set up within the school made this an acceptable alternative:

> We stressed right from the start that the appraiser was a facilitator of the process, that they would be responsible for gathering evidence from the key people involved as third party evidence. So if you didn't have your head of faculty, 'please don't think you're having a second rate one' . . . because everyone was acting as a facilitator.

For the appraiser to have specialist subject knowledge was not seen as essential.

Training

As frequently happened in other schools, Casewell School adopted a 'cascade' model, whereby the process began with senior people and rippled down. It started with the head teacher and appraisal co-ordinator receiving LEA training. Mrs Cooper described the observation skills training she and the appraisal co-ordinator had been given by the LEA:

> What it did was to provide us with training materials so that we could work on that in school. We certainly were not exposed to any real training – that I would regard as real training, but we had materials we could use.

They then organised training in-house for the remainder of the staff. To prepare those who would eventually be taking on the appraiser role, the school had focused its staff development for that year on the skills appraisers would need. The overall approach was to start from the skills that teachers were believed to possess already, such as 'negotiating with children', and to develop those. Mrs Cooper did not run a day on appraisal *per se*:

> We never at any time actually said to staff, 'We're going to have an Inset day on appraisal. This is what it's going to mean to you'. We had an Inset day on 'negotiation' . . . we went on to 'interviewing techniques'. We broke it down into training modules.

The skills based days were followed by discussions on different approaches to the process, such as the atmosphere needed for a successful appraisal interview, and these were written into the school guidelines. In this way Mrs Cooper felt they created an ethos of consultation and avoided the feeling that the process was totally imposed.

Structure of school's appraisal process

The appraisal scheme in operation included self-appraisal, an initial meeting, classroom observation with feedback and other information gathering, an appraisal interview including the setting of targets and an appraisal statement. A thirty-six page booklet of school guidelines was produced in which each stage was clearly documented. A copy was issued to all staff, with the suggestion that it be read in conjunction with the LEA guidelines. The rights and responsibilities of both appraisers and appraisees were stated, as were the expectations for each stage of the process, including codes of conduct for the self-appraisal and appraisal interview and suggested forms of classroom observation, with examples of different methods of observation and possible appropriate areas of focus.

The school guidelines also provided a diagram indicating the audience for each part of the process. For example, it showed that only the appraiser and appraisee were entitled to be party to documents collected in the data collection phase, though the appraiser, appraisee and appraisal co-ordinator needed to see the timetable of appointments set at the initial interview, as supply teachers could be brought in for up to four lessons for each appraisal where necessary. The head teacher, chairman of the governors and the staff development officer could only see lists of agreed targets with the teachers' names deleted.

The school used duplicated proformas for each stage of the appraisal process. One of these, completed at the appraisal interview, laid out who was to be responsible for the outcomes of the appraisal. The appraiser's role was to inform all those mentioned at the appraisal interview whose support was necessary for the teacher's further development. If support was not practicable, it was the appraiser's role to re-negotiate with the appraisee what alternatives could be provided. After their appraisal, each appraisee completed an evaluation sheet and the appraisal co-ordinating group (which later became the appraisal quality management group) met regularly to ensure that structures were in place and were charged with ensuring that the targets of any one appraisal would be met.

New members of staff

The school also linked appraisal into its system of induction for new members of staff, including a year-long professional tutor scheme for new staff, both experienced and newly qualified. This involved self-evaluation, setting a focus for classroom observation, and a formal feedback session. The head teacher described this as 'a very comfortable and non-threatening environment' and explained that it resulted in a negotiated written report. She felt this was extremely useful as a familiarisation process for appraisal.

Purposes of appraisal

School's 'official' view

The head's commitment to appraisal stemmed from the benefits that she felt she had gained from its implementation at her previous school. It had, she said, 'made me think each year about what I wanted' and she described it as an 'enriching experience'. In Casewell School the intention had been to introduce an appraisal scheme that would enable all staff to feel valued, supported and listened to – not just as part of a team but as an individual. The school appraisal document stated that:

> . . . at Casewell School we believe appraisal plays an integral part of the professional development of teaching and non-teaching staff. It will lead individuals to an understanding of their own performance and will reflect objectively the commitment and contribution that each member of the staff brings to the school. It is a supportive model and it enables development of the individual within the framework of the school.

This was intended to underline a strong corporate ethos, though not to ignore the fact that appraisal was about better individual performance and development:

> We are engaging our staff in a process which allows them greater satisfaction with their work, and acknowledgement of planning, and that means they can perform better in the classroom.

To this end, the head teacher identified two types of appraisal: one was concerned with the extension of roles and the other she described as 'plateau development'. The latter was for those people who appeared to be happy with their present position but wanted 'enrichment', which she identified as being 'very different from extension'. The school had developed a specific approach for 'extension', stating in its policy that 'appraisal will lead individuals to an understanding of their own performance and will reflect objectively the commitment and contribution that each member of the staff brings to the school'. There had been concern that some appraisals were moving away from a classroom focus, so it was decided to remind staff that this was to be the main element for most teachers.

Appraisers' views of purpose

The three appraisers we interviewed all had differing management responsibilities. One was a head of faculty (Mr Abel), another a head of year (Miss Baker), the third was the head teacher (Mrs Cooper). The first two often echoed the positive views of appraisal expressed by the head, though sometimes with reservations. In interview Miss Baker stressed the advantages that appraisal offered teachers for reflection on their practice:

> I feel quite strongly that it's to allow the individual to take a step back, to look at the work they've been doing, to really review for themselves with the help of somebody else, with objective views.

Mrs Cooper and Mr Abel identified one of the main purposes of appraisal as the recognition of individual achievement and the provision of support to meet teachers' needs. Mr Abel went on to explain that out of these two aspects came a further benefit because 'if you take those two things further, it becomes motivating. So I guess they're the reasons for doing it. I think it's an excellent way of motivating staff'.

However, later in the interview, the same appraiser expressed doubts about the need for formal appraisal, expressing a degree of cynicism about government support:

> Anything that makes people reflect on their classroom will be a good thing. Now having said that, we don't need appraisal to make people reflect on their classroom processes. If we just want to improve classroom performance, there are yet even cheaper ways of doing it. I think it was just felt important that the word 'appraisal' was used, so that industry knew teachers weren't incompetent. . . .
> I think in this school we had effective staff development targeting before appraisal and we will continue to have effective staff development targeting. We have effective classroom teachers, we have classroom teachers who are developing. The bottom line is, if they were serious about appraisal, the government would have funded it properly.

Miss Baker, however, believed that the statutory nature of the scheme was necessary to ensure its proper implementation: 'I think it's got to be done on a formal basis, otherwise it won't be done. I don't think it will be done properly unless it's done on a formal basis'.

Mrs Cooper, the head, again reasserted her view about the corporate nature of appraisal, seeing it as a means for improvement through a formal whole school framework: 'the advantages of the scheme are coherence, consistency – everybody has a similar experience'.

Appraisees' views of purpose

Of the three teachers participating in the project, one, Mrs Duke, had been at the school for three years and held a scale post as Key Stage 3 co-ordinator, responsible for the science programme for eleven to fourteen year olds; the second, Mr Edwards, had moved to education from industry five years previously and was a Key Stage 4 curriculum co-ordinator, responsible for the science education of fourteen to sixteen year olds; while the third, Mr Foster, was a member of the senior management team and held the post of appraisal co-ordinator within the school. The three had developed different ideologies, and only Mrs Duke introduced the notion of 'assessment' during our interview with her, although this was in the context of self-evaluation and was seen by her as a positive outcome: 'To monitor your own progress within teaching . . . it's a way of clarifying you're doing the right thing really. . . . I think it keeps you on your toes . . . and I think it can be a supportive thing also'.

The other two placed appraisal more in a school setting and talked about the development of the individual for the benefit of the pupils and the institution. Mr Foster explained that he saw the advantages of appraisal as: 'first of all, for the support and development of the individual, but also for the benefit of the educational experiences of all the pupils. In other words, you'll get a more highly trained work force'.

Mr Edwards also stressed, in his first interview at the beginning of his appraisal, the importance of placing the appraisal of the individual within the wider school context: 'I think it should be a rewarding experience for the individual and in a positive constructive way should indirectly support the institution we're working in'.

With the benefit of hindsight, however, when he was interviewed for a third time, a term after his appraisal process had been completed, he was less sure how the balance between teacher and institutional needs could be ensured, fearing that pressures to please the 'customers', that is, the pupils, might clash with the needs and aspirations of the teacher:

> . . . even my own knowledge tells me that there's this wonderful overall issue – which focuses on the children, which is fine – to be child centred. But I would argue that the development of the child also needs to be development of the staff. Because if they don't have development, if they don't feel satisfaction, if they haven't clarified their role, their status, their successes, they're not really in a position to encourage children to do that . . . I think appraisal could go in both directions – it could go towards the child's benefit and towards the appraisee's benefit. But I think personal development is going to be somehow pulled back if the appraisal process is lead-ing to child development. I think appraisal is about teaching

performance, teaching skills. I don't say it has to be or **should** be, but I think it is – based on a direction of a customer – that's not the right word. Our aim is to help the child, which is the customer area . . . and I think what will happen is – and I feel this quite strongly – that the personal development side, even the professional side, is going to be limited by that goal.

This fear was not shared by the other appraisees at the end of their appraisals. Mrs Duke felt it had benefited her personally to reflect on her teaching, despite admitting to initial doubts about its usefulness. Mr Foster, the school's appraisal co-ordinator, and so someone with a strong vested interest in the process, was keen to stress the personal development aspects of the school's appraisal process:

> Basically I think the process that we've got in place here is a very effective one. It's a supportive model and I think that staff see it in that light . . . We're looking at personal development planning and those issues at the moment.

After the appraisal cycle was over the school put into place personal development plans for staff. Mr Foster felt very strongly that the appraisal process had been extremely influential in the introduction of these plans to the school.

Casewell teachers' experiences of appraisal

Mrs Duke

Mrs Duke was an experienced teacher, Key Stage 3 co-ordinator for the department, and part of a year group tutor team. She felt that the key component of the appraisal process was the classroom observation and during her first interview, when asked about the effect that appraisal would have on classroom practice in general, said: 'It concentrates your mind to think what you're doing if you know somebody else is going to be in the classroom'.

However, she was less sure as to its impact on her own practice: 'I don't know. I think probably when I've been through the process I'll answer that. . . . He might do something I don't agree with'.

She felt confident of the steps involved in the process and initially did not express any concerns about it. At her initial meeting with the appraiser it had been agreed that the three areas of focus would be her work as the Key Stage 3 co-ordinator; work with pupils outside the department; and for the classroom observation, setting work appropriate to the child or group, that is, 'differentiation'. She hoped the feedback on the observation would give her advice on improving her use of differentiation within her teaching. She knew whom she wanted to be consulted as part of the information gathering process and this had been agreed. When asked how she felt about being observed, she explained:

> I don't really mind actually. Perhaps I'll feel slightly nervous on Monday morning! I think, in a way, we're always walking in and out of each other's classrooms anyway and, because equipment's in various places, we're not isolated from each other.

Although the choice of her appraiser, her head of department, was imposed, he would have been her first choice. As was the case with many secondary teachers in this study, she felt it important that the appraiser had close knowledge of the theory and practice of the subject, the department and the way she worked:

> I suppose in an ideal world it would be nice to choose your own appraiser. Having said that, I guess I'm lucky because I would have chosen Tom to do my appraisal . . . I wouldn't have liked to have had somebody outside the science department doing my appraisal, because I'm not so convinced that they would have understood perhaps the pressures, the schemes of work. . . . It's a different subject in as much as it's practical, as well as theory.

She was disappointed in the number of observations carried out. When interviewed on the first occasion, she was not sure how many observations there would be, but thought that probably three lessons would be observed, plus thirty minutes feedback on each occasion. In practice, she was only observed for one double period with feedback of less than thirty minutes. She assumed this was because of pressure of time but was happy with the feedback as it gave her 'constructive criticism', particularly about the use of the resources. That particular period had been chosen because it was a practical lesson (hence the double period). Mrs Duke would have liked a second observation of a theory lesson or another lesson later in the term when she knew the group better:

> I thought . . . I knew he was observing me for a double lesson and I assumed he was going to do another double. I didn't realise that once that was over, that was it. . . . It was almost over too quickly. But again, that's time, isn't it?

Her appraisal interview was conducted during school time in the school interview room. The room has comfortable chairs, and it appeared, on the surface at any rate, a relaxed meeting. There was a noticeable amount of laughter and repartee. About 20 per cent of the discussion was about the departmental heads' course she was already attending and linked the course work she needed to do for that and the allocation of non-contact time for the development of her co-ordinator's role to an appraisal target. Approximately 40 per cent concentrated on her pastoral role and how she would like to develop that, while another 30 per cent concerned the chosen focus of her classroom practice. The rest dealt with practical matters such as the wording of the targets and statement. Overall Mrs Duke was happy with her appraisal. When asked whether it had affected her practice she said: 'Not in a major way, but in some ways, yes, it has. It wouldn't change the structure of the way I actually do lessons. It would change little areas'.

She cited the benefits of the appraisal as the confidence she had gained from knowing 'how much people think of you', and felt she was now more aware of differentiation. In retrospect she had found the process worthwhile:

> I have found it useful actually. It makes you think about your teaching, it makes you think about what you're doing. I wasn't so convinced I would find it useful. At one point, I thought I'd find it a drag, you know – just another thing to go through really.

Mr Abel, Mrs Duke's appraiser, was very concerned that appraisal was being introduced by the Government without adequate funding:

> It's got to be recognised that if you want an appraisal system for teachers, this is as cheap as it gets, and that's nothing to do with this school. The Government has introduced the cheapest possible appraisal scheme and what they're going to get is cheap results!

His original plan of using a variety of observation methods was reduced to making headings of the agreed areas of focus in order to prevent 'drifting in the lesson', but he was happy with the method used and felt it gave him the information he wanted. He felt he already knew his departmental staff well and, therefore, he had not expected to learn much about Mrs Duke's teaching skills from the process. In this he was not disappointed, but commented that 'it is a damned expensive way of reassuring me . . .'.

He had two other concerns about the process – the additional workload it created and the Government's insistence that all teachers apart from head teachers should be observed in the classroom. Although he had intended to carry out the appraisal thoroughly he was still surprised about the amount of time he had actually spent on it: 'It's frightening when you see it all written down'. He estimated it would take about six or seven hours as opposed to the eight hours and five minutes that it did, of which his teaching was covered by another teacher for two hours. He pointed to the ever increasing workload of heads of faculty and the need to give appraisal more time to undertake it effectively:

I am concerned that the workload at this level is just increasing exponentially and there's no flexibility in the system really to allow us the time to do it. . . . I think there's a crying need for people to be given the time to do the job properly. . . . And this is probably one of the most important things that's been introduced in the last five years and we can't afford to screw this up, and, if people feel it's just another chore, it won't be done properly.

He was equally critical of the presence of compulsory classroom observation in the appraisal process:

The Government's insistence on it being classroom based is frankly a nonsense. . . . The reason I'm in this job [head of faculty] is because I'm a good classroom teacher, and so for most middle managers the idea of focusing on the classroom for appraisal is a nonsense! Because what we're struggling on is our management tasks. Because we're not managers! There are very few people in this school who are trained managers. . . . I would say that probably two-thirds of the people who are being appraised – their needs are not classroom based.

Mr Abel explained that he was already confident in Mrs Duke's subject teaching abilities and did not see appraisal as a way of assessing her teaching skills but more in terms of providing the opportunity for her to review, with his help, her wider role within the school. He knew Mrs Duke was a good practitioner but was concerned that she would not receive promotion merely for being a good teacher; promotion was given for abilities outside the classroom.

He was not even convinced of the value of classroom observation within the appraisal process for other staff within his faculty:

I could appraise every member of my faculty, I think – quite satisfactorily – on the basis of two meetings a term or two meetings a year. I don't think I need to watch them teaching. I need to see them teach anyway, but not as part of an appraisal process.

Mr Edwards

Mr Edwards was another experienced teacher in the same department who had responsibility for Key Stage 4. He had come into teaching from another profession, in which he had had experience of appraisal. In his first interview, he told the researcher that he regarded the key components of appraisal as his own self-appraisal, third party evidence and 'agreed goal setting with defined action dates'. Although he believed that appraisal would affect classroom practice, either positively or negatively, depending on how it was structured and the support offered, he had concerns about the process itself.

He felt the self-appraisal sheets produced by the school were poor: he would have liked space to ask questions about the process and more time to fill them in. He was unsure about the exact stages of the process, knowing that it involved observation and feedback and 'presumably some goal setting', but he did not know if there was an appraisal interview. He felt there had not been enough communication about the process and too much depended on goodwill: 'the outcome, the expectations are not clear as an individual in terms of career or performance'.

He was unsure as to whether there was an actual start date for the process as he had known who would be appraising him for some time and, being unsure of the appraiser's role, expressed a passing thought that maybe he had already been covertly observed. When asked how he viewed the classroom observation component of the process he said:

> It's not a common experience. We do have support teachers in, so I'm used to having people in. I think it's a good experience. I haven't had it happen very often. . . . In theory, one agrees it might be a good idea between colleagues, but one is usually shooting through . . . 'Have you got those books?' – that sort of thing. So it's not a common experience. I don't mind. What I would like is to know what criteria the observation is based on.

He went on at some length about his appraiser, stressing that she needed to be aware of the aims and objectives of the lesson under observation and that some allowance should be made for the type of subject being taught. For example, science lessons involve certain safety rules that impose on the teaching methods. These concerns seemed to stem principally from the fact that his appraiser, Miss Baker, came from another subject area and was his appraiser simply because she led the year group team of which he was part.

Certain of his early concerns were addressed in the initial meeting and, though some proved groundless, his actual experience of the process raised other worries. He had only one combined feedback of the two observations, and even this was delayed due to a school activity taking precedence:

> I didn't have a de-brief on the day, which was a bit sad. The priority wasn't to de-brief on the day – there was some other school activity going on, which was the school production. Costumes had to be sewn up.

The other feedback had not occurred because school photographs were taking place. This caused Mr Edwards to question the value that the school were placing on appraisal:

I did feel it took the edge off the whole process. It has meant that it didn't have the profile and priority that I thought it should have, because of those two things. . . . I was disappointed that it didn't have priority.

Although he did not expect the whole process to take place within his teaching time, he felt that more acknowledgement of the time involved would indicate the priority it was given by the school.

The feedback, when received, was both positive and constructive, but Mr Edwards wondered whether it was based solely on the observations:

I don't think it was untrue, but I think inevitably it was subjective in nature, because of the position of the appraiser as my line manager in my year group, the physical situation of my appraiser in an office next to my lab. . . . And it brings me back to the point of only having one appraiser who was not within my subject area.

He had earlier indicated that he felt that each appraisee should have two appraisers – one chosen by the institution and one chosen by the appraisee 'more as a critical friend'. He went on to stress: 'You could choose them on the relevance you think they've got either to the focus you want to be observed, or to your general fieldwork, or your experience. And I think that's very important'.

At the initial meeting it was agreed to focus on his role as a resource for his pupils. He felt that several aspects of his teaching were not commented upon. He was happy with the general outcomes of his appraisal, but not with his statement:

. . . because I had no input to that. Although I could have sent it back and discussed it, it had taken so long arriving that I was so busy, and I'm quite happy to accept that I was too busy to make even more use of it.

A term after the process was completed, he appeared to be fairly positive about his own experience and the way in which appraisal was developing in the school as a whole:

I think it's very worthwhile. It needs developing. It needs more evaluation, I think, from the appraisee. We have now set up appraisee induction and appraisee training which we didn't have. I didn't have any of that. But that's come, which is valuable and that should be compulsory in a way. . . . And, of course, appraisers are of a different calibre. I was very happy with mine. I thought it worked well. Good effort went in.

However, he reiterated his reservations about the classroom observation component and also questioned the purpose of the appraisal statement:

I wasn't happy with the observation. I wasn't sure what the observation was about. I had no feedback on the observation really. I had feedback on the third party evidence. Um. . . . And the final statement was a sort of review of my historical journey into teaching, focuses, and a confirmation that all is well – because a third party said it was fine anyway and I shouldn't really worry about it . . . or that it wasn't a major issue. And it was a confidence building statement which was fine. But I wasn't sure what the observation was about.

Miss Baker, his appraiser, also felt that self-appraisal was a key component, saying in interview: 'It's the important starting point. Without that, you would have no focus'. She linked the self-appraisal to the appraisal interview, which she saw as an opportunity for the self-appraisal to be supported or questioned by evidence from others. She agreed with Mr Edwards that appraisees should chose their own appraiser 'because it's got to be someone you feel comfortable with'. She believed strongly that the process should be led by the appraisee. This belief shaped the way she conducted Mr Edwards' appraisal:

In the initial interview I hopefully intend him to do most of the talking, rather than me questioning him on self-appraisal. There are just a couple of things that I noticed that could be foci, but it's his decision in the end.

She also negotiated the methods of observation and saw the appraisal interview as a presentation of all the collected evidence and a forum for the negotiation of the statement. Although Mr Edwards did not dominate the interview, most of Miss Baker's interjections were for clarification or requests for expansion of points he had made. While Mr Edwards had claimed that the statement had been written with no input from himself, there was evidence from the transcript of the appraisal interview that, in the wording of the targets at least, Miss Baker had been at great pains to make the wording wholly acceptable to him.

When asked how she felt about taking on the role of appraiser, Miss Baker expressed herself as happy with the responsibility, particularly the classroom observation:

I enjoy it. I frequently go and do that – observe classes as part of my head of year job. Well, not as part of the job, but because I like doing it – as long as they don't mind and generally they don't.

Perhaps this familiarity with the process made her, in contrast with Mr Edwards, far more positive about the place of classroom observation within the appraisal process:

I think it's actually got a central role. . . . Because classroom teaching is a major part of our jobs really and I think we can all, no matter how long we've been teaching, can always benefit from an objective observer coming in and giving us a bit of feedback, whether or not they're looking for anything specific. [It's] . . . sharing ideas and expertise really. . . . And to a certain extent it's made me think about my teaching. It's a two-way process, I think.

However, like many others, her main concern about the appraisal process was finding the time to carry it out properly and she was worried that her own classes would suffer, concluding: 'I feel it's a very worthwhile thing to be doing as long as there is understanding that something else may go'.

Mr Foster

The third teacher we studied in Casewell School was Mr Foster, a member of the senior management team and also the school's appraisal co-ordinator. As appraisal co-ordinator he had played a large part in the development of the school's appraisal system. He was also undergoing appraisal for the second time and so had more clearly defined expectations than the other appraisees: 'I'm on my second run through and it certainly has helped me considerably from the last time. I feel that appraisal has finely tuned areas of weakness really . . .'.

For his second appraisal, he was keen 'to look at all angles' of his teaching. However, the main focus of his appraisal had to be his management role, although both he and his appraiser saw the classroom observation element as being critical to the process. Indeed, Mrs Cooper, the head, was his appraiser, and she was keen to stress the importance attached to classroom performance by the school for all teachers, including senior management: 'We mustn't forget that's what we're about!'

The appraisal process followed the scheme described in the school guidelines very closely, which perhaps is hardly surprising, since the two players were the appraisal co-ordinator and the head teacher, and both were being observed by an external researcher. There was a long initial meeting held in the head teacher's study in which there was detailed discussion of the self-appraisal sheet that Mr Foster had completed. This was largely concerned with his change of role since his last appraisal and also the outcomes of various applications he had made for deputy headships. Mrs Cooper's desire for this to be one focus of the appraisal caused some conflict during the discussion. Interestingly, in her first interview, when questioned as to whether she had any reservations about the role of appraiser, she said:

The concern sometimes is, as his line manager, that I bring pre-conceived items for the agenda, that it isn't as discrete as perhaps it ought to be at this level. . . . We know our working practices so well. I suppose it could be a very good process because I've been involved in the formative bit in a very regular way. . . . I've been keeping him on target as far as his action plan is concerned. So it could be very healthy in some respects. But in other respects, I could be thinking: 'Now I want to tackle so and so in his appraisal . . . and so' . . . that's my reservation. Too close, almost.

The transcript of part of the initial meeting, when Mrs Cooper was seeking to make Mr Foster's lack of success at interviews for deputy head posts one focus of the appraisal, confirms that Mrs Cooper's concern was well founded. Indeed, the initial meeting became a striking example of what can happen when an individual comes under close personal scrutiny from a superior, as the discussion became increasingly confrontational:

Mrs Cooper: What kind of person do you think they are looking for?
Mr Foster: In that particular school they were looking for someone . . . that I am! But which they didn't appoint . . .
Mrs Cooper: But can you put that into descriptors, rather than . . . ?
Mr Foster: No. I can't. (Pause) Because you and I know . . . I don't want to touch on this subject particularly, because I've visited it once and I really don't want to visit it again.
Mrs Cooper: I understand that.
Mr Foster: So I don't see any mileage in this.
Mrs Cooper: Well, I'm just sort of . . . What I'm trying to do is to see whether there are one or two indicators there that are areas that we can test out here, so you can be reassured that you can demonstrate those qualities on a day to day basis to other colleagues, and therefore get a concept of how you can project in on another occasion. . . .
Mr Foster: I really don't want to talk about it particularly. It upset me and I don't really want to revisit. . . .

This conversation continued for some time, with Mrs Cooper pressing to discuss areas of development for Mr Foster which might facilitate his securing a deputy headship and Mr Foster continuing to resist. The transcript may appear to be a case of badgering someone who is reluctant to talk, but she was keen to provide some positive comment:

Can I give you a little bit of feedback about the type of person that you portrayed here [in the self-appraisal] and the one that I've been nodding to all the way along – somebody who is steady, reliable and is always there for people. . . .

After this the conversation became less confrontational and Mr Foster did succeed in removing his deputy headship applications from the appraisal agenda. When interviewed later, Mr Foster blamed himself and the heavy cold he was suffering from at the time for the conflict which occurred during the initial meeting: 'The initial meeting was my fault. . . . Because I wasn't 100 per cent. And I gave her a hard time – if I'm straight'.

Mrs Cooper, while also pointing to the part played by the appraisee's health, suggested the presence of the researcher played a part in making the tone of the meeting strained:

> I was rather concerned after our initial interview . . . clearly my appraisee was not well and it might have been better. . . . I think had you not been here, we might have just put it off for the day. It wasn't as relaxed as it should have been. We both agreed that both the appraiser and appraisee can bring something to the initial interview. . . . But we went through an uncomfortable time which shouldn't have happened. So I think it's a combination of not feeling well, and perhaps an additional tension by possibly . . . another person's presence as well.

She did not believe that she had been misguided in pressing to discuss the issue of Mr Foster's lack of success in applying for deputy headships. Both she and Mr Foster felt that the rest of the process had passed very smoothly.

In the end, the major focus of Mr Foster's appraisal was his role in supporting the pastoral team within the school and in the classroom his relationship with the pupils. It was agreed that the criteria for the observation should be based on the criteria used by the Office for Standards in Education, and that two separate classes would be observed. It was also agreed who would be approached for third party evidence and exactly what they would be asked to comment on.

Two observations were carried out, each of forty-five minutes. Feedback was given within twenty-four hours on both occasions and was quite detailed. Mr Foster was a modern languages teacher and conducted the vast majority of his lessons in the language he was teaching. Mrs Cooper was the head teacher and therefore worked closely with him in his management role, but she was not a language teacher and did not speak the language the children were learning during the classroom observation lessons. Neither believed this to be a problem, as it was teaching skills and interaction with the pupils that she was observing. Other teachers and appraisers have argued, however, that his subject knowledge – for example, the accuracy of his own and the pupils' spoken word in the target language – should also have been scrutinised.

The appraisal interview was carefully structured and, despite the head's assertion of the importance of classroom teaching, mainly focused on the development of Mr Foster's management role. Only ten minutes was spent on the outcomes of the classroom observation. Although expecting appraisal to affect his practice, in his second interview he admitted that it had not:

> I think my classroom practice will change as more and more technology comes in with National Curriculum . . . is embedded within schemes of work. But I would say that that is a natural organic thing. It's not going to be something that I've learned from the appraisal that I'm going to change.

Interestingly, when he was interviewed for a third time, a term later, his perception had changed and he indicated that he felt that focusing on his relationship with pupils had affected his classroom practice, although he did not articulate how.

The targets set as a result of the appraisal were large and complex but Mr Foster was happy with them:

> Certainly the targets that I've got are huge, but are achievable – with a lot of work. And I think that's what it's about, you know, being stretched. And I think that I've got something that is going to stretch me and maintain the interest, the buzz that I get out of being here.

At the end of the process, he said he had got 'tremendous satisfaction' from it and he emphasised his belief that both individual and institutional needs were important:

> It will be not only to the benefit of me, but to the benefit of the school as a whole, and will enable us to be a 'growing' institution. As long as that is in harmony, as long as one grows with the other . . . then I think it's a superb process which we have invested a vast amount of effort and time in, and one hopes that it will have spin-offs for this institution. I think it will.

Finding the time to carry out the process was identified as a problem by both Mr Foster and Mrs Cooper. Mrs Cooper discussed the problems it posed for a busy head teacher but indicated that she gave the process priority and said she felt it to be 'a worthwhile commitment for my team – quality time'.

Comment on Casewell School

Casewell School provides an interesting insight into how the perceptions and intentions of school managers are not always reflected in the actual experiences of teachers. Mrs Cooper, the head teacher, had drawn a picture of the school's appraisal process as a highly organised and well thought out procedure in which staff had been fully consulted. Yet two of the appraisees studied were confused as to the actual stages of the process. Mrs Duke had not known how many observations the process was intended to contain and Mr Edwards expressed himself unsure about many aspects of the process. This may in part have been the result of a lack of appraisee training, although the head teacher believed that the training provided by the school had been of a high quality.

Mrs Cooper had also stressed that the appraiser should be seen as a 'facilitator' and, therefore, it was not necessary for the appraiser to have subject knowledge. Mr Edwards, however, definitely felt it to be a disadvantage that his appraiser worked in another curriculum area. This affected his attitude towards her feedback to him, making him more negative and less respectful of what she had to say. Furthermore, although the head teacher had stressed her commitment to appraisal strongly throughout her interviews with the researcher, it was the experience of Mr Edwards that in terms of priority it took second place to other routine school activities.

While stressing that the agenda for appraisal should be agreed mutually at the initial meeting between appraiser and appraisee, the head teacher had herself become embroiled in a confrontation concerning areas of focus when appraising a member of the senior management team. In a hierarchical setting, such as that adopted for appraisal, power relationships can become an inescapable part of the process. However it may be dressed up in banter or skilful interpersonal relationships, superiors are appraising subordinates, with some degree of control over their career. Self-confrontation, especially where it concerns some aspect of failure, can be a painful business, as Mr Foster found when his lack of success in obtaining promotion appeared high on the agenda with his head teacher, even though she was trying to boost his self-esteem.

Casewell School had given a great deal of time and thought to the appraisal process, more than was the case with many schools. The head teacher and appraisal co-ordinator had both been through appraisal, which allowed them to shape the process on the basis of experience. Yet this case study shows that, even with these advantages, there can still be misunderstandings, differences in emphasis or perception and disagreements about the importance of subject knowledge or what should be the area of focus. It is no criticism of Casewell School that these occurred. Appraisal brought together the members of a large community, already with conflicting pressures on their time, energy and priority setting, and placed them into another web of complex interpersonal relationships. What is told here about Casewell, therefore, represents the craggy reality of appraisal in practice, rather than the clinical hygiene of policy statements or regulations.

Chapter 6

Teachers' views of appraisal

In the previous chapter we looked at the appraisal process in one particular school. This chapter will discuss teachers' perspectives on appraisal as they emerged from our interviews and observations of the twenty-nine case studies of primary and secondary teachers in Study 3 of the research project. Their perceptions often broaden and deepen the generalities which emerged from the national questionnaire survey described in Chapter 4.

PURPOSES OF APPRAISAL

From the very first interview appraisers and appraisees had been asked what they thought was the purpose of appraisal and also what advantages or disadvantages they saw in having a formal scheme. They found it difficult to separate their answers to these two questions but they did distinguish between what they felt to be the Government's aims and the purposes that they felt appraisal could serve if carried out properly.

Some concern was expressed about the introduction of performance-related pay and the role appraisal might play in its introduction. However, most teachers seemed happy with the reassurance they had received from the LEAs and their own senior management that this was not the hidden intention, so their responses were mostly based on the scheme that they were being presented with and not hypothetical developments. Their subsequent answers ranged along a continuum, with those referring to the assessment of teacher performance at one end, and those using the language of staff development at the other.

Appraisal as assessment of teacher performance

A number of teachers identified the aim of appraisal as the summative assessment of their classroom practice. These responses could be split into identifying incompetent teachers, or as an opportunity to 'celebrate existing strengths'. A small number of appraisees believed that the Government's sole motive for introducing appraisal was the assessment of classroom practice with a view to 'weeding out' poor teachers. For the majority of these, 'weeding out' meant removing poor teachers from the profession. This stance reflected an acceptance that 'all barrels contain some bad apples', and some made reference to teachers who brought the profession into disrepute:

> Originally I saw it as a way of getting rid of the worst teachers . . . which really I was in favour of . . . because I have come across some bad teachers and I think they have . . . done an awful lot of harm. . . . From a parent's point of view, if you've got a bad teacher and your child is with those teachers, I mean there's nothing you can do about it. And it's just a case of sitting there for a whole year and hoping you'll get a better one next year. And that's not a good thing for the profession.

One teacher used the term 'weeding' more specifically, in terms of identifying less competent teachers for remedial action, so that they could be targeted for help: 'There are some teachers who are not necessarily poor, but they're bogged down and don't know where to go for help, and schools and staff are often so busy. Appraisal will help them'.

Teachers' perceptions were often affected substantially by their own prior experiences of being assessed. We observed and interviewed one secondary teacher, Mr Chumley, who had taught in the private sector before joining a comprehensive school staff. He had been teaching for some years, though he had only just completed his probationary year. The LEA adviser who had observed him during that year had written a negative report which he considered to be unfair. He perceived the purpose of appraisal as 'to check you're doing your job properly', about which his feelings were ambivalent.

While indicating that he felt appraisal should be used to identify and remove bad teachers, it was clear that Mr Chumley felt personally threatened, explaining that, prior to training, he had thought appraisal would be 'a lot of inspectors coming in and telling you off all the time'. He believed the training had made him feel more positive about the process, and that he now saw it as an opportunity to redress the balance and to prove to his head of department, who was also his appraiser, that he was a good teacher. His view of appraisal as assessment made him feel particularly anxious about the process:

> I feel under pressure to produce excellent lessons, simply because I know everyone else will be. It seems a rather false situation and you can see the people who are totally incompetent . . . spending several weeks preparing an excellent lesson, whereas I might spend

one evening preparing a decent appraisal lesson and then at the end of it they come up with a better appraisal, simply because I've been more conscientious and I've been spending time preparing all my lessons, but all they've been doing is preparing one lesson for the last three weeks.

Appraisal for improvement and celebration

A number of appraisees saw appraisal more positively, as a tool for teachers to evaluate their own practice with a view to its improvement, and indeed to celebrate what was good. In this way the role of the appraiser was not so much that of an assessor but more one of support in self-evaluation. The purpose of appraisal, therefore, was to create an opportunity for teachers to gain feedback about their classroom practice. This would enable specific targets to be set and the support needed to achieve their goals to be identified.

One Year 2 infant teacher was concerned that her teaching of physical education was not up to the same standard as her provision of the rest of the curriculum. She did not instinctively know, as she felt she did in maths and English, how to move children on to higher achievement once they had grasped the skill she was teaching:

I'm hoping to know whether . . . I am providing sufficiently interesting lessons . . . with my own enthusiasm not really being there. I still feel after all these years in teaching, I still feel I don't know where I'm going in the sense of a complete structure for PE.

Another Year 2 infant class teacher was working with a team of colleagues in an open plan school. She wanted to focus on discipline in her multicultural class. She was unsure whether problems she was having with the class reflected discipline or language problems:

I want to encourage them to talk all the time – so you need to be friendly and encouraging. But on the other hand, particularly at this time in the year, they start to go the other way and they start to take advantage. . . . It's hitting the right line really and that's what I'd really like to explore.

As she had taught an acknowledged difficult class the previous year, she had lost confidence in her ability to provide the right kind and amount of discipline. She saw appraisal as the opportunity for her appraiser to observe her teaching in a variety of types of activities and then give her feedback about her perceived discipline problems.

The debate as to whether classroom observation should have a specific or general focus had been addressed by many LEAs in their guidelines to schools, as we described in Chapter 3. The majority of these recommended a general observation for the first lesson, with a specific focus for observation two. There was a view that a specific focus should emerge naturally during the feedback session following the first observation. One modern language teacher in a comprehensive school felt that a specific focus was inappropriate: 'I think that an appraisal that is too sharply focused in one area is meaningless. It needs to be about the whole job, if it's going to be meaningful at all'.

She took a somewhat authoritarian view and queried the value of letting teachers choose their own focus for appraisal as this avoided a review of their whole practice. She quoted examples of other professions in which pay and promotion depended on a form of appraisal and she could see no reason why teachers should be afraid of exposing themselves to a similar system. Other teachers quoted examples of professions where 'promotions boards' were an integral part of staff advancement and the introduction of a formal appraisal scheme for teachers could only increase their professional credibility.

While many teachers discussing appraisal as assessment talked in terms of it highlighting areas for improvement, some teachers mentioned the important role appraisal could play in 'the celebration of a teacher's strengths', a phrase that had been promoted by a number of LEAs. Mr Abel, the science teacher described in the previous chapter, was suspicious of the Government's intentions, but saw one advantage as being:

> to recognise people's achievements . . . it's an excellent way of motivating staff. It sets up a formal system within a school, through which people's achievements can be recognised. And it's terribly *ad hoc* in most schools – you know even in this school . . . and this school is very good at many things, but we were never good enough, I think, at recognising achievement.

Development of the individual

Teachers who took the view, stressed by both Government and LEA guidelines, of appraisal as a tool for staff development, mentioned different aspects. First, there were the purposes it would serve for individual teacher development, both for the appraiser and appraisee, and second, there were issues of whole school development. Some appraisees saw appraisal as an opportunity to reflect on their own individual practice with the help of an experienced colleague, the latter acting as a mirror. A young, enthusiastic teacher in her second year of teaching, who was keen to learn from her more experienced colleagues, saw appraisal as an opportunity to develop her own practice and reflect on different approaches through interaction with her appraiser:

I'm hoping that it's going to sort of point me in areas that I'm a little concerned about. . . . Just hopefully reassure me in certain areas, and if there are areas – of which I'm sure there are many – that I need to pick up on, that we'll talk through how they might be overcome. So I'm not just left with a list of things, but perhaps talk about how to get on and deal with them.

Some teachers saw development in terms of a career review. They wanted to identify the specific skills and experiences they would need to develop in order to gain promotion, either within their present school or elsewhere. Often this approach was at the instigation or suggestion of the appraiser, as happened, for example, with Mr Abel and Mrs Duke described in Chapter 5. Part of the appraiser's role was seen as being to facilitate the advancement of members of their departmental staff. Sometimes this was in conflict with how appraisees saw their own needs.

Development of the whole school

Whereas some teachers emphasised the individual aspects of staff development, others stressed the corporate view taken in the Government and many LEA guidelines:

Appraisal should be set in the context of the objectives of the school, which will generally be expressed in a school development plan. Appraisal should support development planning and vice versa. The school objectives in a particular year should be linked with appraisal, so that, for example, professional development targets arising from appraisal may be related to agreed targets and tasks in the development plan. Similarly appraisal targets, when taken together, should provide an important agenda for action for the school as a whole. Targets set during appraisal should therefore meet the needs of the school as well as those of the individual appraisees. Setting appraisal within the framework of the school development should also ensure that targets are realistic and make the best use of available resources.

(DES 1991b: para. 11)

From the interviews with the head teachers, it was apparent that they were increasingly regarding appraisal as a tool to evaluate their policies and practice, looking at the school's strengths and weaknesses as a well managed institution. By the end of the project, schools were beginning to approach appraisal within a whole school context, rather than as a purely individual process, and subsequently were using appraisal targets as a way of informing their school development plans, a relationship acknowledged by appraisees as well as school managers. Mr Edwards from Casewell School went as far as envisaging appraisal as a two-way process that supported the institution as well as the individual:

> I think it should be a two-way dialogue. I don't think it should be hierarchical, coming from the top down. I think it should be a way where there is reciprocal input to the experience, and the appraiser should be prepared to take information into the system, the institution. I think it should be an opportunity to consider the appraisee's position in relation to the institution and vice versa.

Some schools saw appraisal as a way of identifying the school's in-service needs and considerable co-ordination structures were in place to make sure that once set, targets could be met. It was felt that there could be a genuine benefit to the school as a whole if there was some co-ordination in the setting of targets. In their final interview several teachers commented on how the introduction of appraisal was leading to a fairer and more efficient use of the in-service training budget.

The extreme form of corporatism occurred in a small rural primary school we studied. The head took the view that the school staff were a team and appraisal should not only benefit the individual but also the efficient working of the team. He decided that all teachers should have the same single focus. This, he believed, would take pressure off any individual. He expressed concern that appraisal would be seen as insulting to his staff if they were asked to identify a focus for that appraisal from their own practice. He felt it best to appraise a corporate initiative in the school and the teachers' performance within it:

> Each teacher should fit into the school as a whole unit, rather than just as an individual, although they should be allowed an individual voice. Teachers should not be put on the spot, therefore appraisal should be global.

THE IMPLEMENTATION OF APPRAISAL

The case studies revealed considerable diversity in the way appraisal was carried out. National initiatives often suffer the effect of 'Chinese whispers', as regulations, circulars and guidelines are filtered, interpreted and wittingly or unwittingly distorted down a complex communication matrix to individual teachers, as we showed in earlier chapters. Even when circulars have been distilled through local authority filters, they still have to pass through different kinds of school organisations, past individual keyholders and gatekeepers, until they are finally negotiated into practice by the individual teacher and appraiser.

School organisation

One factor that proved vital in how the teachers experienced appraisal was the differences in school organisation. In some schools there appeared to be no appraisal management structure at all and a distinctly *ad hoc* ethos prevailed. Other schools had very clearly documented policies and the infrastructure to back up the whole appraisal process. They had either set up a staff working party to co-ordinate the practicalities of appraising the whole staff over a two-year period or had appointed an individual co-ordinator at a senior level to take on this task, as in Casewell School.

In some schools that appeared on the surface to manage the process implicitly, however, the process did not work at all well and staff were left feeling they had very little control over events. In one of the case study schools, Bigchester College, an appraisal co-ordinating group was set up, but its senior management, in particular the two deputy heads, controlled the timetable of each process. In order for there to be minimum cost to the school, their prime intention was to maximise use of staff non-contact time for each appraisal process. Appraisal meeting times were imposed, times being notified no more than a week in advance. This was justified as it was not known from week to week who would be needed to cover other absences. As a result, appraisers and appraisees felt that they were given no choice as to when these meetings took place and which of their own lessons they would miss:

> Students losing teaching time – personally I see that as the most worrying of all. It should not be at the cost of the students. I have found on several occasions that I have been timetabled for some or other part of an appraisal, when I had one of my last few extremely valuable lessons with Year 11 – for their oral, for example.

The outcome appeared to be alienation and a loss of confidence of both appraisers and appraisees in the process – they talked about appraisal being 'done' to them, rather than in terms of being full participants in the process.

It was in secondary rather than in primary schools that giving high priority to administrative considerations caused aggravation. In another secondary school in the sample the decision had been made that all appraisals would be carried out during the second half of the summer term, when the pupils in Year 11 had left. Such a concentrated effort created pressure on individual appraisers and one observed appraisal had to be re-started the following term. The teacher involved was part of the senior management team and it had not been possible, because of his and the appraiser's other commitments, to complete his appraisal during the summer term. Rather than try to remember exactly what stage they were at after a six-week break, they both felt it more appropriate to start again.

Matching appraisers and appraisees

As discussed in Chapter 3, most LEAs had identified the appraiser/appraisee relationship as being pivotal to the success of the appraisal process, and the case studies underlined the importance which teachers attached to this delicate and potentially threatening relationship. The influence of individual appraisers on the process and outcomes of appraisal was seen to be large. In the first interview questions were asked to discover teachers' opinions on how they felt appraisers should ideally be chosen. Their responses showed two concerns: the process by which the selection of appraisers should take place, and the qualities which they felt to be important in the appraisee/appraiser relationship.

In our national questionnaire survey we showed that slightly over half the teachers (51 per cent) said that their appraiser had been imposed, compared with 22 per cent chosen by them and 26 per cent negotiated. The majority of appraisees in the case studies were very clear about their own preference for choice:

> I think you need some freedom over your choice. I'm not sure that I would appreciate my appraiser being chosen for me – for whatever reason. I think that if it was someone who perhaps you have a personality clash with, or you didn't have mutual respect for, it would be difficult to treat them seriously.

Many appraisees advocating freedom of choice insisted that this would not be an 'easy option' and stressed that, as they wished to benefit from the process, they would choose an appraiser who would be able to provide valid feedback:

> I would fight very hard for the right to choose who appraises you. And I think if you were being honest and fair you would choose somebody who knew you. . . . I would always select people who I felt had been on the receiving end of what I do.

By way of contrast, in one secondary school where teachers were permitted a free choice of appraiser, some appraisers were not convinced that this was the right course of action. One teacher, who had actually chosen his own head of department because he considered this to be the 'obvious choice' as he 'not only has the most contact with you, but also knows the subject as well', appeared to feel that appraisees could not be trusted to select an appropriate appraiser:

I don't think it should be totally open to the choice of the person that's doing it. . . . I would feel particularly narked if I was a head of department and someone that was in my department chose somebody else, because they thought they would get an easier time.

Most interviewees regarded professional respect as being a key criterion when choosing an appraiser. Excellence in classroom practice was seen as imperative by some: 'You've got to admire the person who's going to appraise you. Because if you reckon they're a rotten teacher . . . I mean, you wouldn't listen to a word they said!'

One deputy head, in an authority which had been a pilot for appraisal, emphasised that respect was commanded by successful professional experience:

They have got to be a well respected and experienced colleague. We found this in the pilot scheme where, though not initially, everybody was trained as a support teacher and people were being appraised by somebody who had only been teaching for one or two years and they just didn't have enough credibility.

In addition to trust and respect, another factor that had been noted in the national questionnaires was often mentioned. This was the need for appraisers to have a good level of knowledge and understanding of the context, especially of the subject and age group, within which the appraisee worked. In most cases the advantage of this kind of specialist knowledge was seen as allowing the appraiser to undertake more informed observation and be in a position to offer advice and guidance.

A number of the case studies undertaken involved appraisal by someone without that specialist experience and knowledge, and it would appear that whatever other benefits accrued, non-specialist appraisal was less effective in changing classroom practice. Different curriculum areas and age groups often involve different approaches to teaching and where the appraisers were unfamiliar with those ways of working their feedback was likely to be general, and was sometimes even disputed by the appraisee.

Some non-specialist appraisers, perhaps because of a feeling of operating on unfamiliar territory, appeared less confident and were more likely to defer to the appraisee's interpretation of events. Others shifted the agenda on to territory where they felt more at home. In schools where appraisers had been given the assignment because of other managerial responsibilities, for example, their pastoral role, the emphasis of the appraisal would tend not to be on classroom teaching, and other aspects external to the classroom would become more prominent. For some appraisees this was preferred, as they wished to focus on their other responsibilities, but for others it almost offered a 'cop out', in that they felt that there was no need to accept the feedback given, as the appraiser had no intimate knowledge of the context.

The appraiser shifting the agenda on to familiar territory was not always a one-sided event. Mrs Gardner was an infant teacher being appraised by her head teacher. In completing her self-appraisal pro-forma she was surprised how little she had written about her classroom practice and how much was about her management concerns. She particularly wanted her appraisal to focus on her management skills, as she was applying for deputy headships. She chose the implementation of the National Curriculum physical education programme as her area of focus for the classroom observation, as it was a subject area in which she felt less confident. The head was an extremely experienced teacher and taught music within the school, but she too was less confident about her skills in teaching PE. She commented that the staff expected her to be expert in all areas, but she herself was unsure about the value of any feedback she could give in this subject area.

As a compromise the head asked for, and was given, a very detailed plan of the lesson by the appraisee, who made explicit exactly what she wished to be observed. In the final interview the appraisee described her classroom observation as a 'red herring'. She knew she could produce a good lesson if she prepared well, but under normal circumstances she would not spend that amount of time preparing one lesson. The rest of her appraisal, which concentrated on her management skills, she found extremely useful. In the end the appraisal shifted on to common secure ground by mutual agreement.

Hierarchical v. peer appraisal

Although all the case study schools usually followed the principle of hierarchical appraisal endorsed in the official guidelines, it was clear from the comments of several appraisees that they did not believe that the qualities they desired in an appraiser were guaranteed by higher status in the school hierarchy. As this teacher with eighteen years' teaching experience stated:

> I don't think it should be line managers, necessarily. My line manager is the head of department – who has had five years of teaching experience. And whilst, I wouldn't say for one minute that she hasn't probably got a lot to offer me . . . nevertheless, I think that could be awkward.

The examples of peer appraisal tended to involve members of senior management teams appraising each other. In primary schools there was a tendency for it to be taken for granted that the appraisers should

be the head and deputy, although a small number of appraisees indicated that they could have exercised a right of veto. In secondary
schools, most appraisees felt they had a degree of choice over who was
their appraiser. In some schools they exercised this choice through a
right of veto, but it was more common for negative preferencing to be
used, in which appraisees were given a list of three or four possible
appraisers and asked to indicate any who would be unacceptable.

There was some ambivalence over the respective advantages and
disadvantages of peer and hierarchical appraisal. Teachers saw a peer
system as providing a more relaxed and non-threatening context for
appraisal, or even allowing teachers to tackle sensitive or difficult
aspects of their teaching. One primary school teacher explained
how her school had experimented with the approach for classroom
observation:

> We actually went in and observed each other in a situation where we
> were not comfortable. . . . We found it helpful. And, in fact, we ended
> up feeling better about what we were doing – we were doing it better
> than we thought. In both instances, it was definitely reassuring.

Some, however, expressed the more cynical view that peer appraisal
might lead to the reinforcement of poor or inadequate practice, questioning whether it was possible for teachers who work closely together
to offer objective feedback on classroom competence. There was also
anxiety about the effect peer appraisal might have on staff relationships:

> It could work well – someone who's on the same level as you and
> knows the day to day ways of working – but it could be difficult to
> be totally honest.

> It's quite difficult. In a way, I suppose, people are put into a position
> where . . . it could be seen as the appraiser knowing more than the
> appraisee does. So people maybe feel threatened by that. I think if
> you're in a school where . . . people don't visit each other's class-
> rooms, it can be a very difficult situation.

One possible compromise between peer and hierarchical appraisal
was described by a deputy head of a primary school which had been
involved in piloting appraisal:

> I am in favour of it [peer appraisal], providing the people who are
> doing the supporting are of sufficient experience and standing and
> well regarded amongst the rest of the staff. It was a system that we
> piloted with a lot of success. The interview was still conducted by
> the head, but the actual classroom observation and support was
> given by peers and it really did work – because it was not threatening.

This deputy head felt that for most staff the most threatening aspect of hierarchical appraisal was their head coming into their classroom, making them feel as if they were on teaching practice again. However, she personally welcomed the head's presence in her classroom: 'I just feel it's going to be an eye opener in my situation for the head to actually see what we have to put up with all the time. It will do him good'.

The main drawback of the peer appraisal model identified by teachers was that appraisers would not have sufficient 'clout' to ensure future in-service needs identified were met, or to facilitate career development:

> Personally, I think because I'm looking for progression within the profession, I'd prefer somebody higher up, because it will help me sort out what I need to do.

> If I spoke to my peer about facilities in the room, nothing would change. If I speak to Mr Harrison [senior staff member] I might possibly get something done. It depends on where you are in the structure. I mean, I could appraise the head and it would be a very valid appraisal if it was on something for which I didn't need any power or authority behind it, but if you wanted any changes brought about, it would be useless me doing it, because I don't have the authority or power or status to make changes.

Power and control

Although issues to do with power and control are commonly played down in schools, they are inescapable. Most schools stressed the collegial nature of appraisal, both in their literature and in conversation. It was shown earlier in this chapter that some heads exercised direct managerial influence over such matters as the area of focus. Appraisal can easily become a powerful form of managerial control over process and outcome, especially when it is designed as a hierarchical exercise in the first place. In most of these case studies teachers themselves were centrally involved in negotiating the focus and method of observation, but it was predominantly the appraiser who exercised control over the way the process was conducted. Sometimes control was covert, in that appraisers imposed their agenda, whilst overtly stating that the appraisal was appraisee-centred.

In Littlevale Primary School the appraiser was the head teacher. She made the judgement that it was important for the appraisals to take place over a short period of time, in order that feedback and outcomes would be relevant. She carried out each appraisal within forty-eight hours. One appraisee was the deputy head, and only one observation was carried out instead of the required two. The observation had a general focus, even though the appraisee had expressed her preference for concentrating on her teaching of the humanities curriculum, as she was concerned that her subject knowledge had been ignored.

The head appeared to have pre-determined that, as the deputy was relatively new to the school, her appraisal was an opportunity for her to tell the head more about her background, something the deputy was particularly keen not to do. The head also held clearly articulated ideas as to how the role of the appraisee should develop within the school, and that a deputy head should be acting as a particular kind of role model for other members of staff. This requirement eventually became one of the targets set, much to the deputy's amusement, as the head had spent some time assuring her that the appraisal was to focus on her needs and would not be spent discussing 'school business'.

In other case studies, the control of process was even more explicit, with the appraiser asserting that there was very little interpretation allowed of the given guidelines. Sometimes this appeared to derive from their own feelings of insecurity in the appraiser role. In other cases it was because they did not see them as guidelines, but more as a set of procedures that had been laid down to ensure uniformity of experience. For example, the structure of meetings or seating arrangements suggested in LEA guidelines to encourage a comfortable, relaxed atmosphere sometimes became a major preoccupation. Timings, given as a rough guide, were adhered to rigidly and suggested agendas were used as though they were mandatory.

Mr Illingworth, a rather nervous deputy head who admitted that he did not take on the role of appraiser willingly, was the only appraiser interviewed who said that he really did not like observing teachers. When carrying out the appraisal he made constant reference to the LEA guidelines at every stage of the process. He placed them on the table at every meeting with the appraisee and would quote from them, following the word as opposed to their spirit. This became a problem when he wrote the summary statement in what he regarded as 'official' language, using such phrases as 'satisfactory' and 'competent' which upset the appraisee. She felt the use of such cold terms was disparaging, so she took her concern to the head teacher who intervened before the statement was signed.

In another case a deputy head, appraised by her head teacher, commented to the researcher that she felt her statement was unrepresentative of the appraisal interview: 'I didn't feel that it accurately portrayed the interview. There were certain points that I really feel that I did not say, and there were some where I thought his interpretation . . . was way off mine'.

When the head was asked by the researcher if he would change the statement in the light of his deputy's reservations, he indicated that he would, but rejected her objections:

> She felt it ought to be more specific. But that's Annabelle. I mean, in the past she's the only person who ever questions her summary statement, but whenever she questions it – she has on the last three occasions – we've never changed it.

His perception was that the deputy merely wanted clarification of certain points. But in interview she pointed out a number of points within the statement with which she strongly disagreed. However, the appraisee once again did not insist that the changes be made. The final power and authority lay clearly with the head in this instance. A number of other appraisees who had been appraised by their head teacher felt unable to voice disagreement with their statement, although they commented in private to the researcher that they were unhappy either with its content or the way it had been written.

Appraisers' feelings about their role

Despite the issue of hierarchical power and control, in practice most appraisers felt accountable for the process that they were involved in and took great pains to satisfy the appraisee's expectations. Sometimes this was because of their own experience of appraisal. If their expectations of their own appraisal had not been met, they were keen that in their role as appraiser they should perform well:

> My own appraisal took nine months! And it was a disaster, because the deputy head didn't give it priority. . . . If you ever go through a bad appraisal yourself, the first thing you say is, 'If I ever do an appraisal, I shall make sure they don't have the same experience'.

The appraisers we interviewed could be split into two groups: those who felt confident in their role and those who were unsure what they personally could offer to their appraisee. It was relatively rare for head teachers to express doubt about their ability to carry out the role of appraiser, but a number of middle and senior managers seemed insecure about how they could make the process beneficial for their appraisees:

> I want both Tim and Clive to come through this feeling that it's been worthwhile and beneficial. Hopefully, they will be open enough to me to let me know how they feel it's gone. But until it actually happens, I suppose I've got to be a little apprehensive.

For a number of appraisers, the classroom observation component of the process was of particular concern. In the majority of these cases, the appraisee was perceived by the appraiser to be already a competent teacher and the appraiser, therefore, felt uncomfortable about having to identify areas for development:

> I don't know whether, with a person like Paula – who's taught for longer than myself, and by all accounts is a very successful teacher . . . I don't know how much I can offer her in the way of advice. With Paula, I can't see myself being able to add an awful lot to what she's already doing.

In contrast, one appraiser was concerned that he was going to find it extremely difficult to find anything positive to say about the classroom performance of one of his appraisees, though he subsequently welcomed the opportunity that the formality of the process offered him to gain access to the appraisee's classroom and to talk to him about areas for development: 'I have a member of my department who is almost incompetent. That could be a very negative experience and quite worrying for that member of staff'.

Underlying some of the appraisers' greatest insecurities about their role was their lack of experience of methods of classroom observation:

> I'm concerned about getting it right, giving the best advice possible. Am I going to do the observations the best I can, pick out the most important things? Am I good enough for that? I could have done with more training.

One head teacher was critical of the role played by the local education authority in the provision of support and training:

> It requires a lot of skill. And I think it's skills that are not necessarily under the belt of head teachers, any more than it would be under the belt of other teachers. . . . To a certain extent I don't feel fully prepared to take on this role. I think that the support that has been given [by the LEA] has been very minimal.

Some interviewees articulated their concerns about the damage appraisal could do to staff relationships. One head teacher, who had set up staff development interviews prior to the introduction of statutory appraisal, felt that the formality of the new system was likely to make teachers feel much more threatened and believed his role would be more difficult:

> I am very concerned for me as an appraiser. I feel quite nervous about the actual process. I am anxious about appraising the staff, because I know they are anxious about being appraised and I want to make

the situation as comfortable as possible. . . . I mean the staff development interviews are totally different. They're comfortable, they're
easy, because there is no formality.

Other appraisers, however, felt positive about their role. They saw
appraisal as a two-way process with benefits for the appraisee but also
for themselves:

I enjoy it. I enjoy the chance to talk to staff that I work with and to
find out the things that they've been doing. And, actually, I feel it's
helping their development too.

I feel very easy about it. In fact . . . 'excited' would be an exag-
geration, but I'm looking forward to it. I'm looking forward to watching Sally this afternoon and talking to her about it afterwards. It's
dialogue about what you're doing. It has to be enlightening.

I enjoy it immensely, simply because I'm finding out so much about
another colleague . . . another colleague's perceptions. And, on the
whole, they will be positive, so you get a very good feeling about
another colleague.

That's my job. Forget the appraisal scheme, forget what the Government have introduced, it's what I should be doing normally. This
just gives a level playing field to everyone, so everyone across the
school is being appraised.

OUTCOMES OF APPRAISAL

There appeared to be a considerable variation in the outcomes of
appraisal. It seemed that many of the targets set were not comparable.
There was confusion in the minds of some teachers over what the
targets were meant to achieve. This was sometimes articulated as an
inbuilt 'lack of fairness' in the system. Were the targets set meant to be
performance indicators, in which case what would be the repercussions
if they were not achieved by the review meeting, or were they aids to
professional development, only relevant to the individual concerned?
If the latter, some appraisees queried the use of target setting in which
the targets would have been achieved anyway without the appraisal
process.

As described earlier Mr Chumley, the former private school teacher
who had received a negative report during his probationary year, found
the whole idea of appraisal stressful. His poor report had increased
his concern about proving his competence to his head of department.
His appraiser was also extremely anxious to carry out the appraisal
'properly' and his aim was to help the teacher develop his practice. He
extended the number of observations he carried out of Mr Chumley's

teaching to include field trips and lessons on personal, social and moral education.

At the appraisal interview, which was lengthy and wide ranging in its discussion, they agreed six targets. One of these was to conduct a class assembly, which Mr Chumley admitted in the follow-up interview had been planned previously and would have been performed whether it had been one of the appraisal targets or not. A second was concerned with his extra-curricular role of running the school's Duke of Edinburgh award scheme. The target was to continue the work, developing it to enable those pupils already involved to move on to the next stage.

The appraiser felt that it was justified to set targets on work already planned as it was not his principal aim to add to the teacher's workload, but rather to focus Mr Chumley's reflection on his own practice and so improve his performance. Mr Chumley's concern was that since such activities were named as targets, they then became part of his job description and therefore mandatory, ends in themselves, rather than aids to his personal and professional development. Although he was pleased to have his commitment to extra-curricular activities recognised, there was no financial reward for it and it was done in his own time. If this work became an expectation, rather than a voluntary extra, he felt it would change his attitude to it and his relationship with the children concerned.

Other teachers were set targets that involved large amounts of extra work, like the writing of policy documents. In one case, it was felt by the teacher concerned to be an imposition and not part of his role. In another, the teacher was pleased to be given the responsibility as part of her career development and took it on enthusiastically. In a third, the teacher took it on willingly, only to find on returning after the summer break that the head of department had already done it, therefore raising questions about the target as an indicator of his performance.

From the national questionnaire data we found examples of targets which seemed relatively slender, such as 'keeping a tidy desk' or 'trying to write more neatly on the blackboard'. Whilst such targets may have been relevant and important for the individual teachers concerned, they do seem to be adrift from the much more demanding and complex personal and professional targets set for other teachers. Concern expressed by some appraisees about the fairness of this diversity, particularly in relation to uncertainty about the consequences if targets were not achieved, would appear to be justified.

Obstacles and constraints

Time, money and energy were mentioned over and over again as working against the process of improvement. Nearly all appraisers and many appraisees indicated that they found the amount of time required to undertake the appraisal process a major drawback: 'It's actually desperately under-resourced in terms of time. It's particularly at the minute when people are up to their eyeballs in other initiatives. And it deserves better, I think. It's a good scheme, if it's allowed the time'.

To be completed thoroughly, appraisal required a large amount of time. There was a great amount of diversity in how time was allocated. Some schools tried to avoid imposing on teachers' own time, whereas others took the opposing view and used only non-contact or out of school time. The strategy adopted often depended on the generosity of the LEA's financial support. One case study school had £100 per appraisal to pay for the cover of teaching, whereas another only had £19. Despite its best efforts, the second school could do little more than offer cover for the classroom observations, if they could not be completed in the appraiser's non-contact time. The first school felt it could allow staff to carry out appraisal interviews and meetings during the school day, if they wished.

When some interviewees were asked about their expectations as to the completion of the process within their contracted hours, this did not appear to be the main issue. Several were more concerned about losing time with their own classes than giving up their own time. In one school this was a major concern of both appraisers and appraisees:

> I don't like missing my lessons . . . After Christmas I had my own appraisal in that half-term, and then the next half-term I had to appraise somebody, and I missed the same class, the same period three times – which infuriated me! . . . I would prefer to be kept off cover time rather than miss my lessons.
>
> (An appraiser)

> It's been an enormous upheaval. I hate missing lessons for this kind of thing. I think it's wrong in principle. I would have gladly given up free time, if it had to be done. I don't think it's fair to the children. . . . I would have been willing to stay after school or do it in my lunch hours, or give up free periods.
>
> (An appraisee)

The experience of a head teacher in one primary school exemplifies the time pressures placed on primary heads who are often undertaking up to four appraisals a year. In response to the researcher's question about the appraisal interview held the day before, this head teacher said:

> It could have set off to be very frustrating, because I had had a busy lunchtime and lots of things had happened and I'd been in great demand and I was very sort of uptight, and then there we were, two minutes later, supposedly setting off to an appraisal interview,

and you know, you didn't have time to prepare yourself. But, as it happens it was fine.

She felt that it was all very well for LEA guidelines to say that time must be found to carry out the process effectively and that it must be an interruption-free process, but she questioned how she could find that sort of quality time. She had even considered holding the meetings away from school, but felt that she was already absent from school too often, attending courses and other meetings. This head teacher had already put in place, prior to the introduction of statutory appraisal, staff development interviews and she felt very strongly that these were a much better use of time. One of her appraisees agreed:

> I'm not sure we've achieved a lot more, except that we've got an official thing now about my targets, but I'm not sure they weren't already there anyway. I'm still dubious whether all the extra time, plus the fact that the observation was a red herring, has gained any more than we normally gain with our staff development.

Loss of momentum was of concern in one secondary school, which had aimed to carry out all appraisals within one term and then found itself falling behind the deadline:

> It's taken much longer than we allowed. . . . We're rapidly approaching the end of this half-term. But next week is activities week so it could be that we're looking at the last week of term to complete it. And really we do need to complete it before we go away for the summer, because after summer it's going to be very difficult to gather momentum again.

While the amount of time required for the appraisal process was identified by the majority of interviewees as a major problem, most appraisers felt afterwards that the time had been well spent. One head teacher who had expressed concern about the time factor when interviewed at the beginning of the process, said at the end of it: 'I think in all honesty it was a good use of time. I think to actually talk on a professional [level] one to one in a formal situation like that – it was very useful and very good'.

The opportunity for discussion was also valued by many appraisees. Not only were they able to reflect on classroom performance, but it also provided them with a forum for considering career progression, which was not necessarily available to them elsewhere.

Confidentiality

Another area of concern for some teachers was that of confidentiality. It is interesting that this was seen both in a positive and negative light.

The process had been presented to teachers as being totally confidential and one over which they would retain control. It is clearly stated in the regulations and accompanying guidelines who has, and does not have, right of access to all or parts of the appraisal statement. The guidelines also stress that:

> all those with access to appraisal statements should treat them as confidential. The regulations specify who is entitled to access to the whole or part of the appraisal statement. Beyond this statements should not be disclosed to any person or body without the consent of the appraisee.

(DES1991b: para. 55)

At the beginning of this project several teachers and appraisers wanted to be clear how involvement in the research would protect confidentiality, which is why all the names of teachers and schools in this book are fictitious. In the national questionnaire, questions were asked about targets and, even though these were completed anonymously, some appraisers and appraisees refused to answer the question on the grounds of confidentiality.

In one school the deputy head was actively discouraged from discussing his appraisal with other members of staff because the head felt that a precedent should not be set. One appraisee, who had no qualms about being open about her own experience, was concerned that she was breaking the rules. The head's reaction was that if it helped individual teachers to discuss the outcomes with others either publicly, in the staff room, or privately, that was up to them, but he felt that for senior management, and the first member of staff to be appraised, open discussion could set up a precedent that dismayed other staff.

The majority of teachers interviewed, however, did not mention confidentiality as a major personal concern, and some were extremely open. One deputy head, when explaining the different stages in the appraisal process to her appraisee, got out her own appraisal statement to show the appraisee an example of this type of document. In another school, where all appraisals were taking place within one term, it was common for appraisal experiences to be discussed. This was seen as a part of the supportive ethos which the institution was endeavouring to establish. Where anxiety was expressed, it was not only about the fate of the appraisal statement but also about the process itself:

> I wouldn't mind anyone seeing mine. I mean, if the inspectors came in and they saw . . . I'd probably be thinking, 'Oh my God! What are they thinking?!' But really, you know, I think if you've got a good one, it would be nice to use it in job interviews. . . . But if you

had a bad one, the last thing you want to do is get it out at an interview.

I think they make a great play about the confidentiality of the appraisal statement, which personally I think is immaterial. I'd like to feel more confident that the process of the appraisal was more confidential, but I'm not sure that it is. So I'd think very carefully about who appraises and I'd think more carefully about what I chose and why and what I want them to see and things like that.

The confidentiality issue is therefore a complex one. Head teachers and appraisal co-ordinators were determined that confidentiality should be ensured, but there was evidence that some teachers were keen to share their appraisal experiences with colleagues, stressing that this provides support and an open professional climate. However, this does not mean that they considered their statements should be freely available.

Although all schools saw appraisal as being individually based and not a comparison of teachers, this was brought up during the interviews as an issue that could not be ignored. Some schools were having to make teachers redundant and in such schools there was a concern that appraisal could influence the choice of who stayed and who went. Similarly there was concern about how it would affect opportunities for promotion or performance-related pay within an institution, though some teachers were in favour of the latter. Teachers being appraised by their head either saw it as a threat or as an opportunity to shine. Once an appraisal had been carried out, to ignore it would be the equivalent of telling a jury to disregard a piece of evidence it had already heard. As one head put it: 'Am I honestly going to stand up there and say, "After I've read your appraisal report I can assure you it will have no influence on any decision I make"?'

The word 'confidentiality' developed an elastic set of meanings in the context of appraisal.

To change or not to change?

The national questionnaire replies showed that teachers divided roughly 50/50 into those who said they changed their practice after appraisal and those who claimed they did not. The practicalities of lesson observation will be covered in the next two chapters, so as a bridge between this chapter and what is to come, we describe briefly how one primary teacher, Andy Barker, despite initial scepticism, did change his teaching, and how a secondary teacher, Caroline Davies, who began optimistically, did not.

Andy Barker

Andy Barker originally saw the main purpose of appraisal as a device to get rid of incompetent teachers. At first he wondered whether he would get much out of it, as he had been teaching older juniors for years, saying, 'I've been doing it too long to change too much'. Yet he was a reflective teacher who liked making notes, or even using a dictaphone at the end of each lesson to record his thoughts.

He was appraised by the head of his primary school, and was observed twice for thirty minutes each time, once doing group work and once whole class teaching. Before the first observation the appraiser recapped the two main purposes of the process: to improve children's learning by helping teachers identify strengths and weaknesses, and to work on these in a positive way.

Andy hated having to list his strengths on the self-appraisal prepared by the deputy head, finding it 'most distasteful', but was persuaded of its value in creating a positive climate. His appraiser commented on the high level of activity amongst pupils and that Andy never needed to raise his voice. They discussed how to engage brighter and slower pupils and the use of computers during lessons. In the appraisal interview he was encouraged to comment on the head's performance running the school.

Following the appraisal it was agreed that Andy should try to make better use of the classroom space. Looking back several months later he welcomed the two-way nature of the process, and though he felt it had been long-winded and stressful for some teachers, his own reaction was positive:

> There's a lot more letting children go to other places – the library – and small groups going off to do research. I am letting them do a lot more, which was one of the things we talked about as a target.

This is a good example of how the high credibility of the head as appraiser, the perceived worthwhileness of the targets, as well as skilful interpersonal relationships on both sides, led even a sceptic, albeit a reflective one, to change what he did in his classroom.

Caroline Davies

By contrast, Caroline Davies, a secondary school German teacher with twenty years' teaching experience, began positively. Her head of department was much younger than her and less experienced, so she asked if she could be appraised by a maths teacher with more teaching experience. The appraiser spoke no German, but Caroline felt that this was not a problem, as both of them had a positive attitude to appraisal.

Meeting in her lunch hour to avoid the need for supply cover, Caroline decided to focus on 'differentiation'. Her appraiser knew the class concerned and felt able, even as a non-linguist, to observe with, as he put it, the 'eyes of innocence'. The forty-five minute lesson seen on a Friday afternoon was not one of her best and she said subsequently that, had it not been a formal appraisal, she would have said, 'Oh, this is rubbish, let's stop'.

In the discussion after the lesson the appraiser commented on her good relationships with pupils, describing the ability to keep that particular class busy on a Friday afternoon as 'masterly'. Caroline was not satisfied with her lesson and told her appraiser, 'I don't think you've really seen enough to comment'. The appraiser agreed and they resolved to arrange another lesson observation. It never took place.

The appraisal interview was amicable, but the appraiser found difficulty with target setting, saying, 'I must confess, I don't know what they (the targets) can possibly be. You will know'. Caroline decided to adapt her language materials to ensure better differentiation and to see how other teachers dealt with the issue, but she commented: 'My target comes out of experience generally, not out of that lesson particularly'.

Reflecting on the process months later, she did not believe that appraisal had helped her 'one little bit', and felt that what had happened since would have taken place anyway. She felt the appraiser had not been able to help, beyond 'pulling out something kind'. The appraiser's own reaction was: 'I haven't done this very well'.

This is a good illustration showing where the process went astray. Initially Caroline decided her pride would be injured if she was appraised by a younger person. Length of service was given precedence over subject expertise. In the event the appraiser's reaction to a request for advice was simply to look bereft and apologise or defer. After only one observation they tacitly called the process off. This and the case of Andy Barker illustrate clearly the critical nature of the actual classroom observation and its penumbra, and it is to this important topic that we now turn in more detail.

Chapter 7

Preparing for observation

The introduction within appraisal of a formal system for observing teachers teaching was for many teachers the first time they had been officially observed since they were trainee teachers or probationers. Primary teachers, more than their secondary counterparts, are used to having other adults in their classrooms, in the form of supply cover, parent helpers, classroom assistants, or through team teaching. However, until appraisal was introduced, it was rare for teachers to be observed with the specific purpose that their teaching should be analysed and commented on. The twenty-nine case studies of primary and secondary teachers undertaken in Study 3 allowed the research team to witness at first hand and analyse several aspects of the classroom observation component of appraisal.

Most teachers were well aware of the daily 'loneliness' of the classroom teaching part of their job, and the likely emphasis on 'performance' in the unusual presence of an observer. Some were, none the less, keen to be observed. so that their appraiser would be better informed about what they actually did, especially when it came to writing references:

> Teaching can be a potentially lonely task, can't it, where you're involved in the classroom and you're not really able to see how you're performing compared with other people. You're not really aware of whether your skills are the best skills that you can employ. So appraisal is very much to do with seeing how other people feel you're performing.

> Well, for example, Gerry [the appraiser] has never watched me teach, ever. I think that's really important – that he saw me teach and saw the way I work, for a start. It's also meant that he seems to give me credit for science teaching. . . . I mean I went for jobs and so he was able to comment on science, because I do want to go specifically for science jobs.

In these circumstances the observation aspect of appraisal provided many teachers with a unique opportunity for development and distinguished it from other staff development schemes that were already in place in many schools.

Both appraisees and appraisers who participated in the case studies were asked about their views on observation. Observation should be a key aspect of appraisal as it is the opportunity for an appraiser to gain an insight into a teacher's actual classroom practice, based on first hand experience of their teaching. One appraiser saw himself as a means of reflecting back to teachers images of themselves: 'I see it as a mirror for people to see themselves more clearly, so that their practice then improves. We don't have time for reflection in education and this forces us to reflect on our own practice'.

The findings of the national questionnaire suggested that the overwhelming majority of teachers were happy with their choice of appraisers, even in situations where this choice had been imposed upon them. However, in addition to being happy with the appraiser on a personal level, the responses reported in Chapter 6 confirmed that it was important that teachers also respected the person as a competent professional:

> I saw Martin and I said to him that in no way did I want a certain person appraising me, because I had no confidence whatsoever in them, and I would have been really uptight having somebody who I considered cannot cope in a classroom, being in a position where they might be criticising the way I cope in the classroom.

PERCEIVED ROLE OF OBSERVER

To some extent how teachers reacted to being observed depended on how they perceived the process. In the last chapter it was pointed out that some teachers saw it as aiding their personal and professional development while others worried about redundancy or performance-related pay. For teachers who saw the possible negative outcomes of appraisal it was a more threatening process, as these four appraisers were all too aware:

> For some staff the fact that we are seeking evidence of all sorts, including classroom observation, puts them under pressure. I feel that's a real disadvantage for some staff. . . . I can think of a member of staff or two – simply because of the people they are and the anxiety they carry – who will find it threatening.

> I'm quite worried that it could lead to all sorts of mismanagement by possibly unscrupulous heads. . . . I'm worried about the fact that

you're going to get teachers up against each other and if you get somebody who's maybe not very popular with a head, then maybe it might be a good way of getting rid of that person through a bad appraisal. So, yes, that does worry me. I think we're very lucky in this school . . . that that would never happen.

The difficulty is going to come for any appraiser, where they are appraising somebody where there are difficulties . . . that's a real onus on the appraiser. There's going to be a really difficult decision for the appraiser to make. What do I do about somebody who I feel is – I don't mean 'really incompetent' – not fulfilling the minimum requirement?

I think the Government are out to hammer just about everybody, and the teachers are the next in the firing line. I can see some useful aspects of it. I've always felt that teachers that can't cope should not be able to continue in the job. They have done in the past. We've had people here. So it would weed those out . . . it would make sure that people are up to the job.

Several teachers who had apprehensions associated being observed with either a crisis or with being a beginner. Even those who were accustomed to having other adults present found it hard to shake off the image of 'novice teacher':

I'm used to people, especially support, but I've never liked having somebody else in the classroom. Because I've been teaching for eighteen years so it's only this last five or six years that I've had people in the class at all. So even though I'm now used to it in this school, it's not something I'm used to as a longstanding teacher, apart from when I was a probationary teacher. In a way it's like being a probationary teacher again.

I think everybody is bound to be concerned. In a way, you're put back into the situation like you were on teaching practice, there's another person in there who is taking notes or observing you. I think everybody feels like that. You're bound to feel like that. I feel happy with the person who is appraising me, but it could be different if it was a different person in a different school.

This awareness of being observed caused nervousness for some, especially in the first lesson, and some tenseness in the second:

I think the first one was more a sort of experiment. I felt that it wasn't very well structured. You know I felt more nervous in the first one. The second one seemed to be much more formal, because we had agreed the rules. I did, I must say, feel at one time during the second observation that I was being, sort of, slightly examined.

The issue of appraisers' prejudices and subjectivity generally was also in the minds of many teachers, especially those who feared dismissal or the introduction of performance-related pay. A few teachers commented in interview that they thought their own appraiser had been too subjective. One teacher felt that this could be overcome if more funds were available to enable a system of 'triangulation' or cross-referencing to be introduced, but he thought that this was unlikely as appraisal had been done 'on the cheap'. He was even more convinced of the necessity for this after his appraisal had finished and outlined it when describing how he would approach his next appraisal:

> I would tend to make sure that I could get a different set of viewpoints. I would like this notion of triangulation, where you get another source of reference, get someone else to observe, because the more points of reference you get the truer the picture you have. [My appraiser] will come to my next appraisal with a kind of predetermined perspective of what I'm like and it might be more beneficial to have somebody with a clean sheet on me.

PERCEIVED BENEFITS OF OBSERVATION

Even though teachers were conscious that there were possible misuses for the observation element of appraisal there were also many who were well aware of the benefits and how it might help their own personal and professional development. Those who accepted appraisal could see how observation would allow them to gain insights into their teaching. Both teachers and appraisers were also keen to place it within a positive context and use it to offer teachers encouragement. The national questionnaire showed how teachers seemed to need personal attention, as this appraiser in one case study school confirmed:

> Just seeing how people work and being able to say 'God, that's a really good lesson. I was really interested in what you were doing and I was interested in the way that you planned it'. I think positive stroking is one of those things that teachers don't get enough of and this is a really good excuse for doing it.

Observations were not only used to provide the opportunity for feedback on teaching. In schools where teachers felt they wanted to highlight an area of classroom life to senior managers and those responsible for decision making in a school, observation was a convenient way of deliberately drawing the attention of such keyholders and gatekeepers to aspects of classroom life which they considered required action from them. One teacher felt that the department he worked in was under-resourced and his teaching suffered because of this. He deliberately made one of the primary purposes of his appraisal to ensure that the appraiser recognised these constraints. It was not the official agenda, but it became the major item on the hidden agenda, as observations were transformed into a device for improving the facilities within the department. This ruse was something that a number of appraisers recognised, and in some cases welcomed:

> It changes your view when you see somebody in their normal working environment, and you see what problems and constraints they work under. Things like equipment, text books and all those other things which, when you're beavering away somewhere else, you're not aware of. You suddenly realise that having one book between two is very inconvenient in some instances, or a lack of test tubes in a lab . . . as an appraiser you would not be aware of these necessarily, and there is no mechanism by which you can easily get to know this. . . . But the classroom observation element is certainly a really worthwhile one.

AREA OF FOCUS

The national questionnaire described in Chapter 4 showed that school management, class management, teaching methods and differentiation were the most common areas on which teachers chose to focus during their appraisal. The likely outcome of their appraisal was an important consideration for many when they chose their observation focus. One appraiser voiced what he perceived to be the potential problems associated with hierarchical appraisals when it came to the appraisee choosing the area of focus: 'There could be more mistrust and an unwillingness to really focus on your weakness and the things that you really want to improve because you didn't want your line manager to know them'.

Not all teachers felt threatened within their own school, though a number mentioned that while for them personally it was not a problem, they could see how it might be in a different school. Teachers are more likely to opt for a 'safe' focus if they are being appraised by the head within a threatening environment, or are unsure what their appraisal will be used for. This concern came from appraisees and appraisers alike, though they often expressed fears about other schools rather than gave descriptions of their own.

For some teachers the lesson observations did not go as they had expected and although not always unduly concerned, they were disappointed that their teaching had been portrayed in an unfavourable light. Not surprisingly a few teachers deliberately minimised the possibility of this, and one teacher described how it had become part of the folklore: 'I'd been told by several people to choose in my first appraisal cycle to focus on something that I was very confident in'.

In a later interview this appraisee reiterated the same point, at the same time emphasising that, although his choice of focus had been something he had felt confident in, this did not mean that he believed the appraisal had been pointless:

> I wanted to choose a focus for the first time round that I felt very confident in already. I was encouraged to do that by everyone involved, so I did. I think that my practice has improved, but not necessarily because of appraisal. I think that it would have done anyway. I'm not saying that appraisal was not valuable, it was very valuable.

His appraiser had not been concerned about the selection of an area of focus that the appraisee already felt confident about, because he had his own concerns about how appraisal was going to be used in the long term:

> How might people start to manipulate it? People might drop themselves into something that they might regret later on. I subscribe a little bit to the conspiracy theory, rather than the cock up theory. I think there's a lot more people want to manage, have control.

If teachers wished appraisal to be beneficial to their classroom teaching, they needed to focus on something that could be developed, but if appraisal was in any way perceived as threatening or judgemental, either by the appraisee or the appraiser, it was more likely that the focus would be concentrated on an area of strength, which could not subsequently be used against them if redundancies or performance-related pay became an issue. One appraiser felt some concern about this aspect of her role, stressing the place of trust:

> I don't want to waste people's time. . . . I hope there's enough trust between me and my appraisee so that we can do worthwhile observations. . . . It's a waste of time when people play safe on things and say 'Oh come and look at whether X is working for an hour'. You want something concrete to come out of it, so it depends on them being able to open up and say, 'Well I'm not very good at questioning', or 'I want to be able to improve my groupwork skills'.

However, as with many other aspects of appraisal, appraisers did not always perceive their role in the same way. One appraiser was more concerned about the difference between improving practice and assessing or diagnosing competence:

It's actually quite difficult to separate helping with development and identifying the development – in the sense that you need to talk it through and try and tease out where the focus really is. And there is a danger that you try to start and solve them – whatever it is that wants improving. Rather than spending the time appraising.

This neatly illustrates the uncertainty felt by some teachers and appraisers over the principal purpose of appraisal. The tensions which arise are to some extent based on the tension between 'appraisal as professional development' and 'appraisal as a management tool'. Ultimately, it could be said, the outcome should be the same, namely the improvement of teaching. But in the one case it is through discussion and consent, in the other, appraisers play a more interventionist and directive role, in accordance with, as they would see it, the school's needs. Mistrust of appraisals and their outcome was not necessarily allayed once a teacher had experienced appraisal. A few teachers felt more suspicious after appraisal than beforehand, or saw the need to become smarter about who they had appraising them in the future or what they chose to focus on. Other teachers wanted to be observed teaching in what they would categorise as 'difficult' circumstances, but some were subsequently disappointed when their lessons then did not go well.

Within some LEA documentation there was strong advice that the focus needed to be 'observable'. We encountered examples of conflict when teachers chose a focus which appraisers believed they could not observe. In some cases appraisers were unwilling to agree to a focus, believing that it was not possible to observe this type of focus within a classroom. One appraisee explained how her choice of focus had been affected by the appraiser's reaction:

My initial concern was that I set two [areas of focus] and . . . Tom decided that he didn't think that they could be observed and I had to completely disagree. They were originally 'differentiation' for top level special needs and 'positive reinforcement in the classroom'. . . . Tom felt that 'positive reinforcement' couldn't be observed because of the observer effect, and that 'differentiation' for top level special needs I could just do that without being appraised on it. . . . He implied that it was just a question of planning that I didn't need to discuss really. He then suggested something a bit more to his liking really and I said 'Fine', and 'positive reinforcement' he felt was a bit more of a non-observable management issue – which I disagree with, but there you go.

This is another striking example, as described in the previous chapter, of a power relationship where in the end the more dominant person, in this case Tom the appraiser, overrides the perfectly defensible judge-ments of the less powerful appraisee, who in the end has to defer to him with reluctant resignation. As a result this teacher, like many others, still felt that she had benefited from appraisal, but not specifi-cally within her classroom teaching. She believed that her relationship with her appraiser had improved and the observation had enabled him to see some of the pupils' behavioural problems and the way she dealt with them. She was determined, however, to learn from her experience and back her own judgement in future:

> Ultimately [next] time I know it would be my total decision and I'd have the confidence to say, 'No, I don't want to do that', which I didn't have the confidence to do last time. Because I know what is involved now and I know how I can use the appraisal process to the best possible advantage to me.

There was a distinct difference between teachers who had a clear idea of what they wanted to focus on and those who opted for very general or non-specific observations. The choice was often influenced by factors such as the preparation undertaken by the appraisee before the initial meeting, who took control of the meeting, the perception of the purpose of appraisal, and the willingness of the appraiser to support the chosen area of focus.

In the above example of conflict, the eventual choice of focus had been influenced by the appraiser's own strongly held opinions and his unwillingness to observe the appraisee's choice of focus. In some cases the opposite was apparent and appraisees had gone to the initial meet-ing hoping for guidance from the appraiser, because they found it diffi-cult to select one specific aspect of their classroom teaching to focus on. One teacher who would have preferred to concentrate on her management responsibilities commented in the third interview, three months after her appraisal:

> I found the classroom observation very difficult. So the answer is that it was too vague, I suppose. . . . It was what I wanted but at the end of the day it was so general it just became a nothingness.

This teacher too was keen to learn from her experiences. She was determined she would not select such a general focus for her next appraisal and would be far more specific.

LESSON SELECTION AND TIMING

The choice of focus could also affect the selection of lessons to be observed. Which lessons were eventually picked out was often related to how teachers, both appraisees and appraisers, perceived the purpose and outcome of appraisal. The issue of whether to choose a 'good' class or a 'bad' class emerged in all the interviews with case study teachers. They were each asked by the researcher how representative of their teaching they felt the observed lessons had been. The issue of representativeness is important for, among other reasons, the validity of classroom observation. Validity is sometimes queried on the grounds that it is not a 'natural' setting when an observer is present, as it may affect teacher and pupils. One appraiser echoed some of the general criticisms made about the representativeness and 'normality' of appraisal observations:

> I think there's no harm in them being put under pressure sometimes and I think it can have a very positive effect. The cynics have said, 'well at least the kids will get two good lessons in a year!'. You know, because they will be the two when they are being observed. I don't think that's a sensible view to take.

Appraisers tended to prefer a lesson that had not been subjected to any extra preparation or planning, but was as close to the appraisee's normal teaching as was possible. Those who took a developmental view felt that this would allow the appraiser to identify areas for improvement. A few teachers responded positively to this and tried not to plan a special lesson for the observer's benefit. One teacher even claimed in interview that he had forgotten that his appraisal observation was taking place.

Whether the lesson was typical or specially conceived was sometimes affected by factors out of the direct control of the appraisee. These factors included the effect on the children of another adult in the room, usually one holding a more senior position in the school than that of their teacher. Another factor was the timing of the lesson, the stage of the week or the term at which the appraisal took place. Timing could be a sensitive matter for some, and one teacher complained bitterly about every conceivable aspect of lesson selection:

> They [the two observations] were both totally inappropriate lessons to come into, I felt, because we were straight after half-term. One group as you know, were completely new and a different mix . . . and the other group, that was a class that I am quite used to, and are a bad class anyway, and both were coming in for introductory lessons . . . [and] they were both first thing in the morning.

The national questionnaire survey showed that 38 per cent of teachers chose which lesson would be observed, while 53 per cent negotiated the selection. Ideally many appraisees would have liked to choose freely which lesson they wished to have observed, but the inescapable realities of two people's timetables not matching up, meant that this could not always occur. Certain lesson times are traditionally considered worse than others, such as Friday afternoons, Monday mornings, or the first day back after half-term, but these times were used for observation, despite appraisees' attempts to 'blacklist' them.

On the other hand, teachers who had decided to focus on certain types of issue, such as class management, sometimes chose these traditionally unpopular times as being the most appropriate to explore the problems they were experiencing. One such teacher nominated a Friday afternoon lesson, saying in interview: 'That will be really good because that's a dire session'. After the observation had taken place she was asked about her choice of lesson. She replied that, in the event, it was not at all representative of her normal teaching, describing it as 'really duff'. With hindsight she would have preferred the appraiser to have seen her teaching a successful lesson.

The timing of observations was a factor for appraisers as well as appraisees. Appraisers too felt tired by the end of the week. The role of observer can be an emotionally intensive one, especially for those who are relatively new to it, demanding a high degree of attentiveness. One appraiser felt that fatigue had reduced the value of the exercise:

> I was just too tired last thing on a Friday afternoon – it wasn't a good time to have it . . . and now it's sort of 'Right what are we looking for? Yes, we'll comment on that'. So it's all new. So I would perhaps query our preparation, but I don't know whether our end results are acceptable or not either.

The stage of the school year or term when observation took place was also regarded as an influential factor. Some teachers felt that if their appraisal took place at the end of term its effectiveness could evaporate, especially if it was the end of the school year, thwarting any fruitful outcomes. Several teachers, in the national questionnaire reported in Chapter 4, as well as in the case study follow-up interviews, stated that they could not even remember what their targets were. One interviewee believed that the late stage of the year at which the appraisal took place was a significant contributory factor:

> No I can't remember them [the targets]. I think one of the difficulties was the timing of it – at the end of the summer. It's just a wind down, but one puts it sort of behind one for the summer.

NUMBER OF OBSERVATIONS

Most of the teachers in the case studies appeared to be aware that there should be at least two observations lasting for at least an hour overall. However, as the national questionnaire survey showed, the amount of time appraisers allocated to their lesson observations did not always coincide with these requirements. Over a quarter of teachers only had one lesson observed, and some appraisers were present for as little as ten minutes, though the vast majority aimed at the minimum requirement, few going over it.

One appraising head commented in interview beforehand that he thought the observation would last about an hour, but also remarked: 'What's interesting about observation is that it might well be that one hour's observation is inadequate and therefore we may well be involved in looking at another hour or even two or three sessions'.

After the first observation the appraisee said she felt that there was no need to do a further observation, as she believed that all her lessons were very similar. This was despite her belief that her appraisal observation had not gone very well. The appraiser was prepared to do another observation but felt that it must be the appraisee's choice. In this case the observation only took place on one occasion and lasted for fifty minutes, meeting neither the statutory regulations nor the recommended guidelines. A number of other appraisers opted to observe only one lesson, sometimes lasting less than an hour. There were various reasons for this shortfall, but it was rare for one of the parties to object. On only one occasion did an appraiser refuse a teacher's request for a second observation.

Not following the guidelines was, therefore, common, but there was no single explanation. Some attributed it to logistical problems, like lack of cover for the appraiser's class. Other appraisers said they did not wish to spend time away from their class or duties, while some teachers equally said they did not want a second disruption. On a few occasions one or both parties involved decided it was simply not necessary to undertake more than one observation. There were also occasions when teachers were seen in a 'double' lesson, which they gratefully designated as two separate sessions. Many appraisers in the case studies, however, did fulfil the requirements.

THE EFFECT OF THE OBSERVATIONS ON PUPILS

A number of the teachers feared that an observer's presence could affect the pupils, some behaving better, others worse. Even where the pupils were better behaved, this was not necessarily perceived as positive by the teacher concerned. In one example the teacher had been experiencing a number of problems with the pupils in her class and one of her desired outcomes from the observation was that the appraiser should be able to see at first hand what she 'had to put up with'. After the observations she felt that the children had behaved better than they normally did and was exasperated that the lessons had not demon-strated the problems she had hoped the appraiser would be able to comment on. In primary schools the appraiser was often the head teacher, and some teachers believed that children were invariably quieter when the head came in.

This effect on pupils' behaviour during the observation was often influenced by how they perceived the role of the appraiser. Pupils were often not aware of why there was an observer in their classroom. When we sat in on appraiser/appraisee discussions and planning meet-ings before observations took place, we rarely heard mention of what pupils might be told about the appraiser's presence, though it was sometimes commented on afterwards if the appraiser had been questioned by the children. Only once did we see a teacher explain to her class the reason why there was an observer present. One appraiser even thought it best if pupils believed they were under scrutiny, rather than their teacher:

> It's more likely that I will move around amongst the groups and although I will be watching what Neil is doing all the while, I'll actu-ally be interacting with youngsters – talking to them and being involved. I think they'll feel easier about that. It's likely that they will feel that I am there to observe them, rather than to observe Neil, which may well help him in some respects, because he will feel that there is no need for them to know that I'm observing him. I'll be there to see them performing . . . rather than him per-forming. . . . That will be the popular myth, I think that will exist amongst them.

Sometimes pupils themselves did comment spontaneously on another teacher being in their classroom. While many assumed that the appraiser was there to monitor their work and behaviour, which might affect how they behaved, a few realised that it was the teacher who was being assessed. One teacher found out after his appraisal that the class had guessed that he was being appraised. At the end of the term, when he left the school for another post, some pupils asked him if he had been sacked.

Older pupils were more likely to work out that a whole programme of observation was taking place, though they were not always aware of its purpose. In one school a more senior class speculated freely and pub-licly amongst themselves at the start of the lesson, with some asking the appraiser outright for reasons why she was there, others wanting to interact with her in her normal relationship with them. This made the appraiser self-conscious about her unfamiliar role as observer, and she commented afterwards:

The only feelings I had about it is that I think we should have told the class, because on both occasions I found the students were sort of, 'Oh, what are you here for?' or 'Hello, I've got my work experience sorted out' and I felt that we really should have said to them, or the teacher should have said to them, 'Right, I've got Ms Wilbey in – she's just watching me, or watching what's going on' . . . and I think if they'd been aware of what was going on it probably would have carried on without them asking me questions.

The ambiguity of appraisers appearing in a different role from that with which pupils are familiar caused problems for other appraisers. Some senior people found it difficult to restrain themselves from taking over the lesson. It seemed odd to be with a class they normally taught, yet not to be in sole charge of it. As the national questionnaire survey showed, about a quarter of appraisers did actually take part in some way in the lessons they observed. One deputy head described the dilemma and the temptations:

I've got one concern actually – about myself as an observer in a classroom. Because when I was observing Janet, I was observing children with behaviour problems, showing disruptive problems and I find it really difficult to be in there as an observer and not actually reprimand those children about their behaviour. I felt awkward and wondered about the effect of that on those children – for them seeing me being involved, as deputy, and them getting away with that behaviour. So that quite concerned me actually. It was something I hadn't thought about.

Yet when teachers were asked in interview how they felt about being observed, many simply accepted someone coming in to observe without demur. Some did say they were apprehensive or nervous, and occasionally this led them to plan too much for the observation, or try to be larger than life, leaving them feeling the whole situation had become too unreal. One teacher who felt that his lesson had gone badly, said later that he was too much influenced by the feeling that he was 'on show'. This put pressure on him to demonstrate his authority over the class from the beginning. Consequently, during the appraisal observation, he had 'tried to put some order down' with his class straightaway by sending two boys out, commenting: 'I suppose when I asked the children to get out . . . it was a bit over the top'.

Some teachers were essentially philosophical, believing that there was in any case no such thing as a 'typical' lesson, so the effect of an observer was just one more variation in a varied professional life, rather than a rude disruption of it:

I don't know if you can have 'everyday' teaching really. I mean, it's part of the nature of the job that it's so flexible and you can teach the same class five times over, but it's never the same lesson.

There are three sets of problems surrounding the presence of an observer: first, whether it affects the behaviour of the children so much that the purpose of the observation becomes invalid; second, whether the appraiser is placed in a difficult position, not able to intervene for fear of undermining the teacher's authority in the eyes of the pupils; third, the effect of observation on the teacher, the person actually being appraised, for whom a great deal may be at stake. We describe the actuality of lesson observation in the following chapter.

Chapter 8

The implementation of lesson observation

The research procedures for recording what happened during the observation phase of appraisal were described in Chapter 5. They involved members of the research team sitting in on the preliminary discussions; watching teachers in their classrooms before, during and after they were observed by their appraiser, noting what happened, recording critical events, taking measures of pupil involvement and deviancy; observing, whenever possible, lessons where the appraiser was undertaking a formal lesson observation in the classroom of the appraisee; sitting in on feedback sessions and appraisal interviews; and interviewing teachers and appraisers.

To give a picture of how this worked out in practice we describe below the classroom observation of Miss Winter, a reception class teacher in Smallville Primary School, who was appraised by Mrs Summers, the deputy head.

THE OBSERVATION OF MISS WINTER

Initial meeting

As in many of the initial meetings between teacher and appraiser, several aspects of the appraisee's job were discussed and observation only formed one part of the meeting. Though the appraiser, Mrs Summers, provided guidance on the possible choice of focus, it was Miss Winter who decided what her two areas of focus were to be. She selected:

1 Whether children, when working in groups, were engaged in their task.
2 Children who were distracting others – to discover why they were doing it.

Miss Winter explained to her appraiser that the pupils in her current class were lively, but immature, and less involved in their task than her previous class had been.

These two areas of focus were then shaped by the appraiser as 'how effective present classroom organisation system is'. The choice of focus was checked twice by the appraiser with Miss Winter, who added that she wanted to know whether there were particular children who were distracting others. On the matter of methods of observation both had ideas, but the initiative lay mainly with the appraiser who checked out possible ideas with the appraisee, saying: 'Well I can go away and think about that and come back to you on how I'm actually going to record it'.

Miss Winter commented that the appraisal observation might lead to a behaviour modification programme, something in which senior members of the school were very interested. Smallville School had formerly been a social priority school, and some of the children had serious problems which often manifested themselves in severe mis-behaviour in class. She also explained that she would have a different class the following term and how that might affect the timing of the observation. Mrs Summers wondered whether it was necessary to come into Miss Winter's classroom beforehand, but then answered her own question by stating: 'No. I know the way your classroom works'. Miss Winter offered information on specific children, but the appraiser declined, stating that an outline of activities would be sufficient.

Mrs Summers clarified with Miss Winter how long she wanted her to observe for, whether she wanted her to move about, whether she would prefer morning or afternoon. They agreed there would be two observations, one all morning, one all afternoon, and Mrs Summers said she would like to talk to a group, asking them: 'What are you supposed to be doing?'. She would then focus on a specific child and consult another member of staff to see whether a schedule was already drawn up to use in observations. Miss Winter agreed to give the appraiser her lesson notes the week before the observation, and Mrs Summers agreed to give the appraisee a copy of the data collection method by then also. They would also try to arrange feedback straight after the lessons.

First lesson observation

When Mrs Summers came to watch Miss Winter teach she arrived before the class, bringing with her a simple observation schedule for focusing on children's misbehaviour, with headings like: 'The behaviour' (What did he or she do?) 'Antecedents' (What do you think provoked it?), 'Background' (Where did it happen?), 'Consequences' (What did you do to stop it?) and 'Aftermath' (What happened as a result of your efforts?). The senior staff of the school were interested in their own version of 'assertive discipline', a behaviour modification programme in which approved behaviour is recognised and reinforced. In consultation with the appraisee, she decided to monitor two particular pupils known to be disruptive, Richard and Mark, noting every three minutes whether they were on or off task over a period of twenty minutes.

In her first observation the appraiser started off by watching quietly from a distance. Then she left her place and moved nearer to a specific group of pupils. She sat quietly observing from a distance to focus on one specific child, Richard. The first part of the observation lasted thirty-five minutes, before the pupils went to watch television with another class. After break the appraiser returned to the lesson, but commented to the teacher that she did not want to stay for longer than fifteen to twenty minutes because of cover for her own class, but wanted a chance to finish the 'on task' schedule.

One of the target children, Richard, had had to leave to have a medical at 10.30 and neither the appraisee nor the appraiser had realised this. Richard returned from his medical crying, so the teacher cuddled him and gave him a tissue to wipe his tears. The appraiser left after twenty-five minutes. Feedback about the lesson had to be re-scheduled for after school, because the teacher had had to see the nurse after the lesson about Richard.

At break time the appraiser commented to the researcher how difficult it was to observe. There were problems with interruptions, such as the TV programme and medical, and one of the children she was observing went off to take the register. She also realised that she needed a stopwatch. She wondered how representative what she saw really was. She pointed out that as the deputy head she often acted in a disciplinary role, and she wondered how this affected the behaviour of the pupils. She believed they had ignored her, commenting: 'It's funny, as soon as they realise I'm not going to react, it's almost as if they forget who I am . . . but obviously I can't start interfering in things, so it's quite weird for me'.

Feedback after first observation

The feedback session took place the same day after school. The appraiser took the lead, with Miss Winter mainly listening and accepting the comments from her appraiser, asking her if she could type them and let her have a copy later, to which the appraiser agreed. Discussion centred mainly on the two disruptive children. Richard, the appraiser commented, had exhibited 'loads of disruptive behaviour' – talking illicitly, kicking, running, making a fuss when he returned upset from his medical.

She said that it was a new experience for her, as she had never actually sat and watched a class before, so she found it interesting. What she was going to say, she felt, was probably 'not going to be any news' to Miss Winter. She explained that she had abandoned doing the on-off task schedule for Richard because he had been 'in such a state' when he returned from his medical. She also said that she had found it really hard to concentrate with all the disruption, though she had found it interesting and had learned from it as well.

Miss Winter informed the appraiser that the doctor had written to the child guidance clinic. The appraiser suggested it would be worth waiting to see what the educational psychologist did the next day. Both agreed that Richard posed a serious problem, even though he would be leaving Miss Winter's class soon. The appraiser pointed out that it would be useful to have some coping strategies none the less.

The second target pupil, Mark, had been well behaved, and no examples of disruption were noted, as he had worked 'really well'. The appraiser had completed the on-off task schedule, but she commented on the complete lack of deviancy: 'I was looking for it, but I didn't get it'. Miss Winter replied with some relief, 'That's good', and pointed out that another pupil, Leroy, was in fact more of a problem. They discussed the kicking and punching of other children that had occurred.

Second lesson observation

Originally the second observation was scheduled to take place from 1 to 3 p.m., but after the first observation the appraiser realised that this was unmanageable and it was therefore retimed to take place from 2 to 3 p.m. The appraiser later found she was scheduled to do something else urgently, dealing with one of the many problems which often occurred in Smallville, so she did not arrive until 2.20 p.m. The observation was therefore decreased, from the original intention of two hours, to forty minutes.

The appraiser came into the lesson quietly and sat three to four metres away from the child she was focusing on. This was not one of the original two children, but the third pupil, Leroy, identified during the first observation. Leroy demonstrated a number of deviant acts during the observation, like breaking wind noisily, jabbing other children, singing and at one point pulling another child off a chair. Richard was also working in the same group with Leroy, so he was involved in some of the same misbehaviour. The teacher intervened and Leroy was made to apologise. The appraiser observed these events in a non-participant role. Richard and Leroy continued to misbehave until the end of the lesson.

Second lesson feedback

The feedback session was again led strongly by the appraiser, who opened the discussion with genuine empathy, saying, 'I don't know how you cope'. They discussed what the appraiser had observed – Leroy switching from one area of the classroom to another, swearing, flicking things, not helping at all, leading Richard into similar misbehaviour.

'He [Leroy] is taking a lot of your time' the appraiser commented, before looking towards possible solutions: modification of the system currently being used to deal with disruption, discussion with the educational psychologist, trying to get some external help, the use of different sanctions. Miss Winter pointed out that the class would be moving to another teacher in five weeks, but the appraiser felt that what Miss Winter learned about the effectiveness of different sanctions and teaching strategies could be useful for the next teacher and, indeed, useful for all the teachers at Smallville.

The appraiser finally suggested that they should set a date by when Miss Winter could try out new ideas, ending the meeting, as she began it, with empathy for the teacher, saying: 'I can see what you are up against . . . I know. It brings you down. It's wearing and it's hard to be positive, so I'll bring it all together next Thursday'.

The appraisal interview

The appraiser again took a strong lead in the formal appraisal interview, beginning the meeting by explaining the main purpose of it – to draw up the appraisal statement. She pointed out to Miss Winter that the data from the appraisal would be kept in the appraisal file, but access would only be to one bit of the file, which she showed to the appraisee. She explained that apart from that particular summary sheet, to which the governors could have access, the rest was totally confidential. She said that it would be typed up and stated: 'You need to be happy that it's a true reflection of what your concerns were, and that you are happy with the targets, and that they are realistic'.

The appraiser then moved on to formalise the areas of focus, concluding first that the discipline focus had been useful because of the need to think about whole school sanctions. Second, she asked Miss Winter to draw up an 'individual education programme' for the 'problem' pupils. If that did not work then, in keeping with the behaviour modification policy of the school, they would look at contracts with children (contracts with built-in rewards). Were there still difficulties, parent interviews, and even exclusion of the child concerned, would be considered. Third, she said that they could both talk to the whole staff about discipline, because it was not just Miss Winter who was experiencing problems. When, at the end of the interview, she offered Miss Winter supply teacher cover, so that she could, if she wanted, go and talk to the teacher who would be taking over the class in five weeks' time, Miss Winter responded: 'That's great, that's brilliant'.

Appraisal statement (written during the appraisal interview)

In order to explain to Miss Winter what an appraisal statement looked like, the appraiser, somewhat unusually, actually showed her a copy of her own appraisal statement. She explained that she would go through the statement with Miss Winter so that she agreed with what she was writing. They drafted Miss Winter's statement together, with the appraiser taking a firm lead. The main elements in it were as follows:

1 Miss Winter's initial concerns – how effective classroom organisation was and the behaviour of specific children who misbehaved.
2 Miss Winter's post of responsibility.
3 Classroom observation, what the appraiser's role and focus had been.
4 Feedback from the observations: that nine out of ten children seemed clear what they were supposed to be doing; that Richard took a lot of time and was disruptive; that Mark had not misbehaved; that Leroy had emerged as one of the most disruptive pupils, even though Miss Winter had not originally asked the appraiser to focus on him; that it was, therefore, Richard and Leroy that the teacher needed to concentrate on.
5 Targets set, following the observation: no problem with general class organisation, so that did not need to be a target; Miss Winter to draw up a behaviour modification programme for Richard and Leroy (this was seen to be the main target and one the appraisee was most keen to meet); if the programme worked, Miss Winter was to explain it to the staff, so it might be used by other teachers.

Mrs Summers, the appraiser, concluded by saying, 'Now I feel that is enough, to be honest', to which Miss Winter replied, 'I think that's fine'. The appraiser commented that she would prefer a modest aspiration, something that the appraisee could actually do, rather than 'a great long list'. She arranged to review the targets with Miss Winter in three weeks' time.

Researcher's observation of lessons

A member of the research team observed Miss Winter teach on five occasions, following exactly our original research design. The first observation took place before the appraiser had visited. The second and third coincided with the two sessions observed by the appraiser. The fourth observation was eleven days after the appraiser's second visit. The fifth and final observation was the follow-up, scheduled to take place several weeks afterwards, by which time Miss Winter's original class had moved on to another teacher and she now had her new class.

There was quite a lot of disruptive behaviour during the researcher's first observation. Although the appraiser, Mrs Summers, felt that her presence made little difference to the pupils, there was a much higher level of involvement in the task and less deviant behaviour from pupils, apart from Leroy and Richard, when she was present, as Table 8.1 shows.

The involvement and deviancy index described earlier is a quantified measure which produces scores ranging from a possible minimum of zero up to a possible maximum of 100. It involves the researcher in studying every pupil in turn for twenty seconds at a time, noting whether the child is showing high, medium or low application to the task in hand, and the extent of deviant behaviour. Although carefully compiled, it is a rough and ready index of application to work and mis-behaviour. As it involves making a sweep of each individual pupil's behaviour, there is no guarantee that the period when a particular pupil is observed is 'typical' for that pupil. None the less it does provide data which can be placed alongside other forms of evidence. Scores were recorded in four out of the five observations by the researcher, the missing one being the appraiser's second visit, when, because of the shortness of the lesson and the interruptions, it was not possible to assemble the full record of individual pupil behaviour.

Table 8.1 Pupil 'on task' and 'deviancy' scores[1] during three observations of Miss Winter by the researcher and one by the appraiser

| | Researcher (before) | Appraiser | | Researcher (straight after) | Researcher (3 months after) |
		(first)	(second)		
On task	62	96	Missing	77	75
Deviancy	16	8	Missing	11	9

[1] Possible range 0 to 100.

Table 8.1 shows that during the researcher's first observation an 'on task' score of 62 and a deviancy score of 16 were recorded. When the appraiser made her first visit, children were more involved in their task, with a score of 96, and less deviant, a score of 8 being recorded. By way of comparison, the average figures obtained for all teachers' lessons observed during the present research project were: 82 for involvement in the task and 9 for deviancy. What Miss Winter's figures mean in terms of pupils' actual 'on task' behaviour is that, when the researcher made her first observation, roughly half the class were fully engaged in their work, a quarter were medium engaged, and a further quarter appeared not to be doing the work set. When the appraiser was present, however, all except two children appeared to be fully engaged in their work. Pupil misbehaviour was higher in the first session observed by the researcher, when five or six pupils exhibited some kind of deviancy, whereas, when the appraiser was present, only two or three pupils misbehaved.

When the researcher made her later observations, more of the same sort of pupil disruption occurred. Eleven days after the appraiser had finished observing Miss Winter, the researcher watched a lesson. Leroy and Richard continued to misbehave. Leroy rolled around on the carpet, teased another child and chanted aloud whilst seated in the carpeted area. Richard was seen kicking another boy. He later sat on a boy's head on the carpet, whereupon the teacher used one of the coping strategies discussed with the appraiser, leading him away by the hand and seating him elsewhere. However, there was less disruption and more attention to the task than had been witnessed in the first lesson, before appraisal. This applied both to the researcher's second observation, with the same class, and the final observation, by which time Miss Winter was teaching her new class.

Comment on the observations of Miss Winter

This brief description of the full cycle of Miss Winter's classroom observation by her appraiser shows that even in a well run school, where teacher and appraiser are committed to professional improvement, the path is not straight. Despite her best efforts, Mrs Summers, originally intending to spend two half-days in Miss Winter's classroom, found her plans thwarted by what are in practice 'normal' interruptions, like medicals and school crises that compete for a senior teacher's time and immediate attention.

Although some of what was witnessed in Miss Winter's case was typical of other classroom observations, there are elements which are different, each case study being unique. Unlike many other appraisers, Mrs Summers used a schedule in which she systematically observed individual pupils under pre-determined headings. Most appraisers merely made freehand notes about whatever caught their attention. Furthermore the observations were related to a particular view of behaviour modification the school was trying out, in order to cope with children who behaved badly, of whom there were several.

Mrs Summers was a benignly despotic appraiser, taking a strong lead, determining and controlling the agenda. She was concerned about her dominant influence, worrying that it might affect the pupils' behaviour. In the event she did not feel her presence in the classroom influenced what happened, but there was less disruption and more application when she was there. Miss Winter seemed happy to play a subsidiary role and be guided by her colleague's controlling style and the school's policies on pupil behaviour.

The observation part of the appraisal seemed, in this instance, to have made a positive impact on Miss Winter's teaching. She tried to carry out the suggestions made by her appraiser, and though disruptive behaviour continued, subsequent observations by the researcher suggested that it seemed to be at a lower rate than was noted before appraisal. Moreover, a situation which could easily have become perceived in a negative light – that Miss Winter was having discipline problems and could not cope alone – was skilfully turned into a positive agenda. By empathising with the appraisee and arranging for her to discuss her difficulties with others, so that her experience was shared, the appraiser seemed to evoke a positive response.

However, when interviewed four months later, Miss Winter confessed that she had done little towards meeting her targets. It was not that these targets were not still considered to be important, more a case of many pressures in the school on both her and Mrs Summers, so that some of the original impetus had been lost by the appraisee and appraiser.

THE DYNAMICS OF CLASSROOM OBSERVATION

Mrs Summers' classroom observation of Miss Winter's lessons illustrates how this important part of the appraisal process was carried out in one case study primary school. Not all appraisers had given as much thought to observation as Mrs Summers, however. In Chapter 2 several possible approaches to classroom observation were described, yet the questionnaire data reported in Chapter 4 suggested that many appraisers just 'sat and watched', and were most likely to use freehand notes. During the case studies we saw what teachers and appraisers actually did before, during and after the observation of lessons. Lack of variety in methods used by appraisers could reflect the area of focus chosen, a particular methodological perspective, or a lack of training in observation skills.

Some appraisers were critical about their training in lesson observation, finding it to be perfunctory, or even insulting. Observing videos did not always translate into reality:

There was nothing on the observation, that was the worst part of the training for me, because I was just being told and I felt – I was actually being told what was on bits of paper, and since I learned to read many years ago, I feel slightly insulted when people do that to me. . . . We were taken through the observation schedules – very little that you could just immediately pick out and use. I think they were relying on the fact that we were all going to be quite good observers anyway.

We actually did have a meeting and I think we had a video but it didn't stick up there [pointing to her head] and I think in some ways it would have been useful to have had an Inset where we were going through what we were looking for. So the concern is: have I done it efficiently or not . . . and I've nothing to measure that by. . . . So it's the depth that we need to be getting into.

Not all appraisers were so negative. One appraiser, who had received no training at all in observation skills, did not feel that this had disadvantaged him. His view was that observation should be kept simple, something that any experienced practitioner could do:

I don't think that [observation] is a problem for me. You can give me research evidence to suggest there are easier ways that people can be given observation training. . . . Teachers are very perceptive. I mean you are teaching thirty people at once. You've got to have eyes everywhere and I think they [teachers] are pretty good as a profession. . . . I don't think we need it for the depth and sophistication we are aiming at this time round.

Methods of recording

There had been little evidence from the national survey to suggest that appraisers used any technical aids, such as stopwatches, video or tape recorders, most (89 per cent) preferring to record notes on paper, usually within an unstructured timeframe. This was confirmed in the case studies in Study 3 of this research. Most appraisers found a discreet place in the room from which to view the lesson and wrote notes as they observed. One teacher found her appraiser's attempts to blend discreetly into the background somewhat impractical:

He was huddled in a corner trying to disappear – well it looked perfectly ridiculous – he was trying to be unobvious . . . but you can't. You might as well sort of introduce yourself to the children and say: 'Well I'm here to do XYZ, please don't interrupt me while I'm doing whatever I'm doing'. If you tried to disappear in here the children wouldn't have it. They always interrupt.

By contrast with Mrs Summers at Smallville Primary School, one appraiser was much less discriminating, saying: 'I wrote and wrote – everything I saw I wrote . . .'. However he also recognised that even comprehensive note taking was not without problems. After the observation of one lesson he wanted to discuss the teacher's use of sarcasm. Unfortunately, even his copious note taking turned out to be too parsimonious, so he had not recorded any examples of sarcasm:

> It's quite useful to have bits of evidence, so that when you're feeding back you can say, 'You know, as in such and such' . . . which is what I didn't do when I [mentioned] the 'sarcastic comment' . . . I hadn't written any of them down. But it's nice to have evidence so I tend to write quite a lot.

There was also an instance where an appraiser used neither a structured nor an unstructured framework, choosing instead to make no notes. This head teacher explained why he favoured the method he did, which involved sitting and watching, but without making any notes until after the lesson had finished:

> You can't go in there and make notes and things like that . . . It all had to be done most subtly I think. I think it's got to be very relaxed. You can't be sitting taking notes. I think you've got to get the feel and perhaps go in in a very open way. That's also very difficult. You've got to consciously forget about the preconceived ideas that you might have about what that classroom's like.

A few appraisers did favour using schedules, and in one school the teachers who had been on appraisal training got together and devised an observation schedule which was given to all appraisers as a framework for their observations. In practice, only one of the two appraisers we studied in that school actually used it. The other preferred to devise his own system for observing the appraisee, to make it more appropriate to the focus.

In only one of the case studies did the appraiser and appraisee opt to video record one of the observations. In this instance the use of a video camera was prompted in the discussion about how the appraiser was going to observe:

> And when I'm an observer what would you like me to do? Would you like me to sit and take notes . . . or a video so you actually get to see it afterwards. It might be quite interesting. . . . It would be interesting to see how you start and how you progress.

On this occasion it was agreed that the appraiser would observe and make notes in the first observation and video record the second observation, which they could then both watch and discuss. In spite of the benefits of the teacher being able to watch himself at work, more suggestions about future practice actually arose from the non-recorded lesson. It was also interesting that after the appraisal was finished, the video was retained as a departmental resource, and was even shown at a curriculum evening for parents.

Although this was the only case study that used a video recording technique in the observation and there was little evidence to suggest that it was any more common in the national questionnaire findings, another appraiser wondered after the appraisal what benefits might accrue from video in future:

> I wonder how much can be done by video camera. Small little video cameras set up could probably have given me as much information less intrusively. But I think, I would hope in the future staff would have an option – that type of option.

In the case study where the video camera was used, the appraiser actually felt that it affected the behaviour of the children rather than the member of staff: 'The kids played up to it. They saw it there. Although we thought it was going to be quite a good place for it to be, it was actually quite obvious. It was very noticeable'.

Although it was usually the appraiser who took responsibility for such decisions, in one of the case studies it was the teacher, herself an appraiser, who demonstrated much more knowledge about observation methods than her appraiser, articulating this in great depth:

> **Teacher**: So, if I said to you, just make a note of sort of how often I talk, how often they talk, how often they introduce a question or how often I introduce a question, then that might not give me the information I want on how I'm dealing with these interruptions. . . . If you have a list of the half-hour by minutes, or even by the half-minutes. . . . So if you prepare a time sheet allowing two or three lines for each half-minute and then on that thirty seconds you can just reflect back over . . . I mean I've tried using things like Flanders Interaction Analysis, but it's almost impossible to fill it in accurately I think. You can try using that one if you want . . . but it's very diffi-cult from your point of view to fill that in.

> **Appraiser**: Besides I don't know what the Flanders Interaction Analysis is . . . (laughs).

In this example the appraisee was quite clear about how she expected the appraiser to conduct the observations and her own experience of being an observer informed the discussion. In spite of this, at the end of the explanation the appraiser felt it was his duty to regain control over the method of observation to be employed. This did not please the teacher, who felt she had been ignored, commenting to the researcher: 'I think he manoeuvred what he was doing round to what he wanted to do'.

Consulting pupils

Talking to pupils about a teacher's competence is a controversial subject, as we have pointed out earlier. Yet pupils are present every day, so they clearly spend much more time witnessing teachers at work than is feasible for appraisers, who have their own job to do. Some appraisers sought to amplify their own observation by conversing with pupils in appraisees' classes. The official circular was not too specific on such matters, stating:

> The regulations require the appraiser to consult the appraisee if he or she is going to consult other people to obtain information which is relevant to the appraisal. During such consultation, appraisees should be given the opportunity to express their views about the principle of collecting information from the particular people involved and the method of collection.
>
> (DES 1991b: para. 38)

This implies that appraisees should be told if any other parties are to be asked to comment on them – pupils, fellow teachers, or anyone else – but they do not have a veto, merely the right to be consulted. Some teachers in the schools we studied knew that the children were going to be asked for information, but were not sure of the detail. One accidentally intruded on just such a conversation between his appraiser and a class he taught: 'I came across the meeting. I was looking for Jenny one lesson and found her talking to Year 9 kids, and she said 'Go away, go away'. But I don't know how many she saw'.

The written document produced by one appraiser's LEA suggested that 'the principle of agreement underlies the whole of this scheme, and it is recommended that the operation of observation be no exception. Good practice involves agreement on the time and place of the observation, the focus of the observation and the method to be used'. Yet the appraiser himself was more concerned with his own perception of what made sense, or even of pupil expectation, than whether the appraisee might want to know what method of data collection he was likely to use: 'I'm going to leave it to my commonsense as to whether to wander around, talk and ask what's going on, I think. Because, not least, they would expect me to usually, the kids'.

A teacher, on the other hand, whose appraiser did talk to pupils during his lesson felt very strongly that he should have been the sole focus of the appraiser's attention:

> I didn't agree with her [the appraiser] getting involved with the group. I thought that wasn't the thing that appraisers should do on the observation. Because if you're talking to youngsters, then you're actually not observing what is going on, and she was there to observe me.

This teacher also remarked that he had not known beforehand that she was going to talk to the children, nor did he ever discover what it was that the appraiser had spoken to the children about, or what she had done during the rest of the observation: 'I don't know how she actually observed me, or if she used any sort of recording techniques or anything other than just, sort of, visual observations'.

What appraisers observed

In some cases both teacher and appraiser were clear about what was being observed and how it was being done. Most commonly in these instances the teacher had asked the observer to focus and report on a particular aspect of teaching, as one teacher described:

> We are concentrating on the beginnings and endings of lessons. . . . I honestly think it's a good thing for me as a teacher to do that sort of thing, because I just know for myself personally, after a while you get into a routine and bad habit, sort of lazy ways of teaching can easily happen.

This harmony of purpose, it must be said, was by no means the norm. Indeed, uncertainties about observation were much more common. Relatively few appraisers claimed to be secure about what they were trying to achieve and by what means when they were observing. Some did appear confident about classroom observation, but the majority ranged from uncertain to bereft. We encountered several cases where the teacher did not appear to have a clear idea either of what it was the appraiser actually did in the classroom or of how it was being done, and this opinion was not necessarily better informed after the feedback session or the appraisal interview: 'I was very conscious of the fact that he was sitting there. I was conscious of him writing his notes. And that's as far as I know what he was doing'.

Some appraisers freely confessed to having few ideas of what to do while they were observing. Once they were in the classroom the speed and complexity of events could overwhelm them, as these two appraisers, with the benefit of hindsight, admitted:

> I got totally side tracked by what was going on in the lesson. So I didn't do that very well. I got quite into what he was doing with

them. I watched a few things about his teaching style and how he talks to the group. I've seen him work with them before, quite often. And I got quite interested in the content of what he was doing. . . . So I was actually a participant.

I should have focused a lot more on what he was doing, instead of what he wanted them to do.

In one case study school there was a somewhat bizarre example of a huge confusion of purpose. The appraiser lost sight of what he was supposed to be doing and became a participant in the lesson, trying to learn what the pupils were doing by actually joining in himself. Watching a lesson in which information technology was being used, he became so engrossed in using the computer himself, it was questionable whether he observed much of what was going on. The appraisee had said in interview that he had deliberately chosen an area in which he felt especially competent – the use of computers in his own subject. The appraiser was a senior teacher who worked in the same subject field, but was not as familiar with the use of computers as the appraisee. The teacher was aware of the problems his appraiser had experienced, trying to critique a lesson in which his own knowledge and expertise were slim, but was bemused at what happened:

It didn't really affect me. The only thing was I didn't know quite how to react when Jim [the appraiser] was falling behind. We talked a lot about it afterwards but . . . this lot are pretty skilled in using that software and Jim wanted to bring his own skills up to that level, but I didn't know whether I should stop and help him or not. A pupil was helping him a bit.

However, when asked in interview whether the observation was carried out as expected, his first comment was that it was, but when asked for further information he said: 'He said that he wasn't going to . . . he wouldn't be using the computer . . . he would be going around seeing what the others were doing'.

Afterwards this appraisee felt he had only learned about the remunerative structure in the school, as the appraiser shifted discussion to more familiar territory. He did not feel he had learned anything that would actually help him improve his teaching.

Though some observers confessed to a feeling of cluelessness when faced with actually having to observe a lesson, others allowed the agreed area of focus to act as their principal guide. The method of recording was often unstructured and involved making freehand notes, but this would still primarily relate to the focus. What happened more frequently, in practice, was that appraisers would combine the area chosen by the appraisee with one of their own concerns. One appraiser was quite happy to go along with the appraisee's choice of focus, but was concerned at the pupils' lack of opportunity to make decisions:

> Well I wrote one or two notes, only very basic things. We went slightly away from the [focus], because the focus was meant to be Karen's language, but you know I felt that the way that she approached it from a language point of view was not an area that I believed anyway and we didn't get involved in that a great deal, you know, where you could say there were grounds for great development. So in fact what did interest me. . . . Well, you know, what interested me. What interested me much more, was a very tight teacher-controlled lesson . . . how you could increase the positive role of the children.

This represents a real clash of ideologies. The teacher wishes to teach in a didactic manner and chooses to focus on language. The appraiser seeks to temper the didacticism, so he shifts the focus away from language and towards pupil involvement. In the event he did not make many notes during his observations. Once in the feedback session there were few grounds on which Karen, the appraisee, was able to take issue except for the verbal account offered by the appraiser. When discussing the observations with the researcher, Karen commented that the appraiser had discussed 'what he'd actually found out, not the way he had gone about it'. In this case only one observation took place and therefore the original focus could not be revisited. Karen's appraiser was aware of the intrusion of his own priorities, commenting that, if he were doing it all again:

> The observation method that I used probably would need to be more focused . . . the awareness on my part probably needed to be heightened. . . . I find it easier to observe lessons when I'm completely neutral. That means it's in another school with a teacher that I don't know very well and children who I don't know. . . . I mean observations in those situations, I can get a greater focus.

Although at the end of the process he still recognised the role of observation to be important, he had also realised how difficult it was to carry out, especially when he knew the people involved.

Addressing the area of focus chosen by the appraisee was not the major problem. Some appraisers were anxious whether what they observed was simply too trivial and superficial, not penetrating beneath the surface of classroom life. It was even harder for those who only did one or two appraisals and, not having had the opportunity to witness a range of teaching styles and competence, felt the lack of reference points for comparison:

Well, I went into the lesson and I took the areas of focus that we had discussed at the initial meeting and I looked at that and also wrote down comments on peripheral things. But it's the in-depth bit I would question. Does it need to be more in-depth? Have I missed a lot? You know that's where I wouldn't know, because I've not seen what anyone else has done. I've not got anything to match it with. I've not seen a really good one.

Feedback after the observation

The effectiveness of classroom observation was intended to be enhanced and assured by its becoming part of the teacher's professional and personal development. A key element of this was meant to be the feedback session after a lesson observation had taken place. The guidelines suggested that appraisal feedback should take place within forty-eight hours of the observation, and our national questionnaire revealed that about three-quarters of teachers did indeed receive feedback within this time. As with other aspects of appraisal, time was often an important consideration.

Within the case studies many appraisers conducted a feedback session which took place immediately after the lesson that had been observed. This immediacy may have been affected by the presence of a researcher, since we had asked to be present at the feedback session where possible. On occasions when the appraisers had undertaken a structured observation, using timed segments, categories or sub-headings, the discussion was also more structured. Otherwise it tended to be a general discussion based primarily around the teacher's area of focus. When appraisers did spend a lot of time discussing the observations in a separate feedback session, it meant that they were less likely to spend time discussing it at the appraisal interview.

While some appraisers spoke in general terms about what they had seen, others were very specific, pointing out tiny details about what had transpired, or what was the area of focus. One appraiser commented that the teacher had not been going to the children in the order in which they had put their hands up, and that some of the children who had put their hands up had then put them back down when the teacher had not gone to them. She had also noted that some children had had their hands up for 'quite a while'. This was mitigated by: 'It's very difficult to be aware of everything at once'. Some of her comments were prescriptive: 'You need to keep saying, "Sit down, put up your hand and I will come to you"'. She also gave advice on strategies to stop interruptions when the appraisee needed to spend time with a specific child, on classroom rules and the use of reinforcement.

The two main media through which the feedback was offered were oral discussion and written notes. The choice primarily appeared to lie with the appraiser and often depended on the format chosen for recording the lesson observations. One teacher, who had been given verbal feedback, felt afterwards that he would have preferred it to have been written:

> I don't think that it was done thoroughly enough and fed back in a thorough way. One way to improve that would have been to give me a written account of that feedback, rather than a few notes and a chat.

However, in another case study, an appraisee wished to have verbal feedback, but the appraiser had felt written feedback was more appropriate and consequently this was the way in which it was presented. Ironically this teacher was herself an appraiser in the school, and when she undertook her role as an appraiser of other teachers, she found that time constraints prevented her from giving any feedback at all, either written or verbal.

Recommendations in local authority guidelines often suggested that the notes made by appraisers during observations should be shared with the appraisee, but this did not always happen. The tone of the meetings also varied, but there was a heavy emphasis in most on reassurance. Though not always intentional, some appraisers sounded negative or judgemental, usually to the dismay of appraisees.

Perceptions about the meetings and the advice given varied between appraisees. As most teachers perceived appraisal to be developmental, they usually had expectations before their classroom observation on areas of their focus about which they expected feedback. If appraisers intended that their words after the lesson should act as encouragement, then many teachers said they did indeed feel reassured during feedback:

> We looked at relationships within the group and I think I was reassured in many ways that the things that I aim to do within the classroom happen. I think that I was able to put in what I call 'equality of opportunity' within the lessons, which I always try to do. That was reinforced in what was fed back to me. . . . There was nothing that came out of it which I felt, 'Heck, I should address this possibly!'

> . . . I felt that overall the appraisal showed that I wasn't doing anything particularly wrong and so [it] was reassuring that what I was doing at the moment was all right and there wasn't any particular bombshell that he brought out and said, 'Look you're not doing this and you ought to . . .'. So it was reassuring that I was doing the

right thing anyway and also that he had been able to write down and see that I was doing the right thing.

Sometimes teachers felt that the appraiser had been positive merely to encourage them and promote their self-esteem. One teacher acknowledged the positive nature of his feedback, but realised that the personal boost his appraiser was giving him went beyond the observed:

> It confirmed some opinions I had already of my teaching style – positive ideas. . . . Positive highlights that gave me a 'feel good' factor. Generally it was very positive, constructive and, within the limitations of the observation, it was probably all that she could come up with. It seemed a little more positive than you could have gained from those two observations. I think that it wasn't just based on those observations.

Positive feedback is not inevitably virtuous. Although many appraisers were glad of the opportunity to praise someone they valued, uncritical responses may foster complacency. Some teachers expected a critical analysis of what they were doing and how it might be improved, especially since a senior member of the school staff was doing the observations. They wanted something constructive, and were quick to criticise if they did not get it. One teacher was particularly scathing about the lack of insights from his appraiser:

> I don't feel that I have learned anything from the feedback today. I would expect if someone, especially a deputy head on his salary, has spent an hour of his time in my class observing a class that he himself has taught, that he would somewhere along the line have some constructive suggestions about the way forward. . . . He hasn't really given me any feedback about whether he thought that I was particularly effective. . . . I would hope that somewhere along the line I'll get some constructive comments.

His deputy head appraiser was unaware of this teacher's expectation, assuming that the principal need the first time he observed somebody was to be entirely positive, to overcome possible anxiety and resistance. He had spotted several negative points, he explained, but had chosen to ignore them for the present. Indeed, he was not really impressed by what he had seen:

> Because I want to keep this process a positive one, the negative comments were non-existent really. . . . There are things that one needs to address in terms of classroom management, handling youngsters, which I think I'll rightly address, but not in the context of this particular process. . . . I want him to feel positive about going in tomorrow morning as well, not thinking, 'Heavens, he's just here

to pick holes in me!' That was my intention and I hope I achieved it. I don't think he felt badly about the lesson – that I felt was not very good. . . . I thought it was poor, to be honest.

The appraiser further explained that the children were being taught lessons that pupils three or four years younger could have coped with and were not being challenged in any way. In spite of this he explained that he would rather broach this with the appraisee via a different route at a later date, possibly by suggesting a meeting to discuss these issues once the appraisal was finished with both the appraisee and other members of staff in that subject area. Yet the appraisee, in interview, said that he trusted all issues regarding his teaching would be dealt with within the privacy of the appraisal process and not publicly in departmental meetings. After the process had been completed he commented:

He'll tell you what he wants to say, to be positive and to get things moving. I think, had I been in there very much longer on the Friday, if he hadn't had to shoot off, then one of the things I probably would have said to him was: 'Are there any things that you think are bad about my teaching . . . that need to be addressed?'. . . . Well I've got to take it on trust. I think the fact that he teaches within the [same] department . . . if there was anything that he thought was going wrong, I think he would have said before that. . . . I think that I've got to take it as read that the fact that he hasn't mentioned anything like that means that there isn't anything that he's seriously worried about.

The teacher had not picked up the insincerity of the appraiser's approval. The perceptions of the appraisee and the appraiser in this case study are at considerable variance. The appraiser thought he was being positive by avoiding discussing the teacher's low expectation of the pupils with him, while the appraisee assumed there was nothing wrong since the appraiser had not mentioned any negative points during the feedback. The appraiser felt it would be better to confront the problems generally within a departmental meeting, while the appraisee trusted that if the appraiser had anything to say he would already have raised it beforehand in private.

Other appraisers had difficulty with negative comments within their feedback. One teacher felt that the feedback after her lesson observation had been negative and a bit critical. After having initially said that her teaching was 'only OK', the appraiser conducted the subsequent appraisal interview in a more positive manner, which cheered up the appraisee. Another appraiser checked with the appraisee at the end of the feedback that he was happy at the outcome, saying: 'I hope you

don't feel that there's a sort of undervaluing of you at all'. In this particular instance the feedback had been perceived as useful by the teacher,
who made light of the appraiser's concern by stating: 'That's all right.
I'll go off and jump off a bloody cliff somewhere'.

What emerges from studying lesson observation and the feedback
that follows it, is that appraisers face an inescapable dilemma between
providing reassurance and being critical. This conflict highlights the
complexity of the appraiser's role and the varying demands and requirements from appraisees, many of whom want both reassurance and
criticism:

> He's very good in that he does try and look at the optimistic and the
> positive side of everything, but there are some times when you feel
> like saying, 'Yes but what's the bottom line? I appreciate all this
> positive feedback, but what do you really think?'

Negative comments following observation were particularly bruising
for senior teachers like deputy heads and heads of department. One
head of department was reluctant to be observed at all, saying that her
management role in the school was much more important than her
classroom teaching:

> My concern is that we identify a focus and then we have this class-
> room observation and the two don't relate. I know we have class-
> room observation because it's required of us and I'm not opposed to
> observation . . . but I'm not sure why we are having it.

When asked about the anticipated effect therefore on her practice she
remarked:

> I mean, the two lessons observed are never going to be repeated
> anyway, so this is why I think the classroom observation is an
> oddity in itself. If I felt I delivered the same lesson sixteen times a
> week for a year, then you might say this is really going to affect it,
> but you're not. You can teach the same subject but it's never the
> same lesson.

After the appraisal her views changed. The appraisal had not gone as
she had hoped. The feedback on her role as head of department had
been very positive, but the feedback on her classroom teaching, an
area she had not believed she was having difficulty with, was far more
critical. She rationalised it by saying that the presence of an observer
had affected her behaviour. However, she also accepted the need to
have observations and could 'quite see the validity of it'. In the end
her views came out in confused form, as she tried to reconcile critical
comments that she felt ought to be valuable with a defence that what
had been seen was not typical:

[There was] much more feedback on my classroom teaching than I expected. . . . I wanted it to do with being head of department, rather than a teacher. So that's where my thoughts were going and I was seeing the classroom side of it as being rather secondary. But it didn't come out that way. I felt that it came out the reverse – when it came to the feedback, which quite surprised me. . . . I learned a little bit about me, about the things that people observe in me, which was quite interesting, but as I say a lot of it wasn't necessarily new. . . . What really struck home was how out of context observation is, even when you might come in two weeks successively, because most of what takes place in the classroom is based on relationships and knowing the kids, so one does what one thinks is best in the circumstances with that child and their relationship with you. And that is not something that is necessarily seen by an outsider as the best thing. And I think that's what I've learned through the observation, in fact. But having said that, I also recognise that one is reluctant to take criticism. One tries to justify what one's done. So I would also accept that a lot of what Martin [the appraiser] said is true.

When interviewed for the third time a number of months after the appraisal this teacher was even less positive about being observed. She felt that the appraisal had been affected by time constraints, that she had been part of a mechanical process. She was not happy with the manner in which her appraisal had been conducted. Her views became entrenched as her dislike of the experience added retrospective strength to her conviction that there was too much emphasis on observation during appraisal. With the passage of time she had become entirely negative, feeling that nothing of benefit had come from it:

That's one thing about the observations – they're sort of teaching techniques which really if I didn't know by now, it's a bit worrying! And OK, I didn't do them on that day . . . but it's not the reality. . . . And if you're in a position like myself, where classroom observation isn't really the thing you're worrying about – I wanted to do it really on management and department and team leading, and I've got nothing out of it on that. Nothing at all!

Other high status teachers coped better with criticism. One head, who had appraised a senior science teacher in the school, felt that the appraisee had been starved of feedback during his professional career. He believed the appraisee had welcomed the opportunity to improve his practice, even though some of the criticisms had been fairly trenchant:

Jack certainly found out things about himself . . . the fact he talks too much. A clear case of a teacher going on over the years, not realising that they spend too much time in the didactic mode. No feedback from the children has been given to him, or if it had, he had not absorbed it. He'd felt that lessons should be about talking, sharing knowledge and information. . . . So, on his report, that's one of the prime areas for action. . . . He took it extremely well, was proud of the fact that he had learned about himself and was pleased that the appraisal had given him something concrete to work on. Like lots of scientists, he's a factual sort of person and had feared appraisal would be something airy fairy, rather than practical.

After observation – target setting

One of the required outcomes of appraisal was that teachers should set targets. Sometimes these grew directly out of the classroom observation, sometimes not, as indeed the findings of the national questionnaire also indicated. The issue of the impact classroom observation has on the targets is an important one. In one appraisal it was clear when the teacher was interviewed that his targets had already been determined by his appraiser before the appraisal, without his knowledge and, so far as he was aware, without any evidence from the classroom observations being taken into consideration:

> Now I think that Kieran's got quite a clear idea of what sort of targets he would be happy to set – I haven't a clue what he would want me to set. But maybe after I've gone through the information it will be a bit clearer.

Many teachers did not set targets that were related to classroom matters. Aware that applying for headships and deputy posts often involved scrutiny of teachers' ability to manage some aspect of the school, like resources, a year group or a department, some wanted to make sure that the emphasis was on developing these promotion-worthy skills. Alongside this more attractive option, classroom teaching targets appeared mundane, as one frustrated appraiser commented:

> The way that this present scheme is set up at the minute – where you've got somebody who's a head of department, who really wants to concentrate on their department skills and not their classroom observation . . . then to some extent the classroom observation's a lot of time for relatively little. All I got out of it with Roger is the target that says 'we'll make the worksheets a bit smarter' after two hours of observation! Whereas the hour and a half I spent with the department . . . I could have done with a bit more.

Some local authorities, in their training literature, used the acronym SMART, the letters of which indicate that targets should be 'specific, measurable, attainable, relevant and time-constrained'. This advice was followed by a number of teachers and appraisers. The problem for other teachers, however, was that when interviewed three to four months after their appraisal, they could not even remember with confidence what their targets were, as was the case in the responses to the national questionnaire. This has implications in particular for the recommendation that targets should be attainable:

> I can't really remember my other targets. . . . I mean I should know what they are because that's part of the appraisal – I'm supposed to be working towards them. No, I remember them enough to say that there's nothing there that I don't think I'm working towards.

> The answer's 'No, I can't remember them!' This is terrible, I can't remember what my targets are. . . . In fact, most of the targets, if we actually look at them, would be things that one would do anyway, and I think that the reason I can't remember them is . . . I wouldn't set them as appraisal targets, they are just targets.

Some teachers commented that once their appraisal had finished it was almost as if it had never taken place and even though the experience might have been positive at the time, the momentum was lost shortly afterwards and there was little reference back to what may have been discussed or possible areas for development. Occasionally there was a delay in the receipt by the appraisee of the written documentation. One appraisee felt that, after a long delay, he might as well set his own targets, while another highlighted the need for someone to chase up teacher and appraiser:

> The final sort of statement and targets were not given to me until [two months later] – it was a very long time. . . . And after the half-term I looked at it. . . . I wasn't very happy about it. . . . I didn't actually look for huge changes because by that time . . . I thought that it was awfully late in arriving. . . . The official targets were not very clear . . . and I'm setting my own targets anyway. That suits me to a degree.

> If the system isn't set up properly. . . . If the meetings aren't officially scheduled and reminders sent out and followed up, then the whole thing falls down. You need an efficient co-ordinator who is going to chivvy both parties along.

Another teacher, whose statement had still not been written four months after the appraisal interview, was still in favour of appraisal despite having no targets, but felt strongly that appraisal in her school needed to be undertaken in a much more businesslike manner:

I don't have any problem at all with the notion of appraisal in principle. It seems to me it tailed off a little bit. I mean we don't have to do it again for another two years now. If it's really to be of value, then the targets should hopefully be reviewed . . . the targets should be ongoing. . . . And so I think, it's almost like 'we've done it now'. . . . I'd like to see it being given a more high profile. . . . My fear is that those targets won't be addressed, or they won't be linked to Inset.

Evaluation

Conscious of the need to do appraisal properly, some schools tried to evaluate the process in a systematic way. Sometimes this evaluation was about changes, on other occasions about relationships. One member of the senior management team in a case study school was given formal responsibility for the school's appraisal scheme. He had sent out a modest questionnaire to members of staff. Another school had already undertaken some systematic evaluation and was acting on the information obtained to make sure that classroom observation remained a central not peripheral part of appraisal:

It's a mundane questionnaire from the point of view that it's actually looking at the mechanics of it . . . you know: Are you spending too long? Is it successful?. . . . Is the bumf you get good enough to set you up? They'll certainly come back and say the training's not enough – I hope. Because the classroom observation bit is a real skill, so's conducting an interview really.

We did actually, as a result of questionnaires, we felt that some recent appraisals have been moving away from the classroom focus, so I've asked the appraisal co-ordinator to put on a special in-service training for appraisers to remind them that that is a key focus – improving classroom practice.

Most appraisers had very clear views about the value of classroom observation, even those who had found some difficulties with it, as many pointed out in our follow-up interviews when we asked them to assess its worthwhileness:

I do it [observation] regularly. I enjoy it, I really thoroughly enjoy it. I think it's wholly worthwhile and I wouldn't ever not want to use it. I think it's good anyway and it gives me the excuse to go and see a fellow professional at work . . . and there are lots and lots of instances where you can give excellent positive feedback and appraisal gives you the excuse to do it.

I think at the end of a busy term, it's probably not the best time, but it's been an enjoyable experience, I have to say. I've enjoyed other people's lessons . . . and what it's done for me is actually help me with my own teaching.

Teachers themselves had mixed feelings. As pointed out earlier, personal relationships often determined how people felt about appraisal in general and classroom observation in particular. Some teachers never recovered from a bad start, like the one who was infuriated that his appraiser refused to observe in the area where he most wanted help: '[Pupils over sixteen] was an area I was concerned about, but she wouldn't entertain that at all, which I'm sorry about. But I didn't push it'.

This made a significant impact on how he evaluated his appraiser's classroom observation. He expressed great disappointment with the quality of the feedback he received, when asked about the important points identified during it:

That I didn't know already? Nothing! I was quite disappointed. I must say I was quite disappointed with the whole appraisal. . . . Well it was just a feedback process that didn't really inform me about anything that needed work on. Either I'm the perfect teacher and the perfect head of year, or the appraisal wasn't done thoroughly.

Other teachers gave a more positive evaluation, though often with reservations:

I still think the classroom observation is quite a key component, but I have changed my mind slightly about that because it does depend on the experience of the teacher. Now I'm not saying that experienced teachers can't learn from classroom observation, but I think it may be more useful for newly qualified teachers, in terms of classroom observation, to undergo that. Most of my colleagues I've spoken to who are relatively experienced are saying that the classroom bit is almost irrelevant. In other words they are not actually learning much from that.

Establishing good personal relationships was stressed by local authorities in their training, as well as by appraisers and teachers in interviews. It is in this respect that classroom observation may have had a greater effect than on actual practice, allowing fellow teachers to share an experience normally only available to one of them. This appears to have cemented personal relationships in a number of cases, and teachers were often more enthusiastic about this aspect than about the effects of observation on classroom behaviour. One appraiser felt that both observing and being observed brought him closer to his colleagues: 'First of all, there is empathy – you've actually been through it, and hopefully because of that, you can first of all put people at ease . . . and to say that it's really not that incredibly threatening'.

Some mentioned the opportunity to share ideas and for greater professional collegiality, as classrooms were opened up, when they had previously been closed communities:

> I've always found some very positive things in lessons that make me go away and think, 'I should do that'.

> I think classroom practice will benefit from it . . . for the appraisee and the appraiser. I've found that the two lessons that I've appraised I've actually picked up things that I've adopted for myself.

This second appraiser explained that in her own teaching she had had a problem trying to keep lessons manageable when pupils were engaged in different tasks. The person she had appraised had chosen this same class management issue as her area of focus and the appraiser, by finding a solution for the appraisee, realised that she had also solved the problem for herself:

> It's one of the most valuable things. I certainly learned a good lesson – I could use that one! It's a real luxury that we don't have ordinarily of being able to watch each other work and understanding each other's different methods.

There was one aspect of relationships that we were not able to illuminate through the case studies. The national questionnaire used in Study 2 suggested that all female pairs of appraiser and appraisee seemed less happy with the process than all male pairs. Although there were examples of same sex and mixed sex pairs in the case studies, there was no corroboration of this finding in the smaller scale but more intensive Study 3. It was circumstances and contexts that seemed mainly to determine the nature of relationships. The dimension of gender did not override important aspects like whether appraiser and appraisee respected each other, or whether there was a shared purpose. This particular conundrum, therefore, remains tantalisingly unanswered by the case studies.

THE EFFECT OF CLASSROOM OBSERVATION ON PRACTICE

One of the most interesting aspects of the appraisal process was whether teachers perceived that it would affect their classroom practice. There were certainly other perceived benefits as the findings from the national questionnaire survey have shown, but nearly half of the respondents to the national questionnaire did not see it as actually affecting their classroom teaching. There was a similar trend amongst the case study teachers, which has important implications for a process which contains a statutory observation element and is supposed to be aimed at improving the practice of teaching. Yet most of the teachers and appraisers we interviewed agreed that altering classroom practice for the better was a desirable outcome. As one head put it: 'Well, if it doesn't [change practice], it's not worth doing'.

As teachers were interviewed and observed immediately after their appraisal to see whether their practice had been affected, and also three to four months later, this provided both a short and a slightly longer perspective. As in the national questionnaire, where about 70 per cent felt positive about appraisal, even though slightly fewer than half said they had changed their practice, there were case study teachers who were positive and optimistic about the process without it having made any significant impact on their teaching.

It was not uncommon to find teachers changing their views over the year in which their appraisal took place. One teacher who had thought before the classroom observations that appraisal would 'definitely' affect her classroom practice, felt immediately after the classroom observations that her practice would only be affected 'a little'. However, in her final interview, which took place four months after the appraisal, she had changed her mind and believed, in retrospect, that it actually had had a 'definite effect' on her classroom practice, helping her to reflect on processes, the structure of her lessons and independent learning by the children and to give more positive reinforcement. This suggests that in some cases a period of reflection may be necessary before the impact of appraisal on classroom practice is evident.

Other teachers were simply unwilling to alter how they taught. Some had said beforehand that classroom observation would not really affect their teaching and when interviewed afterwards, irrespective of what their appraiser had observed, did not feel that their practice would alter much, if at all, as these two teachers said a few months later:

It's made me more aware of what is going on. So in a sense, no [I have not changed], because I don't believe that everything wasn't being done before. . . . I **do** vary things, I try and vary things . . . but it's made me more conscious of the need to vary things.

I think, when it boils down to it, you just get on with the job as best you can. I can't see it having a big effect at all.

Even those teachers who were willing to change, were aware of barriers to this development. Most frequently time was cited as the major problem. Several appraisers felt they had simply not spent enough time in the classroom to influence events:

> If you are going to appraise, you can't just go in there for half an hour, you have to do it properly. You've got to spend a day, two days in there.

> I think if one had more time one could probably do a lot more, but presumably there has to be a time constraint on it. You could spend hours doing it otherwise. . . . I've asked a few questions and looked at it a bit, but, you know, what does **that** tell me?

An appraisee who had originally found his feedback helpful, stated four months after his appraisal that he had not gone a long way towards changing his practice in the area of his focus, differentiation. He attributed this primarily to the small number of observations that had taken place, in his case only one, and commented that with only two or three observations it would be difficult to improve dramatically his ability to differentiate.

A frequent outcome, therefore, in the case studies was that appraisal had either not affected the appraisee's classroom teaching at all, or had affected it in a minor way, and this was confirmed not only by the interviews, but also by the researchers' follow-up observations. Few teachers appeared to have made significant changes to well established routines after classroom observation. The greatest claim made was about greater 'awareness'. One teacher pointed out that he had been made more conscious of certain aspects of his teaching, but it was not long before 'I slipped back into my old ways'. The benefits of appraisal to teaching thereby appeared primarily to be in the area of reassuring teachers that they were doing their jobs well and consequently giving them confidence in what they were doing. Revolutionary changes in classroom practice did not occur.

In addition to the interviews, we also had available classroom observation data collected by researchers in the team. Whenever it was possible, the researcher observed every individual pupil in the class to determine whether children were on or off task and whether they were misbehaving. At the end of the research it was possible to combine all these observation data. This allowed a comparison between lessons researchers had witnessed *before* the appraisers conducted their class-room observation, lessons they had seen *during* the classroom observa-tion, when appraisers were actually present, and lessons researchers observed *after* appraisal had finished, both in the short term, a few days later and three or four months afterwards.

Not all appraisers did a second observation, indeed eight out of the twenty-nine appraisers we studied only carried out one lesson observation instead of the required two, which at 28 per cent was exactly the figure we obtained in the national questionnaire for the same matter. Nor was it feasible in every case for researchers to observe all possible lessons. Table 8.2 summarises the breakdown of the 123 lessons observed in the twenty-nine case study classrooms.

Table 8.2 Number of lessons of case study teachers observed by researchers before, during and after the appraisers' classroom observations

	Researcher (before)	Appraisers' observations	Researcher (straight after)	Researcher (3 months after)
No. of lessons[1]	26	43	27	27

[1] Total = 123 lessons.

Insights into changes over time and the possible effects of an observer being present are therefore revealed in these observation data, and Table 8.3 shows the scores for pupil involvement in their task and those for pupil deviancy at each of the stages under each condition. For the very reasons given earlier concerning what constitutes 'normality' in teaching, and the real or imagined effects of the presence of an appraiser, a researcher, or both, these figures have to be interpreted with some caution.

Table 8.3 Mean 'on task' and 'deviancy' scores[1] before, during and after the appraisers' classroom observations[2]

	Researcher (before)	Appraisers' observations	Researcher (straight after)	Researcher (3 months after)
On task	81	85	81	82
Deviancy	8	9	11	8

[1] Possible range 0 to 100.
[2] Total = 123 lessons.

What is astonishing about the figures in Table 8.3 is their consistency. Pupil 'on task' figures for individual lessons showed a considerable range. The lowest 'on task' score recorded in a single lesson was 26, the highest figure obtained was 100, which is the maximum possible score if all pupils are fully engaged in their task when observed. Yet the mean grouped scores in Table 8.3 hover around 81 or 82 with remarkable consistency. When the appraiser was present the score was slightly higher at 85, but there is virtually no difference in any of the scores before or after appraisal took place.

A similar picture emerges with the deviancy figures. The range was again quite wide in individual lessons, with a lowest deviancy score of zero, which means that nobody was misbehaving when observed, and a highest score of 32, which indicates quite a considerable degree of disorderliness. Yet Table 8.3 shows again astonishing sameness under different conditions, with the average close to 9 or 10. The presence of the appraiser appears to have made little difference to this particular factor.

In order to test the significance of these figures we used analysis of variance of repeated measures, with Scheffé gap tests. This allows the mean scores under different conditions to be compared to see if there was any significant difference between them. Although the differences between individual teachers in the case both of 'on task' behaviour and deviancy were highly significant, at the 0.01 and 0.001 levels of significance respectively, the differences at the various stages and when appraisers were present were not at all significant. In summary:

- Although children were slightly more engaged in their work when appraisers were present, compared with when they were not, the difference was not significant.
- There was no significant difference in children's classroom misbehaviour when appraisers were present, compared with when they were not.
- There was no significant difference in children's engagement in their work before and after appraisal.
- There was no significant difference in children's classroom misbehaviour before and after appraisal.

There are of course limitations attached to these findings, as we have pointed out. Engagement in work and misbehaviour are but two of many possible indicators that might have been chosen to compare classroom behaviour under different conditions. Quantitative measures alone do not tell the whole story. Furthermore, there were considerable variations within the mean scores shown in Table 8.3, so in some cases there was indeed less disruption and more application after appraisal. But in other cases the opposite was the case, so these cancel each other out.

Nevertheless the main finding in these observation data was that there was less change through appraisal than people had perhaps hoped for, and this is corroborated by what many teachers themselves said in interview. The major impact of appraisal seems to have been more on beliefs, attitudes and relationships than on action, and this should give considerable food for thought.

Chapter 9

Improving appraisal – learning from experience

MAIN FINDINGS

In this research project the investigators were able to study the appraisal process by operating at three levels. First, the analysis of local education authority training literature showed how national policies were 'officially' translated at local level in 109 English LEAs. Second, returns from over 1,100 teachers and appraisers responding to our national questionnaire revealed how practitioners from all over the country said they had carried out appraisal in general and classroom observation in particular. Third, the intensive study, over a two-year period, of twenty-nine primary and secondary teachers, disclosed some of the intimate detail of what actually transpired at school and classroom level, as observed by members of the research team.

It was shown in the first chapter of this book how appraisal was part of a larger push for public accountability in the 1980s and 1990s. Successive ministers from the mid-1980s either embraced it or avoided it. Sometimes appraisal was seen as an exercise detached from the various reviews of school or teacher effectiveness that were taking place, on other occasions appraisal was linked in discussions of accountability to pupil test scores, implementation of the National Curriculum, sacking incompetent teachers, or rewarding those thought to be especially proficient. In the end, after numerous delays since appraisal had become a statutory requirement in 1986, a lightly prescriptive form of hierarchical appraisal was adopted, with a minimum of one hour's classroom observation, spread over two occasions, built in.

The analysis of local authority training literature revealed several differences and some commonalities. Local authorities varied enormously in the style of their training, as well as in the importance they attached to appraisal. Some LEAs had virtually collapsed and the advisory staff were too denuded and often too demoralised to undertake anything of worth. Other LEAs made every effort to mount training courses of substance. The appraisal co-ordinator was often a crucial player – the enthusiasts displaying energy and imagination, the reluctant merely translating national policy into sparse local documents.

One notable feature was the attempt made by some LEAs to 'humanise' and 'personalise', as they would see it, what could easily become a bureaucratic procedure. While some simply reproduced official circulars and recommendations in their literature, others tried to mitigate the effects of dry documents, using a personal style of address directly to the teacher – 'you will need to . . .' instead of 'the regulations state that . . .'. There was great stress on establishing positive personal relationships between teachers and their appraisers, as many LEAs recognised that, given the threats of boycotts and confrontations from some teacher unions, negative relationships might bring the whole process to a halt.

Many LEAs stressed the need for appraisers, before classroom observation, to be briefed on the context in which the lesson was to take place, something that we later found out rarely happened. Lack of briefing sometimes led to disastrous results. They also frequently recommended that the first lesson observation should be general and the second more specific. It subsequently transpired that this recommendation was rarely followed. Other aspirations included awareness-raising training in schools for appraisers, and feedback from the appraiser within forty-eight hours of a classroom observation, wherever possible. In a further attempt to avoid problems, there was a strong assertion from LEAs that teachers should not see appraisal as teaching practice supervision or as inspection, and that appraisers should therefore play a neutral, non-judgemental role.

The national questionnaire gave a comprehensive account of the actual process as perceived by those who took part in it. Many teacher and appraiser responses echoed what LEAs had stressed in their training literature: that positive personal relationships were important, that mutual respect was vital. In other ways, however, the earnest aspirations of LEA recommendations and Government prescriptions were not always met. Although over 90 per cent of teachers were happy with their appraiser, some 28 per cent of teachers said they were only observed on one occasion, and that the second required observation never even took place. In a third to a half of cases, the appraiser had little or no first-hand familiarity with the age group and/or subject being observed.

Half the sample received their lesson observation de-briefing within twenty-four hours, but a quarter to a third had to wait over forty-eight hours for feedback. Almost all teachers set targets, two each on average, but teachers were divided about the effectiveness of these, and a significant minority were unable to recall them at all. With half an eye on promotion, in some cases, about 40 per cent of teachers had in any case chosen an aspect of school management as their major area of focus.

There seemed to be little sophistication in the methods of observation used by appraisers. Most simply made freehand notes, the nature and contents of which were not always communicated to the appraisees, some of whom confessed to knowing little or nothing of what the observer was doing. About a third of appraisers said that they talked to pupils as part of the appraisal.

After appraisal was over about 70 per cent of teachers said they had derived personal benefits from it, but slightly under half claimed that they had actually changed their classroom practice as a result of being appraised. Many valued the close interest of a fellow professional, and some saw this as the main advantage they had obtained from being observed at work in their own classroom. All-male pairs seemed happiest about being observed and all-female pairs were least at ease. Primary teachers seemed to be less happy at being observed than were secondary teachers.

The intensive case studies confirmed and filled out many of the points that emerged from the national questionnaire. Heads were more likely to feel positive about the whole school gains they believed had accrued, whereas teachers often appreciated more their own personal and professional development. There could be a gulf between what heads and other senior people in the school described and what teachers saw as the craggy reality. Just as there had been a diversity of LEA interpretations of Government policy, so too there were diverse individual translations of LEA guidelines into actual practice. There were considerable differences in the targets set for teachers, for example, some appearing trivial and routine, others substantial and offering a formidable challenge.

At an individual level what was meant by mutual respect often became much clearer, sometimes because of the high regard that teachers had for their appraiser, sometimes because of the opposite. In many cases the appraiser's lack of subject or age group expertise caused real problems, and there were instances of teachers feeling greatly frustrated that they could not get expert advice after their lessons had been observed, just as there were other examples of people appreciating shrewd insights and advice.

Issues of power and control were also sometimes sharply delineated. There were appraisers who determined the agenda, sometimes quite forcefully, occasionally refusing to give way, perhaps by not being willing to accept the appraisee's choice of focus. In one case the head decided the area of focus for the whole school. Some senior managers saw appraisal as a means for translating the school's or even their own policies into direct action. Others were willing to acquiesce and go with the appraisee's aspirations, seeing themselves as a mirror.

Several concerns emerged from the case studies. Many teachers and appraisers talked of time and money constraints. Though some schools were able to provide cover for teachers engaged in appraisal, most were not, and lunch hours and after school were common times for feedback sessions and appraisal interviews to be fitted in when no cover was available. There were teachers who were worried about the possible uses to which appraisal could be put, especially with redundancies being a real likelihood in schools that were short of money. Performance-related pay was also an issue which perplexed some, though others were in favour of it.

The case studies, with a few exceptions, confirmed the haphazard way in which many lesson observations took place. Several appraisers confessed to knowing little about observation, despite their training, and a number of teachers said they had few inklings into what their appraiser was observing or how lesson analysis was being carried out. Even well organised observers felt frustrated by the many interruptions and conflicting demands on their time. Some senior people felt particularly bruised when there were negative comments following their appraisal. In the end few teachers claimed that they had altered their classroom practice, and even those who did, often stressed that they had become more aware of an issue, rather than changed the way they taught. Interview and observation data collected by members of the research team seemed to confirm that the social 'feel good' side of classroom observation outweighed its impact on professional practice.

IMPLICATIONS FOR THE FUTURE OF APPRAISAL

Head teachers, when interviewed at or towards the end of the appraisal cycle, had different views about the future. One secondary head, while welcoming the introduction of formal appraisal and feeling it had not been as threatening as staff had anticipated, and indeed, looking at extending the appraisal scheme to include non-teaching staff, identified a major prerequisite for its long-term effectiveness. He recognised the importance of collegiality, but was concerned that the process had been too consensual, too lacking in real impact, and would remain so, if senior staff were not more able or willing to be more proactive:

It actually needs a very considerable managerial follow-up . . . in identifying support that's needed and so on. And I think that, bearing in mind what we're trying to operate is a scheme that says one appraiser should not be appraising more than four people in any one cycle, it does mean, therefore, that the appraisal process is actually devolved quite a long way down within the management structure. And, therefore, the follow-up by senior management is still something we need to explore a bit more. If I felt, for example, that when I received the appraisal statement and targets, that actually it was too cosy an appraisal, I don't think there is still at the moment any agreed procedure by which I can follow that up. I can follow it up, but not by any agreed procedure.

This head teacher's concern that the process should not be too comfortable was not shared by all heads. It was interesting to note that, although improvements in practice were often the anticipated result of the process, a number of head teachers were at pains to stress the positive and supportive aspects of appraisal. This echoed the 'softly softly' LEA guideline which advised that appraisal should be seen as an opportunity 'to identify and celebrate existing strengths'. The head and deputy head in one case study school supported this approach forcefully, the head explaining:

We are absolutely adamant that this is an entirely positive and supportive process. It's not a judgemental process at all, and our classroom observation is not us going in and making some kind of professional judgement about the performance. All the time, it's to sit down and share.

Their desire to keep the two different processes separate stemmed from a suspicion of the Government's intentions for appraisal:

This business was forced upon us by a Government that wanted it for other purposes. Teachers are extremely good at subverting and frustrating that kind of effort. And I think we are basically subverting their original purpose. What we've done is turn the appraisal about so that it actually suits our purpose and that's professional development.

An opposing view was held by the head teacher of another case study school, who had stated in interview before appraisal began that it 'should have a cutting edge and, therefore, should be tied in with performance-related pay'. When he was interviewed again, after appraisal in his school had been completed, his views had firmed up, and he had become strongly opposed to the *laissez-faire* version of the whole process:

While it's staff development I think it's become very benign. And I think it's laughable when a member of staff can . . . actually decide the grounds on which they're going to be appraised, who's going to give information about them, and what their outcomes are going to be. . . . It's not going to do for my school all that I think a more rigorous system, linked to some advantage, financial or otherwise, would be. My own personal view is that I wouldn't mind it linked to performance-related pay.

After appraisal had finished in a small secondary school, the deputy head expressed support for performance-related pay, concerned that once staff had been appraised, they tended to put it all behind them, and regard it as an administrative chore now completed:

> Lots say, 'Phew, that's out of the way! And surely that is wrong because appraisal is useful. It's to benefit, to help you grow and develop, and it's got to be there, hasn't it? And there is a way that you could link responsibilities, allowances, performance-related pay to set targets. If they become better trained or more aware of their work in an area which is currently weak . . . if they can . . . make the teaching staff a more effective staff body, and therefore the children would be beneficiaries, then I see that as a very good reason to link it to financial incentives.

These two interviewees, however, were in the minority with their wish for appraisal to be linked to some form of reward system. The overwhelming majority were concerned to stress that appraisal should be principally a staff development tool. Another head teacher identified in his final interview how the appraisal of individuals was providing a forum for whole school discussion and training, thereby ensuring consistency throughout the school:

> Appraisal has made us focus in more on what we want as a school. We now talk to the staff more about specifics. It's not just, 'Let's have a course on science', but 'Let's have a course on "Forces" in science for Key Stage 2'. So we've thought more carefully about what we're going to do. . . . We're not very keen to rush into things and to provide things for one class instead of overall. . . . And it is actually focusing us more in our evaluation of practice, which we've never found time to do before. I suppose it has focused us on consistency throughout the school.

Time constraints

That appraisal needs time if it is to be done properly was stressed over and over again. In Chapter 8 we recounted how even an appraiser as well organised and thoughtful as Mrs Summers had difficulties coping with the many interruptions, especially in a school like hers which had severe social problems. Another deputy head made the same point:

It's just finding the time for me to actually go into someone's class-room. . . . I've got a full time teaching commitment. . . . To go into people's classrooms, the time to spend on the interview when you sit down together and discuss what you want to focus on, what you are actually going to appraise . . . then collecting the data, feeding it back, summarising it – it's time consuming.

Not surprisingly many of the appraisers expressing concern about the time involved for themselves were head teachers or deputy heads in primary schools, where non-contact time is rarely available. In contrast, the head teacher of one school had organised time in such a way that pairs of appraisers and their appraisees could be seen together, enthusing about the opportunity this afforded to gain extra infor-mation about staff without adding an overwhelming burden to his own responsibilities:

What's useful is that I've got a way of talking to staff about what they do in their rooms, because when I get the statements I generally see the two of them [the appraiser and appraisee] together, and then, if necessary, I see the appraisee on their own and go through their statement with them. So I have all the end product to talk through without having to go through the process of observing etc. myself.

Funding constraints

To some extent time and money are linked. Time costs money and money can buy time. There was some evidence from comments made by the interviewees that the time pressure factor was being exacerbated by the lack of funding for appraisal. Although most LEAs appeared to be funding appraisal training and the supply cover required to release teachers for that, it was generally felt that the funding available for supply cover for the process itself was inadequate. The head teacher of one primary school explained how she had used a student teacher effec-tively as a supply teacher because of the funding problem:

We're keeping to the budget, not that the budget's huge – but, of course, we've got a student in and that's one of the reasons we're doing the last two in this half-term . . . because we're saving money. It has also meant that we've had more time than we would have had, had we been tied to the budget.

The head of a secondary school described the method she had used – concentrating all the resources on non-senior staff – to relieve the money shortage problem:

We only get the GEST allowance, which doesn't meet our programme at all. It relies very much on the goodwill of the staff. And particular appraisers have to give up a lot of their time, but what we did was to do myself and the senior staff without affecting any classroom activities, so we didn't use up any time on us which actually saved quite a bit of time, so that we now guarantee a minimum of four supply covers to every appraisal process, which has helped. Pitifully small but. . . .

The deputy head of a primary school which had taken part in the original pilot for teacher appraisal, was able to point out the difference adequate funding can make:

We started the pilot nearly seven years ago and then when we had the funding for it, it was running extremely smoothly and was very, very beneficial to everybody. Since they [the LEA] have withdrawn the funding and introduced 'top down' appraisal, it's been slightly more difficult to timetable and I don't think the benefits of it are quite so obvious.

The support available during the pilot scheme had included supply cover for feedback meetings to be held straight after the observations. These were now having to be held after school. This seems another important point to be considered if appraisal is to be given the time and energy it requires.

Outcomes and expectations

Once appraisal was over it was not always possible to satisfy teachers' needs. Several senior managers in case study schools were concerned about raised expectations that could not be fulfilled. One deputy head, who was also the school's Inset co-ordinator and therefore aware of the reality of managing the school's budget, echoed this concern:

It's no good promising people the earth if you can't give it to them, or if you haven't got a cat in hell's chance of providing them with a series of courses, because there isn't the money available. I think you've got to be very realistic.

When interviewed after appraisal was completed, however, the main worry expressed by head teachers was not so much about the lack of funding to meet the targets but the lack of availability of appropriate courses to help teachers improve. The head teacher of a secondary school explained a problem he had already encountered:

You say, 'Ah, yes, Joe Bloggs wants to do a course on statistics in A level. There's a county course on statistics in A level – whoopee!'

In goes an application. Three months later: 'Sorry, he hasn't got on it'. Now what do you do then? He hasn't achieved his target. We've failed to get him his appraisal target sorted out and then you have to go fishing round for another course which may not be available. And I don't know how you manage that one.

There was a general awareness among the heads we interviewed that, however positive they themselves felt about appraisal, the staff were feeling uneasy at the prospect of being appraised, particularly within the classroom, and concerned about the amount of time it would take in an overburdened working life. A common response when heads were asked about their staff's feelings toward appraisal was that there was an atmosphere of resignation that it had to be done. A deputy head described the staff's attitude:

> I think the staff view appraisal like I think a lot of people view most things at the moment that are happening in education – just a lot more put on teachers and a lot more to do. The idea behind it of self-evaluation and professional development and assessing lots of things that you do in terms of what you do in your classroom and thinking, 'Well, yes, this will extend me as a professional' . . . I don't think that people can honestly say that they are feeling that positive about it. . . . It's not something which has been met with a great deal of enthusiasm with people saying. . . 'Oh, great! Here's something that we **want** to do'. It's just something else we **have** to do.

By the time the final interviews were undertaken, there had been a marked shift in the head teachers' perceptions of staff feelings. Most reported positive responses by teachers after the appraisal process, though often it was more a sense of relief that it had not been as bad as people expected. One head teacher gave this explanation for the transformation:

> I think what's interesting is that staff have suddenly realised the difference between appraisal and inspection . . . having gone through an inspection [by the Office for Standards in Education] this term . . . there's a clear difference between the two. I don't think people feel threatened at all [by appraisal].

The deputy head of another school put it down to the way in which the process had been introduced in his school:

> They're welcoming it . . . because it's been introduced as something not to be fearful of, and it was basically for professional develop- ment . . . not a sort of witch-hunt. And we've introduced it gradually and we're a close knit staff and I think people aren't afraid. . . . The

messages from the initial meetings were that it wasn't something to be fearful of. . . . It was going to help . . . to identify areas of good practice . . . as well as weaknesses.

Another head, personally very committed to the appraisal process, acknowledged that her staff had originally been very apprehensive, but were now, to varying degrees, relieved:

I would not say that all staff go wholeheartedly into the experience . . . but on our staff I can't think of anybody who would be obstructive, so there is a general feeling of, 'We'll give it a go'. But everybody who has emerged from it has said, 'That was good. I enjoyed it'. Some of them to a greater or lesser extent than others.

She explained these differing experiences in terms of the quality of the appraiser and indicated that she had identified some appraisers 'who need a lot more support'.

In general, therefore, there was evidence that teachers' anxieties about the appraisal process dissipated once they had experienced it. However, although staff might no longer feel threatened by appraisal, one head teacher believed that a new anxiety had emerged, about the effect of letting down their own class, a fear of proprietorial neglect:

It's now increasingly at risk of upsetting and disrupting classroom teaching. . . . The last appraisal meeting, there were quite a lot of concerns expressed about interruptions to classroom teaching, being taken out of exam classes, exam classes being fouled up. Because although you've got supply, you're not there.

This confirms once more the feeling of being overburdened that many teachers reported. If appraisal is to make an impact on classroom processes, then this needs to be addressed.

Confidentiality

Once appraisal was over, some teachers began to be worried about the possible misuses, as they would see it, of appraisal, and the confidentiality of the appraisal statements was identified by several heads as a major issue for their members of staff. Amongst concerns was the role of school governors, as one head reported:

Staff want assurances of confidentiality, of course, and there's always this fear of governors. . . . I think the staff need the security that non-professionals are not going to get [the statements] . . . it worries the staff that the chairman of governors could have a lot of power if [he/she] decided to take it. It's happened in some schools – but over my dead body here.

In this context, he was particularly anxious about the targets arising from the appraisal process, especially as one particular governor was taking a very high profile:

> A concern is the targets going to the governing body because some of the targets are so . . . will probably be so specific that they [the teachers concerned] will be able to be identified, which worries me because there is one governor who is looking for specific things.

When interviewed right at the end of the researcher's involvement with the school, he reiterated his commitment to confidentiality, revealing, in his final comment, the lengths to which he was prepared to go, aware that the staff trusted him to protect their anonymity:

> I do reassure them constantly that it's all confidential, even though they discuss it with everyone else! They trust me that that will be the case. In fact, during the inspection [due in the autumn] I will take them home, because nobody else will have seen them, other than . . . the Director of Education has the right, but as far as I'm concerned, inspectors don't have the right!

The head teacher of another school had gone so far as to agree that the school secretary would not even type the statements, and that the appraisal statements would be put in a filing cabinet to which only the head had a key.

Appraisal literature and LEA support

The majority of heads we interviewed appeared satisfied with the literature and support they had received from their LEA. The head teacher of one school saw collaboration between the LEA and schools in the formulation of policy documents as a key to success:

> We've been quite pleased with it [the literature received]. It's been clear, concise, quite well thought out. A number of staff within the authority got together to plan and I think that's worthwhile. It wasn't just the authority writing it down. They actually consulted.

The appraisal co-ordinator from another school commended the way in which the LEA had worked with the teachers' representatives: 'I think it's fair to say that the authority's booklets have been accepted within the authority very well by the teacher organisations. They worked very closely with them'.

This school was based in an authority which had been a pilot authority and the head teacher felt this had facilitated the introduction of statutory appraisal, as the teacher unions had been closely involved in the pilot stage.

In general, it appeared that schools were using the LEA policy documents and guidelines as a framework within which to operate their own individual appraisal systems. The head teacher of a small rural primary school was glad that the documentation covered the administration side of appraisal, 'how things have got to be done', as well as giving advice on what to do if problems should arise. He felt this was important for heads of small schools, as it used experience within the LEA to provide a framework within which to work. He indicated that, while he followed the procedures as set out, he still tried to ensure that at each stage he did what was 'right' for his school.

A number of heads believed that the LEA's role in the provision of training was finished. Their perception was that training was necessary for the introduction of appraisal, but that further training was neither on offer nor appropriate. One deputy head stated, 'Now it's up and running . . . I don't think there's any further training'. The head teacher of another school agreed: 'They set us off, but we haven't used them since a great deal'.

Keeping to schedule

The timetable for appraisal was such that schools were expected, during a two year cycle, to ensure that half their staff had completed the first year of the appraisal cycle at some time during the school year (i.e. they must have had their observation and appraisal interview). During the second year all staff were to complete the first year of the appraisal cycle. During the research we enquired whether schools were keeping to these targets. The majority reported that they were. However, some schools failed to meet their targets. The reasons for this varied. The deputy head of one stated:

> I think you'd find that there's still little bits to be finalised. And I can understand that because our day to day work is to be out there in front of the children and teaching. Our appraisals are not that level of priority. So there's little bits to be finalised: written out targets to be typed up.

In another school the head stressed that there was a high level of commitment to appraisal, but she had to report that two heads of faculty had not yet started appraising their staff:

> It's not necessarily through lack of commitment. One had a long term of absence and the other one has been involved in initial teacher training and it has consumed him somewhat this year. . . . Although I said it's not through any lack of commitment, there must be an

element whereby they haven't set it as their top priority, and that's sad, because I know that there are people within their team that are crying out for appraisal. . . . That's why I want to go back and remind them of their management role.

One appraisal co-ordinator explained that the problem was most acute where both appraiser and appraisee failed to give the appraisal process top priority:

It's taken a long time where it's tended to be that both people give it quite a low priority. Because as long as one or other of the pair is keen to get on with it, they usually do get on with it, but when you've got both people happy to let it slide – that's when it takes the twenty weeks.

Sometimes changes in staffing affected the schedule. Many primary heads took a very personal and proprietorial view of appraisal, and one head, who had allowed appraisal to drift, explained that this was because he himself was moving to another post:

I felt it more appropriate that the incoming head should take it on. Although we should have done Anna by the end of this term, I think really the appraisal process is such an on-going process it would seem inappropriate for me to start a process and leave it half-way through, because a lot of it is going to be based on a very personal exchange of views, and I think another person's philosophy and out-look would influence the way the process goes.

The movement of staff was mentioned a number of times as a problem occurring in the undertaking of the appraisal process. The head teacher of another school cited the appointment of a new deputy as a cause of delay within the school. In one case study school a key appraiser left to take up a new post, before completing all stages of the appraisal process. The deputy head explained:

Although all the work had been done, the appraisal co-ordinator didn't get the statement . . . and I've contacted him [the appraiser] since, and he said, 'Yes, it's all somewhere . . . I've lost it'. So they've been through the entire process and I'm still waiting for him – this is two months later – to do what he's promised to do which is to reach down into his mind and remember and rewrite it, because I'm damned if I'm going to ask the poor girl to go through it all again. . . . And that's entirely his fault – not finishing it before he left.

The head of another school indicated that the process was taking longer than had been anticipated, and this had led to a rush at the end of the year:

People are not able to keep to deadlines. Of the thirty-seven – that's the number that should be completed by the end of this term. . . . And we've still got a week to go. . . . There are nine people who were to be appraised this term but actually only one appraisal statement so far completed. I know that there are three others currently in for typing and so on. But it's difficult for people to keep to deadlines, to find the time.

Anticipating problems, some schools actually concentrated on the potentially 'easy' staff in the first year, leaving the potentially 'difficult' teachers till last, as these two comments from heads at the half-way stage reveal:

We keep reminding ourselves that a lot of very awkward characters haven't been done yet – partly because we actually started the scheme saying, 'Would you prefer to go in the first year or the second?'. . . . So the unwilling ones tend to be people going in the second half, which has just started.

Next year will be extremely interesting because, in a hierarchical system . . . those people who maybe, for all kinds of reasons, may have more frustrations, less access to in-service training . . . that may spill over into the appraisal process. We may find that the whole thing begins to twitch an awful lot more than it is at the moment.

While there is evidence that delays were, in some measure, explained by teachers' workloads and unanticipated crises, there is no doubt that the enthusiasm for and commitment to the appraisal process by individual appraisers and appraisees played an important part in determining the priority it received. It is clear that those responsible for the management of appraisals in schools cannot simply set up the system and then merely hope it will run its course. Mechanisms need to be in place to ensure that teachers carry out appraisals as timetabled, and in the manner agreed within the school.

The majority of heads, when asked whether they would modify the school's appraisal process in the light of their experience, indicated that they felt there was little need for change. However, it must be said that only a few schools appeared to be undertaking any kind of formal evaluation, so it would be difficult for them to have a comprehensive view of whether these changes were desirable.

Classroom observation

We have looked at classroom observation in some detail throughout this research project. It has to be said that the observation of lessons was not done with great sophistication by appraisers. Local authorities gave little time to training for observation, one hour being typical, apart from the three-day course offered in just one LEA. Although the use of video-tapes was welcomed by some, others were critical. Appraisers really need to learn how to watch and analyse lessons by actually doing it. Vicarious substitutes for the real thing have a limited place, and a single hour, with emphasis on personal relationships, rather than an exploration of the range of possible approaches, is too rudimentary.

The national questionnaires and case studies confirmed that many appraisers were bereft of ideas when it came to watching lessons. In many cases they did not have the subject and age group expertise to understand from the inside what to look for. On other occasions they had the expertise about the context, but not about the means of analysing it. Lesson analysis is itself a set of skills that need to be learned. The social aspect of appraisal, particularly the need for good personal relationships, mutual respect, support rather than demolition, was rightly stressed, but many teachers were disappointed that in the feedback sessions, after they had been observed, they got little more than general encouragement, valued though this was. As professional people they often expected detailed personal advice about their class-room teaching that was not forthcoming.

In those cases where the appraiser was able to focus on events in the classroom, indicating specifically how teachers might adapt what they were doing so as to improve pupils' learning, there seemed to be a greater likelihood that the appraisee would act on the advice. This could be seen when we followed up and observed them several months later. A sharper, more insightful focus on classroom transactions might, in a future appraisal round, avoid the problem of so many people saying that they had not altered their practice.

Teaching for many years was an isolated profession, unwitnessed by others in many cases. By contrast with surgeons, who seem eager to share ideas about practice and often watch others at work, teachers have rarely been given the time for this kind of mutual professional development. Hence the awkward feeling that many experienced at being observed for the first time for many years, which led to emphasis on avoiding a climate of inspection or teaching practice supervision. Far from being commonplace, having an observer present was asso-ciated with being a novice, or even with being in trouble. Not sur-prisingly the attempt to disarm classroom observation of any real or implied threat could easily go to the other extreme and result in a bland exchange of politeness, lacking the insightful edge that many teachers said they would have found helpful.

Yet in what one of the present writers (Wragg 1994) has called the 'dynamic school', a great deal of classroom observation could be taking place. Teachers might be working with student teachers, helping the next generation acquire a reservoir of skills and fruitful experiences. Equally they might be working collaboratively with their fellows, each trying to improve the other. This sort of sustained peer appraisal seemed to be ruled out by the hierarchical framework in which the first round of compulsory appraisal took place, requiring, as it did, two somewhat brief and ritualised snapshots of classroom life as seen from above. In a genuinely dynamic school, where judicious change is based on reflection, discussion and consent, observation of one another should be as regular as is feasible. In addition, shorter- or longer-term job swaps with someone in a different school, observing teachers in other schools, and exploiting opportunities to highlight classroom processes, are among many possibilities for the dynamic school to develop.

CONCLUSION – DEEP AND SURFACE STRUCTURES – THE IMPACT ON PRACTICE

The principal purpose of appraisal is to improve practice. As we explained earlier, daily teaching consists of hundreds and thousands of interactions, many similar to each other. Changing these practices and habits for the better is not easily achieved, when they have been laid down firmly and repetitively over many years. Even the very best teachers can still improve what they do, yet it is far easier not to change than to change.

If patterns of teaching have been established over a long period, then they cannot be unscrambled during sixty minutes of classroom observation. Teaching is such a busy job that there is very little time for reflection during a lesson, when teachers often decide how to respond to a situation in under a second. Nor does change come about solely through coercion. External pressure may produce surface change, but it will rarely affect the deep structures on which teachers' rapid decisions are based. Changing deeply embedded patterns is a much more complex and intricate business, involving respect between teacher and mentor, insightful and convincing observation and analysis of classroom processes, and the time to reflect and act on what has been found. This must be followed by a positive act of will from the teacher, and where necessary, support from others in the school. Change can indeed take place without these conditions, but it will be against the odds and unlikely to penetrate beneath the surface. For the deep structures of teachers' craft to be influenced, the conditions need to be right.

This research has involved a wide ranging analysis of what happened during the first cycle of compulsory appraisal in English primary and secondary schools. It is clear that the unique management structures, attitudes of heads, teachers and appraisers, and the overall ethos of schools resulted in the introduction and implementation of appraisal taking many diverse forms. The majority of those we watched and interviewed expressed themselves in favour of appraisal in principle, with the proviso that it should be principally a staff development tool. There was evidence that many head teachers felt strongly that the needs of the individual must be placed within the context of the institution's needs.

Only a small number believed that, for appraisal to be worthwhile, it should be linked to some form of reward system. However, even those favouring the introduction of appraisal had concerns about its practical realities. In particular, attention was drawn to the importance of existing staff relationships, the time involved and the extra burden appraisal imposed on already overstretched staff, the limitations of the funding available and the advantages and disadvantages of complete confidentiality.

The role of the LEA in formulating policy and guidelines for dissemination to schools was mostly seen in positive terms, but there was an indication that some LEAs may need to reassess their training programmes, in order to make them more interesting and relevant. Nearly all the head teachers, deputy heads and appraisal co-ordinators questioned reported that their schools had tried hard to keep to the schedule within the timetable specified by the Government for the first cycle of appraisal, although some indicated that lack of time or commitment by a few members of staff had resulted in delays or failure to complete the full programme. Most heads seemed to be confident that their school's existing organisation of appraisal was effective and would only require minor modifications for the next cycle. However, this belief was rarely based on any systematic evaluation.

Experience from this project suggests that a number of points need to be taken into account if teacher appraisal is to be fully effective. These include the following:

- If local authorities are to take the lead in initiating training for appraisers, then the rest need to come up to the standard of the best. There was great variety in what was provided, and while most training courses gained approval from participants, some were heavily criticised. In a few LEAs the support structure had effectively collapsed.
- Greater prominence should be given to the classroom observation aspect of appraisal, in both external training courses and in-school provision. The range of possible approaches to lesson observation and analysis need to be taught not only to appraisers, but also to teachers themselves, so that observation and analysis become a regular part of their professional artillery.

- Greater use of peer appraisal should be explored. There may be a fear that this would not have a cutting edge, but one of the complaints from teachers during this research was that hierarchical appraisal could also be bland, especially when the appraiser did not have first-hand experience of the subject and/or age group being observed. Peer appraisal allows those with empathy and understanding of the context to be involved, and it need not be in emasculated form.
- Consideration should be given to the way in which teachers are asked to choose an area of focus and subsequently to set and achieve targets. Many had clear ideas about both focus and targets, but others were vague, in some cases unable even to recall their targets. The range of demands set for teachers was too great, as some were asked to do something relatively trivial, while others were set huge tasks.
- Appraisal should be properly resourced. In saying this it is not our purpose here to assign blame, as some schools seemed able to provide cover for teachers and appraisers and others did not. However, appraisal needs proper time and money. Too many teachers and appraisers had to discuss lessons almost on the run, and very few reported that they had the time to analyse fully what had been seen in the lessons observed. One of the reasons why so few teachers changed what they did in the classroom may have been because there was not enough time, given the many demands on them, to be fully de-briefed, and appraisers were not freed to follow teachers up to see if agreed plans were actually being implemented.
- Finally, schools should try to evaluate what they did and how effective it was. Some schools did send round questionnaires, but these usually concentrated on immediate reactions to the process. A focus on the extent to which in-service training was available, or being used to help teachers meet the targets set, or, more to the point, whether teachers were actually changing their classroom practice at all, would be valuable evaluation.

Bibliography

ACAS (1986) 'Teachers' Dispute, ACAS Independent Panel, Report of the Appraisal Working Group', London: Advisory Conciliation and Arbitration Service.

Adams, R. S. and Biddle, B. J. (1970) *Realities of Teaching*, New York: Holt, Rinehart & Winston.

Bales, R. F. (1950) *Interaction Process Analysis: A Method for the Study of Small Groups*, Reading, Mass: Addison-Wesley.

Barr, A. S. (1961) 'Wisconsin Studies of the Measurement and Prediction of Teacher Effectiveness', *Journal of Experimental Education* 30: 5–156.

Bennett, S. N., Wragg, E. C., Carré, C. G. and Carter, D. S. G. (1992) 'A Longitudinal Study of Primary Teachers' Perceived Competence in, and Concerns about, National Curriculum Implementation', *Research Papers in Education* 7(1): 53–78.

Bird, T. (1990) 'The Schoolteacher's Portfolio: An Essay on Possibilities', in J. Millman and L. Darling-Hammond (eds) (1990) *The New Handbook of Teacher Evaluation*, Newbury Park, California: Sage.

Bradley, H., Bollington, R., Dadds, M., Hopkins, D., Southworth, G. and West, M. (1989) *Report on the Evaluation of the School Teacher Appraisal Pilot Study*, Cambridge: Cambridge Institute of Education.

Brophy, J. (1981) 'Teacher Praise: A Functional Analysis', *Review of Educational Research* 51: 5–32.

Bryman, A. (1988) *Quantity and Quality in Social Research*, London: Unwin and Hyman.

CIE (1989) *Report on the Evaluation of the School Teacher Appraisal Pilot Study*, Cambridge: Cambridge Institute of Education.

de Gruchy, N. (1991) 'Appraisal as a Sneak's Charter', NASUWT Report 9, April.

DES, HM Inspectorate of Schools (1985) *Education Observed 3: Good Teachers*, Stanmore: DES.

DES (1986) *Education (No. 2) Act*, London: HMSO.

—— (1987) *The Education (School Teachers' Pay and Conditions of Employment) Order*, London: HMSO.

—— (1991a) *The Education (School Teacher Appraisal) Regulations 1991, (S.I. No. 1511)*, London: HMSO.

—— (1991b) *School Teacher Appraisal Circular 12/91*, London: HMSO.

Deutsch, M. (1960) 'Minority Group and Class Status as Related to Social and Personality Factors in Scholastic Achievement', Society for Applied Anthropology Monograph 2.

Dimmock, C. (1987) 'Teacher Appraisal: A comparative perspective from Australia', *School Organisation* 7(2): 163–79.

Elliott, J., Bridges, D., Ebbutt, D., Gibson, R. and Nias, J. (1982) *School Account-ability*, London: Grant McIntyre.

Evertson, C. and Burry, J. (1989) 'Capturing Classroom Context: The Obser-vation System as a Lens for Assessment', *Journal of Personnel Evaluation in Education* 2: 297–320.

Flanders, N. A. (1970) *Analyzing Teaching Behavior*, Reading, Mass: Addison-Wesley.

Gage, N. L. (1978) *The Scientific Basis of the Art of Teaching*, New York: Teachers College Press.

Glaser, B. and Strauss, A. L. (1967) *The Discovery of Grounded Theory*, Chicago: Aldine.

Haertel, E. H. (1991) 'New Forms of Teacher Assessment', *Review of Research in Education* 17: 3–29.

Hancock, D. (1985) 'Staff Appraisal in Schools and Colleges – a View from the DES', Speech to the Education for Industrial Society, London, 22 February 1985.

Hazlewood, P. K. (1994) 'The Influence of Appraisal on the Middle Manage-ment of Secondary Schools', unpublished PhD thesis, Exeter University.

Herbert, J. (1967) *A System for Analysing Lessons*, New York: Teachers College Press.

HMI (1989) *School Teacher Appraisal: A National Framework, Report of the National Steering Group on the School Teacher Appraisal Pilot Study*, London: HMSO.

Hoyle, E. (1972) 'Creativity in the School', unpublished paper given at OECD Workshop on Creativity in the School, Estoril, Portugal, reported in L. Stenhouse (1975) *An Introduction to Curriculum Research and Development*, London: Heinemann.

ILEA (1977) *Keeping the School Under Review*, London: ILEA.

Jackson, P. W. (1968) *Life in Classrooms*, New York: Holt, Rinehart & Winston.

James, C. and Newman, J. (1985) 'Staff Appraisal: Current Comprehensive Schools: A Regional Survey of Current Practice in the South Midlands and South West of England', *Educational Management and Administration* 13(3): 155–64.

Joseph, Sir Keith (1984) Speech to the North of England Education Conference, Sheffield, 6 January 1984.

—— (1985) Speech to the North West Education Conference, Chester, 4 January 1985.

Lefton, R. E. (1986) 'Performance Appraisals: Why They Go Wrong and How To Do Them Right', *National Productivity Review* Winter 1985–6: 54–63.

Lloyd, K. (1981) 'Quality Control in the Primary School: The Head's Role in Supervising the Work of Class Teachers', *School Organisation* 1(4): 317–19.

Lokan, J. and McKenzie, P. (eds) (1989) *Teacher Appraisal: Issues and Approaches*, Hawthorn, Vic: ACER.

Lorenz, K. (1966) *On Aggression*, New York: Harcourt, Brace & World.

MacGregor, J. (1989) Speech to the Secondary Heads' Association, Huntingdon, 2 October 1989.

Mead, G. H. (1934) *Mind, Self and Society*, Chicago: University of Chicago Free Press.

Medley, D. M., Coker, H. and Soar, R. S. (1984) *Measurement Based Evaluation of Teacher Performance: an Empirical Approach*, New York: Longman.

Medley, D. M. and Shannon, D. M. (1994) 'Teacher Evaluation', in T. Husen and T. N. Postlethwaite (eds) *International Encyclopedia of Education*, Second Edition, 10: 6015–20, Oxford: Pergamon.

Montgomery, D. (1984) *Evaluation and Enhancement of Teaching Performance*, Kingston Learning Difficulties Project.

Oppenheim, A. N. (1992) *Questionnaire Design: Interviewing and Attitude Measurement*, London: Pinter Publishers.

Powney, J. (1991) 'The Appraisal of Teachers in Middle Management Roles', *Research Papers in Education* 6(3): 171–95.

Rowe, M. B. (1972) 'Wait-time and Rewards as Instructional Variables', paper presented at the National Association for Research in Science Teaching, Chicago, April.

Rumbold, A. (1987) 'What Has Happened to Appraisal?', Speech to the Industrial Society Conference, London, 5 February 1987.

Ryans, D. G. (1960) *Characteristics of Teachers*, Washington: American Council on Education.

Samph, T. (1976) 'Observer Effects on Teacher Verbal Behaviour', *Journal of Educational Psychology* 68(6): 736–41.

Scriven, M. (1988) 'Duties-based Teacher Evaluation', *Journal of Personnel Evaluation in Education* 1: 319–34.

Sharp, R. and Green, A. (1975) *Education and Social Control*, London: Routledge & Kegan Paul.

Shulman, L. S. (1991) *The Odyssey of Teacher Assessment: Final Report of the Teacher Assessment Project*, Stanford, California: Stanford University School of Education.

Skinner, B. F. (1954) 'The Science of Learning and the Art of Teaching', *Harvard Educational Review* 24: 86–97.

Stenhouse, L. (1975) *An Introduction to Curriculum Research and Development*, London: Heinemann.

Stevens, R. (1912) 'The Question as a Measure of Efficiency in Teaching', *Teachers College Contributions to Education* 48, Columbia, New York.

Stufflebeam, D. L. and Nevo, D. (1994) 'Evaluation of Educational Personnel', in T. Husen, and T. N. Postlethwaite (eds) *International Encyclopedia of Education*, Second Edition, 4: 2123–32, Oxford: Pergamon.

Suffolk Education Department (1985) *Those having Torches . . . Teacher Appraisal: A Study*, Ipswich: Suffolk Education Department.

—— (1987) *In the Light of Torches . . . Teacher Appraisal: A Further Study*, Ipswich: Suffolk Education Department.

Turner, G. and Clift, P. (1985) *A First Review and Register of School and College Based Teacher Appraisal Schemes*, Milton Keynes: Open University.

—— (1988) *Studies in Teacher Appraisal*, Lewes: Falmer Press.

Weber, M. (1947) *The Theory of Social and Economic Organization*, New York: Free Press.

Whyte, J. B. (1986) 'Teacher Assessment: A Review of the Performance Appraisal Literature', *Research Papers in Education* 1(2):137–63.

Withall, J. (1949) 'The Development of a Technique for the Measurement of Social–Emotional Climate in the Classroom', *Journal of Experimental Education* 17: 347–61.

Wood, C. and Pohland, P. (1983) 'Teacher Evaluation and the Hand of History', *Journal of Educational Administration* 21(2): 169–81.

Wragg, E. C. (1984) (ed.) *Classroom Teaching Skills*, London: Croom Helm.

—— (1993) *Primary Teaching Skills*, London: Routledge.

—— (1994) *An Introduction to Classroom Observation*, London: Routledge.

Index